CONNECTED COMMUNITIES
Creating a new knowledge la

# IMAGINING REGULATION DIFFERENTLY

Co-creating for engagement

Edited by
Morag McDermont, Tim Cole,
Janet Newman and Angela Piccini

First published in Great Britain in 2020 by

Policy Press
University of Bristol
1-9 Old Park Hill
Bristol
BS2 8BB
UK
t: +44 (0)117 954 5940
pp-info@bristol.ac.uk
www.policypress.co.uk

North America office:
Policy Press
c/o The University of Chicago Press
1427 East 60th Street
Chicago, IL 60637, USA
t: +1 773 702 7700
f: +1 773-702-9756
sales@press.uchicago.edu
www.press.uchicago.edu

© Policy Press 2020

British Library Cataloguing in Publication Data
A catalogue record for this book is available from the British Library

Library of Congress Cataloging-in-Publication Data
A catalog record for this book has been requested

978-1-4473-4801-6 hardback
978-1-4473-4802-3 paperback
978-1-4473-4803-0 ePdf
978-1-4473-4804-7 ePub

The rights of Morag McDermont, Tim Cole, Janet Newman and Angela Piccini to be identified as editors of this work has been asserted by them in accordance with the Copyright, Designs and Patents Act 1988.

All rights reserved: no part of this publication may be reproduced, stored in a retrieval system, or transmitted in any form or by any means, electronic, mechanical, photocopying, recording, or otherwise without the prior permission of Policy Press.

The statements and opinions contained within this publication are solely those of the editors and contributors and not of the University of Bristol or Policy Press. The University of Bristol and Policy Press disclaim responsibility for any injury to persons or property resulting from any material published in this publication.

Policy Press works to counter discrimination on grounds of gender, race, disability, age and sexuality.

Cover design by Clifford Hayes
Front cover image: Close and Remote
Printed and bound in Great Britain by CMP, Poole
Policy Press uses environmentally responsible print partners

In memory of Ros Sutherland and Gareth Williams, our two much-missed colleagues who both passed away before this book was finished. They contributed so much to the Productive Margins programme and to the development of co-produced research across disciplines and communities. We will remember Ros particularly for her generosity, quiet wisdom and boundless enthusiasm and Gareth for his incisive contributions, calm presence and offbeat sense of humour.

# Contents

| | |
|---|---|
| List of figures, tables and boxes | vii |
| List of abbreviations and acronyms | ix |
| Notes on contributors | xi |
| Acknowledgements | xix |
| Series editors' foreword | xxiii |

| | | |
|---|---|---|
| 1 | Introduction: From the regulation of engagement to regulating *for* engagement<br>*Marilyn Howard, Morag McDermont and Martin Innes* | 1 |
| 2 | Co-production as experimentation: the research forum as method<br>*Sue Cohen, Tim Cole, Morag McDermont and Angela Piccini* | 23 |
| | Interlude: Community researchers and community researcher training<br>*Helen Thomas-Hughes* | 43 |
| 3 | Beyond Prevent: Muslim engagement in city governance<br>*Therese O'Toole* | 49 |
| 4 | Regulating for 'care-ful' knowledge production: researching older people, isolation and loneliness<br>*Helen Manchester, Jenny Barke and the Productive Margins Collective* | 67 |
| 5 | Who gets to decide what's in my fridge? Principles for transforming the 'invisible rules' shaping the regulation of food habits in urban spaces<br>*Naomi Millner, Sue Cohen, Tim Cole, Kitty Webster, Heidi Andrews, Makala Cheung, Penny Evans, Annie Oliver and the Food Working Group, as part of the Productive Margins programme* | 85 |
| 6 | *Life Chances*: thinking with art to generate new understandings of low-income situations<br>*Debbie Watson, Sue Cohen, Nathan Evans, Marilyn Howard, Moestak Hussein, Sophie Mellor, Angela Piccini and Simon Poulter* | 105 |

Imagining Regulation Differently

7      The Making, Mapping and Mobilising in Merthyr project:    127
young people, research and arts activisms in a
post-industrial place
*Emma Renold, Gabrielle Ivinson, Gareth Thomas*
*and Eva Elliott*

8      Regulating engagement through dissent      145
*Greg Leo Bond, Daniel Balla, Ari Cantwell*
*and Brendan Tate Wistreich*

9      The role of community anchor organisations in regulating    167
for engagement in a devolved government setting
*Eva Elliott, Sue Cohen and David Frayne*

10     Conclusion: Towards an organic model of regulating    189
for engagement
*Bronwen Morgan, Morag McDermont and Martin Innes*

Postscript: Engaging the university?     207
*Janet Newman*

References     217
Index     237

vi

# List of figures, tables and boxes

## Figures
| | | |
|---|---|---|
| 1.1 | Greater Bedminster toilet map | 21 |
| 4.1 | Mapping memories, friendships and connections in Southville and Bedminster | 70 |
| 4.2 | Performance of *Alonely* at the Connected Communities Utopias festival, London (2016) | 80 |
| 4.3 | 'Loneliness is ...' wall at the Connected Communities Utopias festival, London (2016) | 81 |
| 5.1 | The Food Utopia feast | 88 |
| 5.2 | From the garden to the city: ten principles for the community-led design of urban food systems | 97 |
| 5.3 | The Somali Kitchen in Easton | 101 |
| 6.1 | Reconfiguring 'family' in *Life Chances* imagery | 111 |
| 6.2 | Changing the landscape | 112 |
| 6.3 | The *Life Chances* logo and jewellery material | 113 |
| 6.4 | Examples of jewellery made in workshops | 114 |
| 6.5 | The original *Life Chances* game mat | 115 |
| 6.6 | Example of one of the *Life Chances* game cards | 116 |
| 8.1 | Composition created by Coexist showing the different spaces and activities contained within the Hamilton House building | 148 |
| 8.2 | Sticker installation, Carriage Works, Bristol (2014) | 154 |
| 8.3 | Still taken from the 2015 film *Keyhole Whispers* showing the coded double doors at the front of Hamilton House and a user of the space on the outside | 156 |
| 8.4 | Photograph of the 2016 social sculpture 'Conversations in Thread' held in the Bearpit underpass in central Bristol | 160 |
| 8.5 | Photograph of a live performance of two people holding a conversation while a Coexist team member makes notes | 163 |
| 9.1 | *The People's Palace: after Magritte* | 183 |

## Table
| | | |
|---|---|---|
| 1.1 | Summary of chapters: field of action, key actors, regulatory domains and methods | 8 |

## Boxes

| | | |
|---|---|---|
| 2.1 | Forum methods | 29 |
| 4.1 | 'Care-ful' knowledge production | 83 |
| 6.1 | Social practice methods | 118 |
| 9.1 | Anchor people | 181 |

# List of abbreviations and acronyms

| | |
|---|---|
| 3Gs | 3Gs Development Trust |
| AHRC | Arts and Humanities Research Council |
| BS3C | BS3 Community (formerly Southville Community Development Association) |
| ESRC | Economic and Social Research Council |
| KWMC | Knowle West Media Centre |
| PM | Productive Margins: Regulating *for* Engagement |
| SPAN | Single Parent Action Network |
| SRCDC | South Riverside Community Development Centre |

# Notes on contributors

**Heidi Andrews** was the projector coordinator for the five-year duration of the programme and a member of the Food Project Working Group. With professional services colleagues, she has published articles on the emergence of the publicly engaged research manager. She is currently a National Health Service (NHS) public involvement member developing training and resources for sharing power in co-produced research.

**Daniel Balla** is an artist, a creative facilitator, a storyteller and an activist. His arts practice explores human relationships with the world and each other through immersive projects of participatory theatre, storytelling and film. He is most excited while collaborating to devise creative protest or utilising facilitation/experiential tools for participatory democracy. He has worked with Coexist since 2011 and founded a sibling project, *CoResist*, which works where arts, activism and education meet. A desire to create more empowering and transformative experiences led Daniel to study an MA in Social Sculpture. His current work explores strategies for 'rebuilding the commons'.

**Jenny Barke** is a senior research associate at the Department of History, University of Bristol. Jenny's research focuses on the methods and ethics of co-producing research with people and groups outside of the university. In particular, her research explores how to engage with, support and train community researchers and considers how new knowledge is produced through collaborative research. Much of her work has drawn on creative and arts-based research methods in collaboration with writers, actors, illustrators, visual artists and directors.

**Greg Leo Bond** gained his PhD at the University of Bristol in the School of Geography. The PhD was funded as part of the Productive Margins research programme. Greg conducted co-produced practice-research, investigating how embodied arts practice can be utilised within engagement strategies. The research contributed to the 'Spaces of Dissent' strand of the Productive Margins research programme. Alongside academic work, Greg continues to work in the community sector, facilitating participatory film workshops and developing engagement strategies with social enterprises.

**Ari Cantwell** currently runs the Coexist Community Kitchen in Easton – a non-profit cookery school where the team use food as a way of bringing people together and as a vehicle to combat issues such as social isolation, self-esteem and marginalisation – as well as just having fun! Ari has a background in the social sciences, completing an MA in Applied Anthropology and Community Development at Goldsmiths University. Ari is interested in how theory and practice are integrated in order to address societal issues in a holistic manner. However, Ari also feels that you cannot do any of this if it is not integrated with colour, fun and tasty foods!

**Makala Cheung** is a Knowle West resident, business manager and Creative Director of Filwood Community Centre, and has worked as a community engagement manager and in other roles at the Knowle West Media Centre for 15 years. Makala is also a music artist (KALA CHNG) Happiness Champion (Happy City and Bristol Post Happiness List) and culture ambassador (West of England China Bureau), and also enjoys participating in street dance and martial arts.

**Sue Cohen** is an honorary research associate at the University of Bristol. She was a co-investigator on the Productive Margins programme and continues to undertake co-produced/participatory research with disadvantaged communities. For more than 20 years, Sue was the chief executive officer (CEO) of the Single Parent Action Network set up under the Third European Poverty Programme, developing a network of multi-ethnic grass-roots groups in the four UK nations and being involved in transnational participatory research exchanges in countries across the EU.

**Tim Cole** is Professor of Social History and Director of the Brigstow Institute at the University of Bristol. His research interests range across social and environmental histories, historical geographies, digital humanities, co-produced and interdisciplinary research, and collaborations in the creative industries. His most recent books are *Holocaust Landscapes* (2016) and *Geographies of the Holocaust* (2014, co-edited with Anne Knowles and Alberto Giordano).

**Eva Elliott** is an honorary research fellow at Cardiff University School of Social Sciences in the Wales Institute of Social & Economic Research, Data & Methods (WISERD), and is a previous director of the Wales Health Impact Assessment Support Unit and the Cardiff Institute of Society, Health and Wellbeing (WHIASU). Her research has focused on health inequalities and their social and economic determinants. She has conducted, or advised on, a multiplicity of large-scale national evaluations of place-based interventions, most of which have had some focus on the need for communities to have the collective power to influence change.

**Nathan Evans** is a community development worker who worked for South Riverside Community Development Centre (SRCDC) in Cardiff and led on the community engagement strand in Cardiff within the *Life Chances* project.

**Penny Evans** is a founding member and one of the directors of the Knowle West Media Centre (KWMC). She leads the development of KWMC's The Factory, a digital manufacturing maker space supporting residents and creative enterprises to learn new skills, experiment and prototype using digital tools and new materials. Penny provides leadership and coordinates across a multifaceted, innovative programme, creating programmes and research that respond to future need. She is a key strategist in KWMC's engagement of local communities, and the development of relevant and bespoke uses of new media and technology. Evans is a Fellow of the Royal Society of Arts.

**David Frayne** is a writer and social researcher interested in the politics and future of work. He is the author of *The Refusal of Work* (Zed, 2015) and the editor of *The Work Cure* (PCCS, 2019). He has worked as a sociologist at Cardiff University and New York University, and has written opinion pieces for *The Independent, New Statesman* and *The Guardian*.

**Marilyn Howard** is an honorary research associate and doctoral student at Bristol University, where she worked on the *Life Chances* and Regulation projects within the Productive Margins programme. Previously, she worked in the women's and disability sectors in policy and research roles, as well as in central and local government. Her experience also includes community social work and welfare rights advice. Her research interests include social security, equality, disability and participative approaches. Recent work with the Women's Budget Group includes the impacts of social security changes on survivors of domestic abuse.

**Moestak Hussein** has extensive experience in working with grass-roots civil society organisations in community development, research, management, delivery of government strategy and stakeholder engagement. Moestak was the lead community partner in Bristol's Single Parent Action Network (SPAN), working on the *Life Chances* project. She is the cofounder of Creating Life Chances CIC, based in Bristol, which works to tackle social and economic inequalities through creative arts and culture, financial education workshops, and skills training. Creating Life Chances CIC has successfully secured a fellowship with anti-poverty charity Toynbee Hall in partnership with the Financial Innovation Lab as part of a cohort.

**Martin Innes** is Director of the Crime and Security Research Institute and Universities' Police Science Institute, both at Cardiff University. He is the author of the books *Signal Crimes* (Oxford University Press, 2014), *Understanding Social Control* (Open University Press, 2003) and *Investigating Murder* (Oxford University Press, 2003). Innes's work has been influential across the policy, practice and academic communities. His current research interests are centred upon counterterrorism, disinformation and new social control technologies.

**Gabrielle Ivinson** is Professor of Education and Community at Manchester Metropolitan University. She develops arts-based methods to attune to what lies beyond the spoken word, enabling embodied affects to become visible through multiple media (as sounds, artefacts, dance, movements and films). She coordinates the Creative Margins network, exploring how to make arts accessible to marginalised young people. Recent publications include 'Anticipating the more-than: working with pre-hension in artful interventions with young people in post-industrial communities', *Futures* (with Renold) and 'Re-imagining Bernstein's restricted codes', *European Educational Research Journal.*

**Helen Manchester** is Associate Professor in Digital Inequalities and Urban Futures, School of Education, University of Bristol. Helen is passionate about doing research that makes a difference. She has conducted a number of innovative interdisciplinary studies that set out to creatively respond to environmental, demographic and technological change in urban settings, including research on ageing populations, co-designing technologies for care settings and exploring cultural value from the perspective of diverse young people in the city.

# Notes on contributors

**Morag McDermont** is Professor of Socio-Legal Studies at the University of Bristol Law School. Her research has been shaped by 15 years of working in local government and voluntary sector housing organisations. She has published two books: *Regulating Social Housing: Governing Decline* (Glasshouse, 2006, with Dave Cowan); and *Governing, Independence and Expertise: The Business of Housing Associations* (Hart, 2010). Besides being principal investigator for Productive Margins, she has recently completed 'New Sites of Legal Consciousness: A Case Study of UK Advice Agencies', a research programme that examined the role played by advice agencies in a rapidly changing legal landscape (see: www.bristol.ac.uk/law/advice-agency-research/about/).

**Naomi Millner** is a senior lecturer in human geography who specialises in the political ecologies of food production and consumption, as well as environmental politics. Her work focuses on the 'people' dimension of sustainability, including: experiences of marginalisation and exclusion in changing regimes of social and political governance; processes of community-led transformation of regulation; and pedagogies for social change, including feminist approaches.

**Bronwen Morgan** is a socio-legal scholar working at the intersection of law and social science, with a strong interest in new and diverse economies, particularly those affiliated with solidarity and the creation of a commons, but also with a focus on digital platforms and sharing economies. She is Professor of Law at UNSW Sydney, with a PhD in Jurisprudence and Social Policy from the University of California at Berkeley, and has previously taught at the Universities of Bristol and Oxford. She helped to co-found the New Economies Network of Australia, now a formally incorporated cooperative.

**Sophie Mellor** is an artist from Close and Remote (with Simon Poulter). Recurring themes in their work are unusual places, unusual suspects, watercolour painting, home-brew virtual reality and what they call 'tiny spectacle'. Their works are observational, not attendant to one method and often based on research (see: www.closeandremote. net).

**Janet Newman** is Professor Emerita in Social Policy at the Open University. After a first career working in local government, she reinvented herself as an academic. Her work has explored different configurations of gender, governance, politics and power. Publications include *The Managerial State* (1997, with John Clarke) and *Working the Spaces of Power: Activism, Neoliberalism and Gendered Labour* (2012).

**Annie Oliver** is the Community Inclusion Manager at Barton Hill Settlement responsible for the SPAN Parenting Support Team, community organisers and a wide range of social cohesion projects. Prior to this Annie worked for the Single Parent Action Network for over 25 years involved in grassroots empowerment projects across the country including the management of the Strengthening Families Strengthening Communities programme.

**Therese O'Toole** is Professor of Sociology in the School of Sociology, Politics and International Studies and the Centre for the Study of Ethnicity and Citizenship at the University of Bristol. She was Lead Researcher on the Muslim Civic Engagement project in the Productive Margins programme. Her research focuses on ethnicity, religion, governance and political and civic participation, with a particular focus on the mechanisms for state engagement with Muslims and the impact of the Counter Terrorism agenda on Muslim civil society organisation. Prior to her work on the Productive Margins programme, Therese was PI on a Leverhulme project exploring contemporary grammars of action among ethnic minority and Muslim young people and a large AHRC/ESRC project investigating Muslim participation in contemporary governance. She recently co-authored a book with John Holmwood critically analysing claims about an Islamist plot to infiltrate schools in Birmingham – the so-called Trojan Horse affair, showing that these were based on misleading and discriminatory claims about Muslim leadership and engagement in the governance of schools in *Birmingham: Countering Extremism in British Schools? The Truth about the Birmingham Trojan Horse Affair* (Policy Press, 2017).

**Angela Piccini** is Associate Professor in Screen Media in the Department of Film and Television at the University of Bristol. She is interested in relationships between the moving image and place. Her research focus has been developed through interdisciplinary, collaborative research that links academic practices with the practices of industry, communities and the public sector. Before becoming a first-generation academic, as a working-class child of Italian and Anglo-Chilean immigrants, she grew up swimming at urban beaches and feeding mussels to sea anemones in Vancouver, Canada – the unceded territories of the xwməθkwəy̓əm (Musqueam), Skwxwú7mesh (Squamish) and Səl̓ílwətaʔ/Selilwitulh (Tsleil-Waututh) First Nations.

# Notes on contributors

**Simon Poulter** is an artist from Close and Remote (with Sophie Mellor). Recurring themes in their work are unusual places, unusual suspects, watercolour painting, home-brew virtual reality and what they call 'tiny spectacle'. Their works are observational, not attendant to one method and often based on research (see: www.closeandremote. net).

**Emma Renold** is Professor of Childhood Studies at the School of Social Sciences, Cardiff University. Inspired by feminist, queer and new materialist post-humanist scholarship, Emma's research explores how gender and sexuality come to matter in children and young people's everyday lives across diverse sites, spaces and locales. In recent years, she has explored the affordances of co-productive, creative and affective methodologies to engage social and political change with young people on gendered and sexual violence (see: www.agendaonline.co.uk), and relationships and sexuality education (see Renold and McGeeney, 2017).

**Gareth Thomas** is Lecturer in Sociology at the Cardiff University School of Social Sciences. He is primarily interested in medicine, disability, stigma, reproduction and place. His PhD was an ethnography of Down's syndrome screening in two UK hospitals, which formed the basis of his monograph *Down's Syndrome Screening and Reproductive Politics: Care, Choice, and Disability in the Prenatal Clinic* (2017).

**Helen Thomas-Hughes** is a senior lecturer and director of part-time programmes in the University of Bristol's English Department. She also leads Community Engagement within the department's English Literature and Community Engagement BA programme. Helen's research is focused on co-productive methodologies in the UK, particularly on: working with and training community-researchers; community-engaged pedagogy in higher education within the UK context; and collaborative approaches to designing and delivering parenting and family interventions. Prior to entering academia, Helen spent more than a decade leading and delivering parenting, domestic violence and education-focused interventions in community settings. Helen has four children and lives in Bristol.

**Debbie Watson** is Professor of Child and Family Welfare in the School for Policy Studies, University of Bristol. She was the lead academic for the *Life Chances* project and is head of the Centre for Children and Families Research. Her research interests include:

theorising children's well-being; the importance of life story, memory objects and narrative identity for children who are care-experienced; and understanding experiences of child and family poverty. She has led numerous projects that have involved multiple disciplines and has a long-term interest in the development of arts-based approaches to research in the social sciences.

**Kitty Webster** was research associate for the research project *'Who decides what's in my fridge?'*. She has an MA in Political Sociology and a professional background in the charity sector. She now works as communications and engagement officer managing events for the Bristol Doctoral College at the University of Bristol, including the flagship 'Research without Borders' festival of postgraduate research.

**Brendan Tate Wistreich** spent six years with Coexist supporting the development of a thriving community hub in a once-vacant office building. He later supplemented this experience with an MA in Strategic Leadership towards Sustainability. Brendan currently chairs a number of community sector organisations. He also leads a community organising project that aims to address inequality within the city by working with residents to build collective power and take action against issues that matter to them. Through his life and work, he is committed to creating new theory and practice to support social justice, sustainable development and the creation of alternative economies.

# Acknowledgements

Large, complex collaborative programmes such as Productive Margins do not just happen; they require enormous amounts of administrative and organisational work to make sure things happen, people get paid, rooms get booked and the needs of the many participants are taken into account in planning and delivering action. We want to particularly thank Heidi Andrews, our programme co-ordinator, who provided support and coordination in such a creative, constructive and caring way throughout, supported efficiently and with great humour by Ruby Tucker and Lucy Backwell.

In addition to all the wonderful participants who remain anonymous in our work, the programme and this book could not have happened without the participation of so many inspiring collaborators – professional services staff, visiting scholars, artists, community organisation workers and Connected Communities representatives. We wish to thank, in no particular order: artists Matt Olden and Joff Winterhart, who contributed to helping the project to think about its own regulatory frameworks; the University of Bristol's Ethics Review Committees in both Arts and Social Sciences; the Institute for Advanced Studies' Benjamin Meaker Visiting Professor scheme, which supported visits by Cheryl Siemers, Henry Daniel and Sharon Irish; participants in Vancouver, Canada, who gave us an international context for this work in our first year, especially Lois Klassen, Margot Leigh Butler, Susan Grossman, Marie Lopes, Am Johal and Jil P. Weaving; colleagues at the University of Victoria, Canada, especially Maeve Lydon, Crystal Tremblay and Budd Hall, and the Lansdown Visiting Speaker award; Tom Sperlinger; Suzy Giullari; Sarah Eagle; Keri Facer; Bryony Enright; and Kathryn Dunleavy.

The Economic and Social Research Council have our particular thanks for being bold enough to support a research proposal that, due to its co-produced nature, did not have the usual clear and tangible outputs in the research bid. We also acknowledge the Arts and Humanities Research Council for funding our participation at various Connected Communities festivals.

Across the research projects that form the basis of the book chapters the following people made critical contributions:

- *Muslim engagement in Bristol* (Chapter 3): Zaheer Shabir, Nura Aabe, Sheila Joy el Dieb, Farzana Saker, Suad Abdullahi, Tasleem Kaurser, Ruby Raja, Tamadour Saliem, Adeela ahmed-Shafi, Shabana

Kausar, Nazmi Rana, Kalsoom Bashir, Therese O'Toole, Aleksandra Lewicki and Sadia Rana.

- *Isolation and Loneliness in Older People Project* (Chapter 4): Ros Sutherland, together with Dr Simon Hankins, initiated and developed the idea in the Productive Margins Forum and remained involved throughout in the working group and day-to-day running of the project. Ruth Naughton-Doe and Cam Elizabeth were research associates working at the Merthyr Tydfil site. Les Dobson, Cluster Manager of the 3Gs Development Trust, worked alongside Cam and Ruth to coordinate the activity in Merthyr Tydfil. The project would not have been possible without the peer researchers that we worked with in the Greater Bedminster element of the work. Steve Franks, Carol Jubb, Alexandra Pickford, Chris Priestman, Judith Moore, Catherine Westcott, Chloe Schofield and Teri Brammah were involved from the outset. They designed and conducted research in their community, alongside Jenny Barke, including designing research questions and focus, interviewing older isolated and lonely people, analysing the data, and working to disseminate the project. They also worked with Adam Peck to co-write monologues on loneliness that some of them then performed in a variety of locations. The monologues are being regularly performed in the city and region – with thanks to Lucy Tuck who directed the performers and put together and designed a coherent piece that works in theatre settings, conferences and other settings. Alan Nye became involved later in the process but then worked with Judith Moore and Jenny Barke to design and deliver a hyper-local retirement programme. Stand + Stare worked with us to design an installation to house our Alonely performers for festivals and other events. In Merthyr, we worked alongside local artists during the project. Artists included: Nigel Pugh, a professional documentary environmental and social photographer; Clare E. Potter, a local poet, writer, performer and educator; and Colum Regan, a musician and writer.
- *'Who decides what's in my fridge?'* (Chapter 5): Suad Yusuf worked alongside the other co-authors in the project working group, developing research questions and methods. The research would not have been possible without the many community members from the Knowle West Media Centre and Single Parent Action Network who participated in a variety of ways.
- *Life Chances* (Chapter 6): Allan Herbert, Eva Elliott, Sophie Mellor, Simon Poulter, Bella Dicks (working group members), Akilah Tye

# Acknowledgements

Comrie, Trasi, Safiya, Saediya and those others who participated as research volunteers but did not wish to be named.

- *The 4Ms Project* (Chapter 7): Adam Griffiths, Geraldine Madison, Heloise Godfrey-Talbot, Rowan Talbot, Eve Exley, Seth Oliver, Dan Jones, Jên Angharad, Jonathan Cox, James Hawker, Ashley Evans, Keith Maher, Leigh Medlicott, the young people and staff from Forsythia Youth Centre, the young people and staff from Pen Y Dre High School, and the young people and staff from Bishop Hedley High School.
- *Spaces of dissent* (Chapter 8): Jamie Pike, Rebecca Baxter, Jonathan Newey, Deborah Ward, Coexist, CoResist, Community Kitchen, Bristol Bike Project, D MAC UK, Artspace Lifespace, PRSC, Easton Energy Group, Imayla and Community CoLab.
- *Weathering the storm* (Chapter 9): Chris Coppock, Lee Davies, Glenn Davidson, Les Dobson, Nathan Evans, Allan Herbert, Mel Jones and Sioned Pearce. We would also like to acknowledge the contribution of all the anchor people in South Riverside Community Development Centre (SRCDC) and the 3GS Community Centre to the production of the data and the artwork.
- *Women and data* (discussed in Chapter 10): Pam de Moura; Dot Baker, Penny Evans and Martha King; Les Dobson; artists Stefanie Posevac, Eliza Lomas and Erica Jewell; and participants from Knowle West Media Centre and 3Gs Community Development Trust.

# Series editors' foreword

Around the globe, communities of all shapes and sizes are increasingly seeking an active role in producing knowledge about how to understand, represent and shape their world for the better. At the same time, academic research is increasingly realising the critical importance of community knowledge in producing robust insights into contemporary change in all fields. New collaborations, networks, relationships and dialogues are being formed between academic and community partners, characterised by a radical intermingling of disciplinary traditions and by creative methodological experimentation.

There is a groundswell of research practice that aims to build new knowledge, address longstanding silences and exclusions, and pluralise the forms of knowledge used to inform common sense understandings of the world.

The aim of this book series is to act as a magnet and focus for the research that emerges from this work. Originating from the UK Arts and Humanities Research Council's Connected Communities programme (www.connected-communities.org), the series showcases critical discussion of the latest methods and theoretical resources for combining academic and public knowledge via high-quality, creative, engaged research. It connects the emergent practice happening around the world with the longstanding and highly diverse traditions of engaged and collaborative practice from which that practice draws.

This series seeks to engage a wide audience of academic and community researchers, policy makers and others with an interest in how to combine academic and public expertise. The wide range of publications in the series demonstrate that this field of work is helping to reshape the knowledge landscape as a site of democratic dialogue and collaborative practice, as well as contestation and imagination. The series editors welcome approaches from academic and community researchers working in this field who have a distinctive contribution to make to these debates and practices today.

*Keri Facer, Professor of Educational and Social Futures,*
*University of Bristol*

*George McKay, Professor of Media Studies,*
*University of East Anglia*

# 1

# Introduction:
# From the regulation of engagement to regulating *for* engagement

*Marilyn Howard, Morag McDermont and Martin Innes*

## Introduction

Regulation permeates everyday life and is yet almost invisible – a network of rules, procedures, bureaucracies and forms that must daily be navigated and negotiated. Regulation is understood as a central role of states – protecting citizens from the consequences of markets and competition – but is nevertheless highly contested. The financial crisis exposed the inability of states to control the financial sector, as has their subsequent lack of action to limit bank bailouts, excessive salaries, fraud and poor risk management. More recently, regulation has become a key target of the anti-statist, anti-expert political discourses witnessed in the 'Leave' campaign to take the UK out of the European Union and the 2016 US presidential campaign of Donald Trump.

Yet, activists and theorists have long argued and fought for an intensification of reforms through regulation: health and safety regulation in the interests of workers; rent and building standards to protect tenants; the regulation of hate speech to protect migrants; and controls on schooling to protect and further the interests of children. Furthermore, as more functions shift away from direct state control, we have seen the proliferation of calls for the extension of state-based regulation to secure justice and protect citizens. For example, the fire in the Grenfell Tower flats in London in 2017, which led to the deaths of 72 residents, stimulated public debate about who should be controlling construction standards, and how. Grenfell Tower exposed what happens when regulatory systems are unable (or unwilling) to listen to the concerns of those whose identities are not necessarily inscribed in bureaucratic power – the residents who could see, and had to live with, the dangers of regulatory failure.

*Imagining Regulation Differently* takes a bottom-up approach to rethinking regulation. Here, we are interested in how societies, not just government, regulate, and so our framing is more holistic and multi-vectored than many approaches to regulation. In this book, we recognise that the expertise of communities at the margins of power structures can produce different capabilities that we believe could transform the terrain and spaces of regulatory systems. In the chapters that follow, we explore experiences of regulation across diverse spheres in ways that aim to support policymakers and community organisations to develop new approaches, while, at the same time, challenging academic thinking. Unlike most studies of regulation, which consider only one or two fields or regulatory agencies, the chapters here explore a broad range of intersecting areas – immigration, social work, food regulation, space and surveillance, older people, ethnicity, and faith – to address the central question of how individuals and communities engage with regulatory regimes and processes in ways that enable conceptions of social justice to become central framing devices. What is exposed is the complexity of regulation in daily life as citizens experience the overlapping and layering of multiple regulatory systems.

This diversity of interests is important, as is the 'point of view' of the chapters. Each chapter critically explores an arena for regulation as experienced by citizens and communities who are traditionally regarded as being 'at the margins'. The actors and investigators in each of the chapters are not the relatively powerful organisations that deliver goods and services; rather, they are communities and citizens generally excluded from decision-making about *how* regulatory systems work but who experience the *effect* of such systems on a daily basis. They create their own regulatory environments and the community organisations play an important role in mediating, brokering and translating regulatory systems. In this book, we explore: projects of mapping, making and mobilising with young people; Muslim engagement in decision-making; isolation and loneliness among older people; the regulation of food habits across diverse communities; low-income families' urban experiences of poverty; and immigration regulation. We aim to answer the question: '*What makes it possible to regulate for engagement?*' The threefold answer, explored in the final chapter, urges the importance of a holistic appreciation of place, the power to reframe the key narrative underpinning a regulatory regime and the capacity to surface invisible or tacit rules through new ways of seeing and knowing. All of this points to a need for infrastructure that can support communities at the margins to become central to regulatory design and practice, infrastructure that allows room for experts-by-experience to emerge alongside more formal understandings of expertise, as key actors in regulation.

This introductory chapter has three aims:

- to set out our concerns with the current state of theories and practice in regulation, identifying a fundamental problem of regulatory practice, which turns more and more inward-looking, shutting out the expertise of citizens who experience the effects of regulatory systems. It was this gap that led to the five-year research programme, 'Productive Margins: Regulating *for* Engagement', which led to this book;
- to outline the chapters that follow, exploring both our methodology of co-production and citizens' experiences of a number of substantive fields of regulatory practice in order that we can begin to see and know regulatory systems differently; and
- to set the scene for our explorations in regulating *for* engagement by illustrating some of the ways in which regulation is discussed – or not – in everyday life by drawing on interviews with participants in the research programme.

## Understandings of regulation

Theories and practices of regulation have developed substantially over recent decades, with a shift from a conception of regulation as centralised and operating through mechanisms of 'command and control' (CAC), to ideas of 'decentred' regulation, 'regulatory space' and 'regulation in many rooms'. A focus on the decentred nature of regulation, and the 'regulatory space' metaphor in particular, has shifted regulation thinking away from hierarchical, top-down concepts of CAC towards a more fragmentary and dispersed depiction of regulatory power. In regulatory space theory, the resources of, and relations between, the various occupants of the space are critical in holding it together (Scott, 2001). We can think of these as 'powers of association' (Latour, 1986), which create interdependencies between human and non-human actors. These are exchanged and bargained as part of the functioning of power (see McDermont, 2007).

However, the ways in which regulation has been operationalised have tended to offer very narrow understandings of who, or what, forms part of the regulatory system. The occupants of regulatory space are generally restricted to relatively powerful organisations: the regulatory bodies, the companies/organisations that are to be regulated and the myriad advisers, consultants, financiers and others who circulate through and around regulatory bodies and organisations. In this form of regulatory space, there is little, if any, room for engagement from individuals and communities, for example, in the decisions of supermarkets as to where to locate and what to sell, or of planning authorities deciding to license fast-food takeaways. Engagement seldom moves beyond establishing a consumer advisory panel, or having a tenant on a housing association board (for example, McDermont et al, 2009). Therefore, although the tendency towards decentred regulation would appear to offer the possibility of opening up regulatory spaces, we would rather point to the closing down that occurs – regulatory space may include a broader conception of 'others', but by drawing boundaries, it also excludes.

These exclusionary tendencies arise from a number of institutional practices. First, regulation tends to function through the exercise of specialist expertise. This makes it attractive for governments (and others) because regulation appears as non-ideological, as politically neutral. This allows regulations to travel globally as 'seemingly fluid and flexible instruments of rule' (Turem and Ballestero, 2014: 3). Therefore, while regulation scholars recognise the fragmentary and constructed nature of regulatory knowledge, with no single actor holding all the information (Black, 2001: 107), the more inclusionary concept of regulation that this generates only recognises the knowledge of *organisations* that are the subject of regulation (and their consultants and financiers) as relevant. The result is to make systems *more* internally referential.

Second, the invention of regulatory systems and practices frequently arises not from a desire to prevent a social harm, but rather as a demand from 'cohesively co-ordinated groups, typically industry or special interest groups' (Veljanovski, 2010: 25), to protect a field from intrusion by outsiders. For example, UK housing associations in the 1970s worked with the government to set up a system of regulation with a centralised state regulator. The design of the regulatory system thus reflects the need of the actors inside the system to create authority and control.

Third, the practices that have become vital in decentred regulation – 'risk-based' and 'self'-regulation – also work towards the narrowing down of the focus and attention of those operating in regulatory space. 'Risk-based' regulation has become a leading influence on the design of regulation, being seen as a way of reducing the 'burden' of regulation by targeting resources. What risk-based mechanisms do is focus resources on the inspection of those organisations that are judged to pose the greatest risk, thus ignoring wider societal risks.

Self-regulation, also in vogue because it seemingly saves state resources, leads to practices and procedures based on internal (organisational or sectoral) knowledge. The many meanings of self-regulation all revolve around mechanisms of regulation that put the organisation – or the sector – at the centre of regulatory practice (Black, 2001). Therefore, self-regulation might mean passing the regulatory function down to the level of the firm, where organisations are required to establish their own departments that monitor and inspect, a sort of 'enforced self-regulation' (Ayres and Braithwaite, 1992), or it might refer to a sector or industry carrying out its own regulatory functions with some oversight by government, sometimes termed 'co-regulation' (Grabosky and Braithwaite, 1986: 83).

Therefore, decentred regulation, and the tools and techniques that this gives rise to, results in spaces open only to regulatory institutions (with a variety of attachments to, or detachments from, the state) working alongside relatively powerful actors: companies, consultants and other intermediaries. This 'decentring' of regulation may have produced more efficient and effective regulation from the perspective of regulators and regulated organisations. However, these multiple, discrete systems that have evolved technocratic fixes to regulatory problems allow little reference to the lived experience of those who typically have to engage with these multiple centres of regulation: the person seeking asylum, living in poor housing or wanting to buy healthy, affordable food.

## Expertise, experience, deliberation and creativity: introducing the chapters

These were the problems of regulation that inspired the creation of a programme of research that attempted to rethink the theory and practice of regulation. 'Productive Margins: Regulating *for* Engagement' was a collaboration between community organisations and higher education researchers to re-imagine regulatory systems in ways that would allow the experience and expertise of communities at the margins to be centrally engaged in regulatory decision-making processes. The method of the programme was *co-production*.[1] We hypothesised that the *co-production* (or *collaborative production*) of new knowledge would bring about new ways of seeing and knowing regulatory systems. These collaborative spaces of knowledge production would enable us to address the central question of how individuals and communities can engage with regulatory regimes and processes in ways that enable conceptions of social justice to become central framing devices.[2]

The programme sought to explore both the tensions around systems of regulation *and* the tensions that arose when trying to rethink regulatory systems through the mechanisms and perspectives of co-production. As a programme, we wanted to challenge assumptions of 'expertise', both within the regulatory systems that we were exploring and within the research process. We came to see that these two aspects were inextricably linked. If regulatory systems were to become more responsive to the needs and demands of regulated *citizens* (as opposed to companies and organisations), they had to develop both different ways of seeing and knowing the practices and impact of their regulation, and ways in which communities at the margins could become engaged in designing those regulatory systems. We hoped that co-production, as put into practice in our programme, could open up such new ways of seeing, knowing and redesigning. Therefore, our insights from experimenting with co-production (in research) were directly relevant to the co-production of regulatory systems.

The design of the programme was thus an experiment in doing research differently. Many attempts at co-production are limited from the outset because the focus of research (the field of enquiry) has been predetermined by the bid for research funding. We wanted to shift that dynamic in order to enable community organisations to bring their expertise into the process of defining *what* should be the site of investigation, as well as *how* it should be investigated. In Chapter 2, we describe how we set up the Productive Communities Research Forum as our site of experimentation. This was our first innovation, being a site in which we attempted to create an equality between academics and community organisations to be partners in the design and delivery of the research programme, a site in which new understandings would arise as we reflected what we think we know against others who brought different perspectives.

A second innovation was to embed arts practice in the research process as a key mechanism to enable those traditionally excluded from knowledge generation to become key producers. We wanted to move away from relationships between artists and researchers whereby the function of artists is to communicate academic research to non-specialist audiences or provide a therapeutic/mediating interface between researchers and publics. Instead, by involving researchers, artists and non-academic publics in artistic practice-as-research processes, we were able to link the production of aesthetic, experiential and conceptual knowledge. We believe that this has created genuinely novel insights.

A third innovation was to involve community members as researchers. In three of the projects, local residents – laypeople without any prior research training or experience – became co-researchers with the academics. An interlude between Chapters 2 and 3, titled 'Community researchers and community researcher training', describes and critiques the research training that was co-designed iteratively between an academic research 'trainer' and the workers in the community organisations that hosted the teams of community researchers.

Chapters 3 to 9 each examine a different field of regulation and consider the various experiments in seeing and knowing differently enabled by the overarching programme. Table 1.1 provides a summary of each chapter, the regulatory domain focused on, the key actors and the methods used.

Chapter 3 focuses on the highly contested terrain of the Prevent strand of the UK government's counterterrorism strategy as a form of regulation, exploring how it was received and implemented in the city of Bristol. Launched in 2007 by the New Labour government and badged as a community engagement 'hearts and minds' approach to countering violent extremism, Prevent set out to partner and engage with Muslim communities to address the causes of radicalisation. However, the approach was severely criticised by Muslim communities, and in Bristol an alternative approach was established through the innovative mechanism of a consultative forum, Building the Bridge (BtB). Through a case study of BtB, O'Toole shows how the top-down regulation of Prevent gave way to a more bottom-up approach that departed in significant ways from its original design and, in so doing, created a new political space for the articulation of Muslim interests in the city that had not hitherto existed. The second part of the chapter, which details the co-produced, participatory research with a network of Muslim women in the city, analyses the ways in which Prevent sought to regulate the inclusion of Muslim women in local decision-making. Muslim women were able to influence decision-making structures in mosques to enable them to play a more central role in mosque governance – this phase is termed 'regulating for engagement' by O'Toole. The third part of the chapter examines the post-2011 direction of Prevent, and particularly its focus on mobilising public sector personnel to identify and report signs of extremism, a phase characterised as 'regulation without engagement'. This approach to Prevent becomes regulation without engagement as regulatory practices are narrowed through procedures and systems imposed by consultants, which come into tension with other sets of regulatory and professional norms across those institutions.

In Chapter 4, the focus is on the regulatory practices of research, and the alternative regulatory systems for knowledge production that

Imagining Regulation Differently

**Table 1.1:** Summary of chapters: field of action, key actors, regulatory domains and methods

| Chapter title | Field(s) of action | Key actors | Regulatory system(s) | Methods |
|---|---|---|---|---|
| 3. Beyond Prevent: Muslim engagement in city governance | Cross-cultural cohesion | • Building the Bridge<br>• Mosques<br>• Muslim women network<br>• Prevent compliance | • Anti-terrorism<br>• Community cohesion | • Interviews<br>• Participatory workshops<br>• Participant-observations |
| 4. Regulating for 'care-ful' knowledge production: researching older people, isolation and loneliness | Older people's experience of isolation/loneliness | • Local older people<br>• 3Gs/BS3C<br>• Local cafes as tech cafe | • Knowledge production<br>• Loneliness<br>• Social care<br>• Local authority/health authority well-being/ageing system/s<br>• Digital technology | • Objects, including a tea trolley as boundary object<br>• Interviews<br>• Intergenerational work<br>• Exhibitions and site exchanges<br>• Devised verbatim performance |
| 5. Who gets to decide what's in my fridge? Principles for transforming the 'invisible rules' shaping the regulation of food habits in urban spaces | Food production and consumption | • SPAN/KWMC<br>• Local residents: Easton and Knowle West<br>• Coexist kitchen staff<br>• Pop-up kitchen<br>• Fridge | • Planning regulations on fast-food takeaways<br>• Social enterprise start up and support systems?<br>• Supermarket corporate planning<br>• 'Commoning' as a means to transform food spaces | • Participatory mapping, photography, group walks<br>• Pop-up Somali Kitchen<br>• 'Taste of Knowle West' event<br>• JDPs and fridge as boundary object<br>• Eating/making food together |
| 6. *Life Chances*: thinking with art to generate new understandings of low-income situations | Life on a low income in urban areas | • SPAN and SRCDC<br>• Immigration, Job Centre staff<br>• Homelessness officers<br>• Social workers | • Immigration/asylum<br>• Work/professional standards and qualifications/discrimination at work<br>• Social work practice<br>• Welfare benefits | • Jewellery-making as engagement<br>• Collaborative sociological fiction writing<br>• Collaborative game design<br>• Interviews |

(continued)

**Table 1.1:** Summary of chapters: field of action, key actors, regulatory domains and methods (continued)

| Chapter title | Field(s) of action | Key actors | Regulatory system(s) | Methods |
|---|---|---|---|---|
| 7. The Making, Mapping and Mobilising in Merthyr project: young people, research and arts activisms in a post-industrial place | • Young people's safety in place<br>• Media representations of community | • 3Gs/Forsythia<br>• Youth workers<br>• Young people<br>• Schools<br>• GIS technology<br>• Welsh government<br>• Local councillors<br>• Police<br>• Citizen's Cymru | • Community safety/urban planning<br>• Youth work<br>• School curriculum | • Film-making<br>• Design/craft workshops<br>• Interviews with young people<br>• Zebras campaign as output and generator of change |
| 8. Regulating engagement through dissent | Internal organisational regulation | • Coexist<br>• Tenants of Coexist | • Organisational governance<br>• Security | • Arts practice as research<br>• Film-making |
| 9. The role of community anchor organisations in regulating for engagement in a devolved government setting | Grass-roots community practices in the context of policy shifts and funding | • SRCDC/3Gs<br>• Welsh government<br>• Community development workers | • Government funding of community organisations<br>• Regeneration and poverty reduction policy<br>• Community development practice | • Interviews<br>• Workshops<br>• Ethnography<br>• Monthly feedback<br>• Arts practice as provocation and dissemination |

Notes: 3Gs = 3 Gs Development Trust; BS3C = BS3 Community (formerly Southville Community Development Association); SPAN = Single Parent Action Network; KWMC = Knowle West Media Centre; JDPs = Junior Digital Producers; SRCDC = South Riverside Community Development Centre; GIS = geographic information system.

emerge from collaborative, co-produced research. Manchester and Barke (with the Productive Margins Collective) describe attempts to develop more equitable and inclusive regulatory systems around the production of knowledge concerning the isolation and loneliness of older people, seen from the perspective of two very different communities in Bristol and South Wales. Building on the work of Tronto and Bellacasa, the chapter considers the ethos of care that must be central to knowledge production. They describe the ways in which the researchers sought to turn around the language, realising that loneliness and isolation carried a stigma that focused attention on self-blame and self-help. In contrast, they sought to investigate mutuality and interdependence, both with the natural and built environments, and between citizens. In one site, participants worked with a photographer; in the other, peer researchers used a variety of techniques to contact and interview isolated older people, including taking a tea trolley into public spaces and care homes. The authors make the case for pluralising research outputs: the interview data are transformed into a series of monologues whose performance (by the peer researchers) then created further fields of exploration through dialogue with audiences; participants sought to harness digital space through setting up 'tech cafes' that would support residents to utilise digital technologies to make connections; and they take the monologue performance into the regulatory spaces of policy intervention through a seminar in the Palace of Westminster. The chapter concludes with a text box highlighting the ten elements of 'care-ful' knowledge production.

Chapter 5 considers the regulatory field of food production and consumption through the research question 'Who decides what's in my fridge?', working with residents in two very different locations of Bristol. Residents in an inner-city area with a significant Somali population worked with an artist and social enterprise (Coexist) to co-produce a pop-up Somali kitchen. In so doing, they brought attention to the healthy (and culinary) characteristics of Somali food alongside the problems created by numerous fast-food takeaways in the area. The residents of an outer estate were engaged in the community production of food through growing and foraging, but they ultimately continued to feel that the lack of a supermarket in the area meant that they had very limited access to healthy, affordable food. The chapter therefore reflects on the planning decisions of local government and supermarket corporations, concluding with their own intervention in the regulatory domain of food production and consumption with 'ten principles for the community-led design of urban food systems'.

# Introduction

The Life Chances project, a collaboration between artists Close and Remote, multidisciplinary academics and participants from two urban communities, is the focus of Chapter 6. Here, the project participants co-produced socially engaged artwork to answer the question 'In what ways do regulatory regimes enact, delimit and inhibit the progress of families on low incomes across England and Wales?' Working with ideas of 'utopia as method' (Levitas, 2013), and through 22 workshops that involved jewellery-making, field trips, game design and writing and performing music and poetry, the group produced the *Life Chances* novel, a work of sociological fiction, and the game of Life Chances, which aimed to enable people to experience the stories of characters from the novel as both embodied experience and as a dynamic, performance-based artwork. Along the way, workshops explored the regulatory terrain of social work, and through engaging with a social worker, social work academic and a family lawyer, participants explored understandings of their rights and practices in relation to the care of children. The chapter text box explores the range of social practice methods deployed in the research. The socially engaged arts methods utilised in the chapter offer important insights into the intersectionality of people's experiences with multiple and often punitive regulatory systems of asylum and immigration, housing, social work, and employment.

Chapter 7 charts the twists and turns of the research-engagement project Making, Mapping and Mobilising in Merthyr (otherwise known as the 4M's project). Here, the 4M's team of academics, youth workers and artists worked with the experiences of some of the young people living in Merthyr who have inherited and must navigate multiple, contradictory and imperceptible forms of regulation that come with living in a post-industrial place. This was not a project that held onto predefined research questions, methods or outcomes, but a project that rerouted when events and experiences emerged that required a change of approach. Informed by arts-based, co-produced practices and activist politics, the chapter describes how the team attuned and responded to place-based concerns, and how what comes to matter gathers significance in unpredictable ways. Harnessing what the team call 'runaway methodologies' (see Renold and Ivinson [with Future Matters Collective], 2019) – an approach based on openness, invention and creativity – the experimental arts-based practices seemed to offer multiple possibilities to obstruct, challenge, bend and rewrite the rules in national macro- and local micro-political ways across three projects: the Zebras and Relationships Matters projects, and *Graphic Moves*. The chapter invites readers to glimpse at some of the processes involved in the making and mattering of young people's creations via films, poems and artefacts, and how they continue to act back on the team and wider publics as they infect forums, festivals, meetings and policy agendas with affects that 'cut' their place and their experience together, and apart, differently.

Chapter 8 explores the role of arts practice in opening up spaces of dissent in order to focus on the internal regulation of Coexist, one of the partner organisations in the Productive Margins programme. Coexist was set up as a community interest company (CIC) to manage a derelict former office block in central Bristol, regenerating the building into a functioning community centre as a means to 'co-create spaces that best provide for the communities that surround us'. As an umbrella organisation, it provides space for hundreds of artists, well-being practitioners, a bike charity, a community kitchen and much more. Coexist aims to create spaces where individuals and groups of people can coexist with themselves, with each other and with the environment. However, over time, the growth of the organisation has led to tensions between radical practice and managing the building to provide a secure space for occupants to practise in. The research project sought to foreground dissent as a form of engagement in order to present a new trajectory within the organisation's regulatory processes. The project used street art, social sculpture, film and immersive installations to generate new ways of thinking about regulating for engagement within the organisation.

Chapter 9 focuses on the role of grass-roots community organisations in the context of a devolved Wales, and the Welsh government's focus on citizen participation as the engine for the improvement of public services and social and economic change. The chapter examines the impact of the phasing out of the Welsh government's flagship regeneration programme, Communities First, on the two Welsh community organisations involved in the Productive Margins programme, South Riverside Community Development Centre (SRCDC) (Cardiff) and 3Gs Community Development Trust (3Gs) (Merthyr Tydfil). Communities First was set up in 2001 as a bottom-up vision for tackling poverty through engaging disadvantaged communities in Wales. However, in 2016, the Welsh government deemed the programme to have failed because it was not alleviating poverty, resulting in the end of significant funding to those community organisations involved in the programme throughout Wales. The chapter documents the role that the community organisations – which the authors have termed 'anchor organisations' – played in providing a structure and focal point for local initiatives, acting as a 'champion for local people' and as a safety net, and potentially mitigating the effects of austerity and welfare reform. However, interviews with 'anchor people' show that without a clear regulatory framework *for* engagement, the engagement of anchor organisations can become regulated *by* the state, de-radicalising the nature of their work. The chapter questions the government's narrative of 'failure' that framed their decision to end the programme, showing that the very concept of the programme as one of 'poverty reduction' was misguided, based on the 'bizarre' notion that area-based policies alone could tackle the structural sources of poverty. The chapter concludes with observations that it is public bodies that need to develop expertise and knowledge in regulation for engagement as community development practices and state demands had become in opposition to each other. In the aftermath, SRCDC and 3Gs now find themselves working to resurrect community-based infrastructures.

In the concluding chapter, we seek to build inductively from the findings of the research projects discussed in previous chapters, summarising their collective implications to answer the question: what makes it possible to regulate for engagement? Key to the findings of the whole research programme is that expertise-by-experience is both sidelined and valuable; sidelined by current approaches to regulation; and valuable for redressing the limitations of those approaches documented earlier in this chapter. Here, we argue the need to move towards an organic model of regulation underpinned by a three-fold dynamic process of effective regulation for engagement. This threefold process is constituted by three factors that build upon and support each other: a holistic appreciation of place; the power to reframe the key narrative underpinning a regulatory regime; and the capacity to surface invisible or tacit rules. Together, these three facets challenge the technocratic conceptions of regulation, suggesting instead a much more organic conception of regulation with expertise-by-experience at its heart. The chapter suggests the implications of such a model for regulators and policymakers, and begins to develop a future agenda for research and action that would enable community-derived perspectives on social justice to be at the heart of regulatory practice.

## Talking about regulation

'Regulation' is a term that is seldom used in everyday talk, being generally confined to lawyers, professionals in various regulatory bodies (such as the Financial Services Authority) and scholars of regulation and governance. In this section, we want to contrast the meanings of regulation taken from academic/expert talk with the ways in which it came to be discussed in the research programme.

Given the diverse, sprawling nature of the literature around regulatory systems, which rarely clearly defines 'regulation', those of us who studied the field proposed the following framing as a way of providing some coherence across the programme:

- Regulation attends to process rather than outcomes.
- Regulation is codified (but not necessarily in writing), in that there are shared understandings of the rules of participation and process that are in play.
- Regulation intends behaviour modification. Either directly or indirectly, the purpose of regulating a process is to standardise how it is conducted.
- Regulation engages regulator and regulatee (both have agency) in the process (this gives it a negotiated character).
- Regulation can be facilitative, enabling experimentation and innovation in terms of how things get done.

As the chapters in this book demonstrate, one of the interesting aspects about regulation is its stretch from dealing with profound and acute social problems through to dealing with far more seemingly mundane and routine needs. At the outset, many working on the research programme said that 'regulation' was a term that they seldom used. However, as we progressed, we became more familiar with the term, finding that it frequently cropped up in the Research Forum and working group meetings (though we suspect that we were using it in slightly different ways). In the rest of this section, we draw upon interviews with individual community members and meeting notes of discussions with community organisation staff to demonstrate the different ways in which we approached regulation. The data primarily arise from the two projects discussed in Chapters 5 and 6. In analysing these data, we found that people talk about regulation in three different, but overlapping, modes, each of which contain some of the elements from the academic/expert definition. The facilitative nature of regulation was discussed as regulation as *protective*, providing the possibility for doing certain things. Therefore, here, we might expect talk of rights, as well as of processes that constrain people/organisations from harming others. The second, and dominant, narrative was of the constraining nature of regulation: that regulatory systems have *power over* citizens. Sometimes, this framing led to a third way of talking about regulation: as something to be *disengaged* from.

## Introduction

### *Regulation provides rule-based protection*

In the UK, citizens tend to view regulation as rules that constrain their actions. However, one of the strengths of the Productive Margins research programme was the diversity of experiences that we could draw upon. Some citizens who had come to the UK from other countries would express expectations about UK systems in comparison to previous experiences. Regulation elsewhere could be seen as more formalised: one member of the food project contrasted the UK with Denmark, where they described more regulation around food and the type of food accessible to people. Conversely, regulation elsewhere could be seen as being more 'open', so people with experience of such countries may not expect to find a particular rule, such as needing a driving licence before driving a car, on arriving in the UK. Community organisation workers noted that for those coming from elsewhere, Britain was sometimes perceived as a safe and regulated space in comparison to the countries they had come from. These narratives demonstrate the contextual and socially constructed nature of regulation.

Regulation talk displayed expectations about levels of procedural justice in comparison to home countries. For example, one community member spoke about the police having no record of a call that she had made:

> 'Because I also come from a system where records are not really kept properly, and the system is more than, I would say, you know, regulated … 'perfect' is not the right word, but I would just say that the system in Britain is far higher because there's record keeping, data protection and all this. It's, it's more effective than the system back home, where, you know, records are not really kept up to date, and so if it had happened in [West African country] and a police officer told me 'We have no records', I'd believe him because I know that records are not kept properly, but not here in Britain.' (Community member)

There was some discussion about the need for rules, but also that greater flexibility and discretion should be applied to take account of individual circumstances such as disability, pregnancy and young children. Two individuals who experienced immigration rules had felt that these were too rigid, without scope for personal circumstances to be considered: "yes, they have regulations but, yes, they have to be guided by their policy or something, but sometimes they've got to look at individual cases on their merit" (community member).

For those who encountered social services, the 'rules of the game' were understood as emanating from legislation, city council procedures for their children's services staff and professional discretion. The rules were not always clear to individuals going through the process, but also open to challenge, for example, as to whether community members could audio-record conversations with social workers. Through engaging with teachers of social workers, research participants learned that this was allowed; making rules explicit (rather than tacit) could facilitate a more engaged, equal relationship between social worker and 'client' (discussed further in Chapter 6).

Other narratives picked up the idea that regulation could be more nuanced and that individuals or organisations might have some power to deploy, or engage with, regulations. Some referred to 'social regulation', encompassing other forms of social control such as norms and self-regulation. This perspective recognised that community organisations could also exert some power in relationships with authorities like the local council; rules could sometimes be 'bent', or worked with creatively. Conversely, being unable to 'play the game' with regulators working to a more formal framework of meetings (for example, agendas and minutes) could mean that opportunities for local action were limited or lost.

Even when talking about a narrower understanding of regulation (as rules imposed by government agencies), community organisations indicated that there was scope for them to affect how regulators interacted with them and the individuals they support: they would know the best person to contact on someone's behalf, or by talking 'organisation to organisation', they could hone in on problems more quickly, helping to 'clear the mist' in order to resolve them. Front-line staff administering the mechanics of a particular system were sometimes felt to have more empathy with individuals than policymakers, and would sometimes also 'bend the rules'.

Relationships between community organisations and regulators may also illustrate this perspective. One role that community organisations played was in 'translation' between grass-roots communities and regulators. This could involve facilitating direct conversations between local people and regulators, or a more 'strategic' role with regulators, such as through networking, communications and fostering relationships, taking up opportunities for wider engagement with them. Some suggested that you could learn how to present yourself at meetings and "be useful to them". Such an approach was dependent on personalities but could get you "more ahead of the game than others". This organisation also used local councillors, which could be "muddy, bureaucratic, takes time, but it can happen". Other forms of 'game-playing' could also involve using a powerful third party (such as the university) to give weight and credibility to the organisations' work.

### Regulation as 'power over'

However, despite views that rules could be protective or even facilitative, much formal regulation that emanated from central or local government was seen to "squash people at the bottom". It was a negative, constraining force that could "knock you back": "people get caught in the crossfire of assumptions about what you can do – vice grip of someone saying 'No' rather than 'maybe'. Just closes in around people" (community organisation).

The Life Chances research project (see Chapter 6) set out to explore 'services which regulate everyday lives', such as the local government, Jobcentre Plus, immigration authorities and children's services. Individuals experienced being subjects of surveillance, generating a sense of insecurity: "whatever benefit or reduction the government's giving you they will, to be honest with you, interrogate you" (community member). In some cases, individuals could experience formal regulation from multiple sources, such as those subject to the 'no recourse to public funds' rule applicable to certain people newly arriving in the UK, depending on their immigration status. This rule excludes people from certain publicly funded systems (such as housing and certain social security benefits) while enabling access to others (for example, education). Reflecting concerns about multiple sources of regulation, one community worker said: "there's a whole mixture of half-realised bits of information and half-intended decisions as well, and they all jumble up in the middle of people's lives. If anything, what we work with day in and day out is those tangled complexities". This perspective on regulation – as multiple regulatory systems that become laminated and so impenetrable as to be a dominating power over people's lives – was often linked to the third narrative of feeling disengaged.

### Feeling disengaged from regulatory authority

A dominant narrative in some (but not all) of the communities engaged in this programme was a feeling of being excluded by, or of being very distant from, regulatory decision-making. In one outer-estate locality, a community organisation worker noted that community members often felt "done to". People felt "left behind by the powers that be", with little control over what happens in their community and outsiders making decisions about them without any idea of how they live their lives:

> 'Some of our earlier conversations were about who's the expert in the room? And, actually, there was an expert in the room. It's this whole quite interesting thing, where you get to the Brexit as well, don't you? And they went, "Well, we don't want these bloody experts". So, what does expertise mean?' (Community organisation)

This negative view of formal regulation may itself be a form of local social/cultural regulation; one community worker said that people may also think that change is someone else's responsibility. Such views may have developed from what one community worker described as "cultural habits":

> 'it's also about cultural habits. There's something about taking action and agency that needs to be in there, isn't there? And that's quite provocative. But it's also why neighbourhood partnerships have failed so badly. Okay, one is the gatekeepers around there, but also other people think somebody else is going to do it for them.' (Community organisation)

Some talked of failures of engagement by regulators, where the "usual suspects" or "self-appointed community leaders" became involved but were not perceived to represent the diversity of the community and so themselves became gatekeepers to others getting involved.

One example given was a Neighbourhood Partnership Forum in Bristol. The Localism Act 2011 introduced a new right for communities in England to draw up a neighbourhood plan, such as through a neighbourhood planning forum. In Bristol, before their closure, neighbourhood forums (NFs) used to take place in about 14 different localities across the city.[3] These were public meetings where residents could meet each other, councillors, council officials and other authorities like the police and work on ideas for changing the area. Anyone who lived or worked in the neighbourhood could participate. However as one pair of interviewees said, this was a "top-

# Introduction

down" form of engagement as NFs had little power or money and were susceptible to being run by self-appointed community leaders who were not accountable or who (accidentally or by default) excluded others. The NFs could also become talking shops rather than achieving change. As one community participant stated, their local NF:

> 'got monotonous because it was the same old thing over and over again. They brought people in, consultants, and we worked with them, and talked with them, and it was all supposed to be going brilliant, and nothing since. And that's the trouble. You see, that's what people say. When you say we're going to have a supermarket ... "Oh, heard it all before. Not going to happen. Heard it all before." So, it's very difficult up here, very, very difficult.' (Food group community member)

In another locality, one community worker described this exclusion as people not knowing "how to make regulatory spaces work".

There are different arrangements in Wales, where devolved government has allowed for more clearly prescribed mechanisms for involvement (see Chapter 9). However, these have been criticised as tokenistic, for example, the UN Convention on the Rights of the Child allows young people to have the right to be consulted, but according to community workers, this has not happened in practice. Other community workers noted a change in neighbourhood involvement over time when statutory public service boards[4] in each local authority area replaced earlier voluntary boards. Rather than local problem solving, community workers felt that the emphasis had changed so that there was now less scope for citizen involvement.

In some instances, disengagement looped back into a desire to set up alternative practices in an attempt to distance oneself from unpleasant or confusing regulatory systems. One example was of Somali parents talking about taking their children back to Somalia for a couple of years to get what they perceived as a better education (because teachers are fully responsible for what happens in school), or at least an approach that they understood better. Such a move also had the added attraction of removing their boys from the possibility of getting into gangs. Another example occurred in localities with diverse populations where cultural and community alternatives to regulated financial systems were practised, such as Caribbean 'partner hand' and Somali 'Kimitee' and 'Hegbed'. These were based on trust and family/community connections rather than formal financial regulation:

> 'so, then, my mother and a few of her friends at that particular point had a sort of like a syndicate, what we call a "partner hand" ... so that you wouldn't give your money to a bank. You would sort of like, each person would put in a certain amount and then when it came to their turn, they would get all the money and that's how my mother bought her first property.' (Community member)

In concluding this survey of 'regulation talk' within the research programme, we would make two more general observations. The first is the striking absence in our data of any 'rights talk'. While some specific rights were mentioned (such as the right to education), they tended to be referred to in connection with people not knowing about their rights or how to complain. In some instances, people were regarded as having no rights (such as for benefits for European Economic Area [EEA] nationals). Terms like 'equality' and 'empowerment' tended to be used more in relation to the aspirations for greater equity in the process of co-production in the research programme itself.

The second would be to observe the similarities between everyday talk about regulation and the way in which the academics framed regulation. The previous examples show that regulation is both seen as constraining and offers the possibility of being enabling. This dual aspect of regulation was well articulated by an example brought to the very first meeting of the programme's Research Forum: a map created by the Greater Bedminster Partnership (a partnership of businesses and community organisations in the Greater Bedminster area of South Bristol). The 'Greater Bedminster toilet map' (see Figure 1.1), primarily designed with older people in mind, shows the site of toilets available for public use (as opposed to being exclusive to customers – see the round headed pointers) and the location of benches where it is possible to rest. The intention of the map is to enable older people in the locality to feel that they are able to get out more, making public space more suitable for their needs.

However, the map is not simply an object; in constructing the map, the Greater Bedminster Partnership entered into regulatory practice but without the state (indeed, it was rather a response to the withdrawal of the state as local councils closed public toilets in response to funding crises). As they negotiated with local shop and cafe owners to make

**Figure 1.1:** Greater Bedminster toilet map

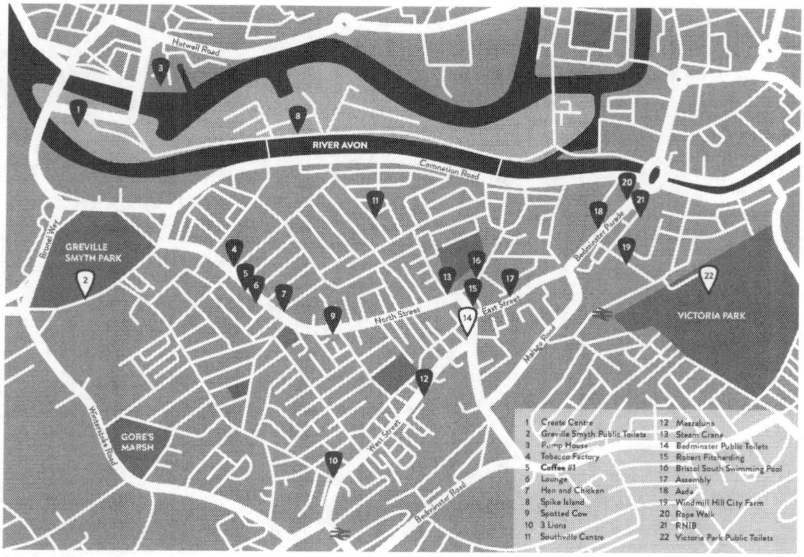

Source: Greater Bedminster Partnership

public use of toilets possible and, importantly, produced a map that would make this visible, the Greater Bedminster Partnership sought to reshape the behaviour of local businesses to become more responsive to the needs of local residents. The map, while not directly coercive, makes visible good (and bad) behaviour, at the same time enabling greater participation in the local area.

## Conclusion

These multiple narratives about regulation appear throughout the following chapters as we describe and analyse the various experiments in seeing regulation differently. These narratives both disrupt and enrich conventional regulation theory, bring in a diversity of voices and experiences, and enable us to look beyond the bounds of institutional practices.

The research programme was designed to present new, practical approaches to university–community collaborative research and to deliver evidence and insights about the conduct of co-production with regard to systems of regulation in contemporary society. By reframing the defining question away from the more orthodox one of 'How do we regulate engagement?', to ask 'How can we regulate *for* engagement?', engagement is no longer a problematic form of social interaction to be controlled and restrained, but rather something that is fundamentally enabling and productive.

We would suggest that, taken together, the following chapters provide three important contributions to our knowledge about how regulatory systems can engage citizens. First, by connecting concepts and practices of co-production and regulation, the multiple and diverse research projects collectively improve our understandings of how co-production engages and integrates specific regulatory mechanisms. This is important as proponents of co-production have hitherto often constructed it in opposition to forms of regulation.

Second, a key contribution of the work is the sheer diversity of settings in which the conduct of regulation and co-production has been empirically studied. Previously empirical work has typically focused upon particular contexts and/or substantive issues. In contrast, our field of vision across multiple situations enables a comparative analysis attentive to highlighting the necessary and sufficient conditions associated with regulations that are co-produced, and co-productions that regulate.

Third, conceptual coherence across this diversity is achieved through the accent upon studying regulation 'from below' in order to understand how it is experienced and received, rather than how it is transmitted and delivered. This opens up a perspective on how those subject to multiple, overlapping regulatory domains can experience it as a stultifying web that restricts and constrains behaviour, rather than encouraging and facilitating it.

## Notes

[1] There is a growing literature on theories and practices of co-production. For an overview of co-production in research, see, for example, Facer and Enright (2016); for an overview of co-production in public services, see, for example, Boyle et al (2010).

[2] 'Community' is a problematic, and overused, term. There are many levels of 'community' involved in this research project. In our practices and writing, we have tried to remain open to this multiplicity, but this is difficult and we recognise that we frequently do not succeed.

[3] In December 2017, Bristol City Council cabinet decided to close NFs.

[4] See: http://gov.wales/topics/improvingservices/public-services-boards/?lang=en

2

# Co-production as experimentation: the research forum as method

*Sue Cohen, Tim Cole, Morag McDermont and Angela Piccini*

## Introduction

> *Experiment*
> NOUN
> *1. A scientific procedure undertaken to make a discovery, test a hypothesis, or demonstrate a known fact.*
> *1.1. A course of action tentatively adopted without being sure of the outcome.*
> Oxford English Dictionary

> *The experimental approach to research is characterised by an interest in learning rather than judging. To treat something as a social experiment is to [be] open to what it has to teach us, very different from the critical task of assessing the ways in which it is good or bad, strong or weak, mainstream or alternative. It recognises that what we are looking at is on its way to being something else and strategises about how to participate in that process of becoming.*
> Gibson–Graham, 2008: 16

In Chapter 1, we described the problem with regulatory systems that self-referentially exclude 'ordinary' citizens from processes of decision-making. We suggested that regulatory systems needed to find ways to bring in 'experts-by-experience' to work alongside technocratic expertise. To produce regulatory systems that are human-centred, we need to find new ways of incorporating the expertise of citizens who experience being regulated on a daily basis, that is, we must work towards the co-design of such systems.

In this chapter, we discuss our experiments in shifting understandings of expertise and in co-producing research that formed the basis of the Productive Margins programme. Those experiments were structured as the Productive Communities Research Forum, a series of gatherings that included all active co-researchers and occurred every three to six months over the lifetime of the Productive Margins programme. Before we discuss this experimental method, we need to ask: who is the 'we' in this chapter? Co-production as a specific set of approaches to collaborative research involves diverse voices. In this chapter, we bring together the Productive Margins principal investigator, community lead, arts and humanities lead, and one of the co-investigators who worked as a link between two projects and the core management group. We have different research interests, forms of expertise, values and standpoints on collaborative working in communities. An example of how these differences can play out was manifested in our development of this chapter, which raised subtle differences in how each of us has been engaging with 'co-production', 'regulation', 'research' and 'experimentation'. Where some of us writing this chapter have come to conclude that 'co-production' has quickly been recuperated by the techno-bureaucratic operations of the academy and we might therefore return to older notions of 'collaboration', others writing this chapter argue that it is precisely the technicity of 'co-production' that catalyses new ways of working with other-than-academic publics. Where some define 'regulation' precisely in terms of structural mechanisms tied to policy objects, others invoke Michel Foucault's understanding of regulation as government, which is developed in his work on biopolitics and governmentality:

> 'Government' did not refer only to political structures or to the management of states; rather, it designated the way in which the conduct of individuals or of groups might be directed – the government of children, of souls, of communities, of the sick. It covered not only the legitimately constituted forms of political or economic subjection but also modes of action, more or less considered and calculated, that were destined to act upon the possibilities of action of other people. To govern, in this sense, is to control the possible field of action of others. (Foucault, 2000 [1982]: 341)

Modes of communication, values, aesthetics and the celebration of co-production itself are clearly regulatory forces in their own right and usefully evidence the importance of affect and emotion in activism and community collaboration (Hochschild, 1979; Anderson and Smith, 2001).

A deep mapping of the myriad definitions and uses of co-production, regulation and research is beyond the scope of this chapter, although these definitions are in evidence throughout this book. We would, however, like to 'stay with the trouble' (Haraway, 2016) that the word 'experiment' suggests. Rather than attempt to settle definitions, this chapter aims to keep those differences live and active in our discussion and, as such, to echo the Forum's processes here, in textual form. The contradiction inherent in definitions of 'experiment' is perhaps useful. It would be reasonable to suggest that an experiment must *either* be a controlled and replicable test that aims to demonstrate a known truth *or* be a course of action undertaken when the outcome is unknown. However, experimentation within the Research Forum both replicated methods and encounters and took courses of action where the outcomes were unknown. The remainder of this chapter discusses this in practice.

## The Productive Communities Research Forum

Research Forum experimentation involved co-producing research questions, methods and outputs with communities at the margins. As a community, the Forum was made up of academics, community organisation workers and the research programme administrators. As a site of experimentation, it was where we collectively identified research projects that could develop regulatory regimes that would engage communities. It was where, in Foucault's terms, fields of action were governed. The Forums had a repeated structure and yet each meeting was unique, with an unknown outcome. The projects that emerged from them arose out of everyday lives rather than from the bureaucratic needs of mainstream institutions. Our methodology of co-production started from two principles: first, that academics and community organisations should be partners not only in the delivery of the research programme, but also in its design; and, second, that new understandings arise when we reflect what we think we know against others who bring to the field different perspectives. The Research Forum was the primary instrument through and with which we looked at the work of the programme 'on its way to being something else' and strategised 'about how to participate in that process of becoming' (Gibson–Graham, 2008: 16).

The Forum first emerged on paper before it was realised in practice. Central to the original research funding application was the idea of a collective space for generating and honing research questions. Somewhat unusually for a research application, we did not begin by defining precisely the sites of investigation or all of the research questions. Instead, there was an intentional space for openness and a process for identifying together what were the important questions to ask. Regular Forum meetings were planned for those conversations among all the members of the project team to take place. The Forum would drive the research agenda and oversee and reflect upon that research. It was much more than an 'advisory group' in that the Forum was intended to comprise all programme participants as an attempt to create a greater equality of partnership.

Over the course of the research, the Forum passed through three broad stages. The first phase was dominated by a year of introductions: of ourselves and the organisations that we were a part of; the range of disciplines and practices across the Forum's membership; and the aims and core programme research focus on regulating for engagement. We adopted a range of methods for this first year. At the opening Forum, we invited members to bring along objects and photographs that were meaningful to them. People brought a wide range of objects, including a model motorbike, a pamphlet celebrating Welsh rugby, a community action plan for Brislington, a photograph from the University of Local Knowledge project in Knowle West and a map of all of the accessible toilets in Bedminster. These performed as 'boundary objects' (Star, 1988, 2010), in other words, as objects with interpretive flexibility, material-structural organising qualities and specific scales. Boundary objects are things that we act with in groups to identify and negotiate our similarities and differences. The objects that we brought with us to the first Forum meeting were used to elicit key themes and concerns held by members and provided entry points for co-investigators to interpret the complex critical-theoretical terrain of regulation at a range of scales.

We intentionally rotated venues around the 'homes' of the different project partners who would host the Forum so as to offer an insight into their worlds. Over the course of the first three Forums, we moved from a large meeting space with views across the city in the University of Bristol, to office and community space in the Gurnos housing estate on the edge of Merthyr Tydfil that is home to the 3Gs Development Trust, and to the farm and kitchens established by Knowle West Media Centre on the urban–rural fringes of South Bristol. As well as getting to know where – quite literally – we were coming from, the Forum meetings in the first year played a key role in finding a common language for the research as the diverse members of the project team came to know – and trust – each other. Key here was identifying a common understanding of co-production. As we discovered, we had different starting premises and assumptions about what it meant. For some, co-production followed Elinor Ostrom's (1996: 1073) definition: 'co-production is a process through which inputs from individuals who are not "in" the same organization are transformed into goods and services'. Others understood co-production in terms of community–university collaboration (Facer and Enright, 2016), as participatory action research (Coghlan and Brydon-Miller, 2014) and as community-based participatory research (see Hall et al, 2015). Although we entered into working together with some understanding of the diverse ways in which all co-investigators understood co-production, these differences shaped – indeed, regulated – the ways in which we understood what it meant for academics and other-than-academics to work together.

This early stage of the Research Forum was challenging for many, both academics and community partners. Many were itching to get started on the actual work of research, and so were keen to settle on precise projects and directing financial resource into on-the-ground working. However, the academic research context had a regulatory force on our working as we needed to use the Forum to develop projects that were guided by robust research questions and methods. In order to get to that stage, emergent groups needed some funding to support meetings and scoping work. Yet, for some, this entailed a certain amount of professional jostling to ensure that their individual and organisational interests were served and to ensure that they could see some return on their investment of time and energy in the process. For other Forum members, there was frustration at the apparent blockage to proceeding to the research project stage, fuelled by an anxiety about timescales and outputs.

A second phase of the Forum began to emerge after a year of meeting together. It was at this point that the Forum moved from being a space for introducing the programme, each other, the places that we come from and the shared language of co-produced research, alongside exploring the research themes of common interest. Now, we began to collectively and actively shape the research agenda. Focusing on the original Productive Margins subthemes of 'harnessing digital spaces', 'mobilising neighbourhoods' and 'spaces for dissent', the second phase of the Forum saw the emergence of clustered interests around poverty, food, resilience and loneliness and isolation. Academic leads for each working group were initially identified, though these changed significantly between this Forum and the eventual confirmation of the projects by the seventh Forum hosted by Coexist at Hamilton House. Over the spring and summer of 2014, the possible working group that focused on resilience fell away and we were left with food, poverty and loneliness and isolation. At this point, we can say that the Forum moved into a third phase.

What is striking is that during the third phase of the Forum, the working groups became the central focus of and energy in the programme. Forum meetings became an opportunity to work productively together in smaller groups but within the shared – and enabling – structural space of the larger group that the Forum represented. It offered a chance for rapid feedback on ideas and the chance to sense-check with the wider group. Moving from the second to the third phase, the locus of power shifted from the Forum having a perceived centralised 'parental' role in distributing money to worthy projects, towards a more distributed structure in which the working groups held the power to direct research and, indeed, to direct the overall direction of the Productive Margins programme.

## Forum methods: conflict and rough consensus

From the outset, Productive Margins sought to embed co-production as both a method of programme management and research design. To that end, the management team invited the different academic and community partners to organise Forums and to use their own facilitation methods to structure the gatherings. The aim was to create a sense of collective ownership and responsibility in order to foster co-production rather than simple engagement, involvement or consultation. It was also to foreground the way in which all attempts at government, even those that are co-produced, involve some form of directing the conduct of individuals or groups (Foucault, 2000 [1982]: 341). Over the nearly 20 Forums that took place between 2013 and 2018, we used a range of methods, including object-based elicitation, mapping, arts-based methods spanning drama workshops to computational art, small group discussions, field trips, collective food making and sharing, fishbowl exercises, presentations, and discussion (see Box 2.1).

Arts-based methods and discussion of artistic practice-as-research generated significant conflict within Forums (see also Douglas, 2018; Pool, 2018). The October 2013 (Knowle West Media Centre, Bristol), March 2014 (Butetown Community Centre, Cardiff), July 2014 (Coexist, Bristol) and January 2015 (Cardiff University, Cardiff) Forums used creative practices as facilitation methods and

# Co-production as experimentation

as subjects for discussion, with mixed results. Productive Margins was committed to the knowledge-producing potential of arts and humanities disciplines and practices alongside the social sciences, and so at the third Forum, we worked with computational artist Matt Olden to experiment with subjecting the regulatory frameworks of the Productive Margins programme itself – its minutes, policies and transcripts of its meetings – to the algorithmic processes of various software packages. For example, earlier Forum transcripts were transformed through automated processes into surrealist poetry. A different approach to creative practice was taken by the Coexist Forum in July 2014, which used crafting (of our own name badges) and drama workshop techniques, such as 'flocking', 'follow the leader' and 'mirroring', as ways to build group dynamics. In other words, in the former event, art itself produced new knowledge about co-production, while at the latter event, art was a method used to facilitate co-production.

---

**Box 2.1: Forum methods**

In addition to our regular methods of small group discussions, brainstorming and reflective reporting via flipcharts and sticky notes, we used a range of qualitative and arts-based methods to facilitate collaboration:

- *Values exercise*: Using structured ethical reflection, based on Brydon-Miller et al (2010), stages of the project are identified (for example, seeking funding, planning activities, communicating) and individuals write on sticky notes the values that they think are most important to the activity (for example, autonomy, transparency, collective responsibility). This exercise helps to manifest commonalities and differences across the group before they become a problem and allows the group to reflect on strategies for managing difference. This is best used at the very start of a project.
- *Object elicitation*: People are asked to bring an object (thing, photograph, text, map and so on) with them to the meeting or workshop that in some way responds to the agenda for the day or expresses their relationship with the group. Using objects can deflect interpersonal issues, provide a way into challenging conversations about group dynamics and effectively express an individual's values, ethics or interests (Willig, 2016).
- *Field trips and residential working*: Taking people out of their everyday working conditions enables us to focus collectively on sites and experiences in ways that mediates clashes of expertise. Two-day residential periods gave the group time-limited spaces in which to focus on writing tasks. While this form of

working requires a budget, it is a cost-effective way to generate a large number of outputs in a concentrated period.

- *Collective making*: From name badges, to lunches, to schematic models of regulation made out of wood and wire, collective making is an established method of facilitating collaborative problem solving. Embodied, material practices with objects, textiles and food present clear examples of pleasurable, radical transformation. If a group can make a salad together, then they can address issues around community food security together.
- *Fishbowl exercise*: The group that has a problem to refine or resolve forms the inner circle. The remaining people form an outer circle and listen to and record the discussions of the first group. The rule is that those in the outer circle can only listen and cannot contribute to the discussion in the inner circle. The inner circle may choose to leave one chair empty so that a person from the outer circle may occupy the chair to contribute a pressing thought, though this is not necessary. Once the inner circle finishes its discussion (lasting 10–30 minutes), the outer circle feeds back to the inner circle what they heard – both as regards content and styles of delivery. This is a useful way to identify problems with group dynamics and to refine the core questions that need addressing. The rule is that those in the inner circle can only listen to and not rebut the outer circle's feedback (Eitington, 1996).
- *Drama exercises*: These are exercises that emphasise group working through elements of echoing movement, for example, flocking, follow the leader and mirroring. There are myriad books with theatre games and drama exercises, as well as online resources (see, for example: http://dbp.theatredance.utexas.edu/teaching_strategies).

---

In other Forums, presentations and discussions about the differences between the role of art in social research to engage, repair and communicate, and the role of art as producing knowledge in itself, raised challenging issues for participants with professional track records in working alongside the arts. Attempts to discuss the differences between uses of art-as-method in the social sciences and art-as-knowledge-producing in the arts and humanities – that is, between art as supplementary to the academic paper as research object and art as the research object in itself – were often productive. University of Bristol Benjamin Meaker Visiting Fellow Sharon Irish, an art historian from the University of Illinois, Urbana-Champagne, brought external expertise in socially engaged art practice to the 2014 Forum in Cardiff; yet, the Forum questioned what they saw as a polarisation between art that is with and for community well-being and art that is both socially engaged and has value as art within an art discourse. Later, a presentation on their initial work for the Regulation project by artists Close and Remote at the November 2016 Cardiff University Forum generated a significant amount of negative response as they attempted to use critical theory as artistic source material rather than following academic conventions of argumentation.

Another site of conflict emerged in those Forums deliberately focused on conflict resolution. Based on the mixed responses of Forum participants to the methods used in the first two Forums in the programme, we decided to work with an external facilitator for the December 2013 workshop at the Single Parent Action Network (SPAN). She used a range of methods to generate productive group discussions; yet, the post-Forum feedback from participants was mixed and while some felt that the Forum began positively, many agreed that it ended negatively and the Forum was somewhat derailed. As the primary objective of the Forums was the co-generation and co-design of individual research projects, it was imperative that the Forum membership address its differences and find ways to move forward in the spirit of 'rough consensus', a term coined in the late 1990s by the Internet Engineering Task Force to enable collaborative, yet pragmatic, decision-making (IETF, 1998).

At the May 2014 Southville Centre Forum, we used a 'fishbowl' approach to support the emerging working group projects in order to identify the areas of their proposed work that needed development and the aspects of their individual and group approaches to collaboration that might impact on their progress. The fishbowl method is used extensively in teaching, management and non-governmental organisation (NGO) conflict resolution (for a history of this method, see Eitington, 1996). Each working group took turns to sit in a circle in the centre of the room, in an open fishbowl – that is, with an additional empty chair. The rest of the Forum sat in an outer circle and engaged in 20 minutes of active listening while the inner circle discussed their projects. If a member in the outer circle wished to contribute, they would enter the centre and sit on the empty chair and then exit once they had contributed. At the end of the 20 minutes, the outer circle then fed back on what they heard and how they heard it in order to develop both the research focus itself and the methods of engagement that the group was using. Critical to this process is the need for the inner circle to listen to the outer circle without speaking back, justifying action and so on. While challenging, fishbowls are successful in other settings. Here, the fishbowl appeared to frustrate some co-investigators who wished to have the opportunity to argue their cases rather than take on board critique while remaining silent.

In short, despite the wide range of methods used, settings and opportunities for different participants to hold and move the agendas forward, the Forums could become mired in the significant differences in values that individuals and organisations held. The tendencies of governmentality could shift the spirit of experimentation away from an open unknowingness towards the illusion of control offered by clear, repeatable structures and situations. Forum participants were, in the main, powerful agents. Some represented communities in their roles as community development workers and there were many organisation directors and former directors in the room, all of whom had a reasonable stake in the distinct ethos of their organisations. There was also a significant and understandable element of competition for resources between organisations.

However, even Forums marked by conflict were productive. The March 2014 Butetown Community Centre Forum was hosted by Nathan Evans and Allan Herbert of South Riverside Community Development Centre (SRCDC). While that Forum was marked by difficult conversations about the role of art in the programme, the Forum also generated the first iteration of the working group projects. The method by which we began to generate the working group projects was a very simple keyword exercise that asked us to brainstorm possible projects from the themes that had emerged so far in the previous Forums. Top-level themes were space, representation, food, isolation, poverty, language, resilience and enterprise. We then added sticky notes to those large themes to explore which could emerge as research projects. By the end of the Forum, the detail of our additional notes pointed towards food, isolation and poverty as the clearest opportunities for co-produced research framed by specific, answerable questions. While some participants were unhappy about the loss of, in particular, space as a focus, it was not possible to frame a specific, achievable research project around that theme, which ended up cross-cutting a number of different projects that we explore in the following chapters.

A year later, we invited Tom Sperlinger (English, Bristol University) and University of Bristol Benjamin Meaker Visiting Fellow Cheryl Siemers (English, University of Alaska Anchorage) to lead the Forum. Tom's background in community-engaged learning and in working in Palestine complemented Cheryl's expertise in Indigenous ways of knowing and her work on community-engaged learning in Alaska. Tom and Cheryl had clear expertise in co-production and in working effectively with diverse communities. Their Forum held in the University of Bristol in March 2015 revisited all the previous events to try to help the group move forward. We told the person beside us in the circle the story of how we became involved in Productive Margins while a 'passions, skills, connections' exercise then enabled us to map what each of us brought into the programme. The results were as diverse as our understandings of co-production and regulation: our passions spanned politics, histories of place, equality, grass-roots transformative learning, legal processes, food and health, play, and families; our skills included social interaction, quantitative research, action research, administration, community development and digital media; and our connections spanned artists, computer scientists, activists, higher education institutes, community organisations, ethnic communities and local government. The next exercise invited participants to move around the room to read and add comments to the posters that the management team had made that summarised the Forums so far, using the Forum reports, photographs and other materials. The two exercises together usefully contextualised the challenges that we experienced in trying to reach even rough consensus on the research questions that would frame our individual projects. The Forum summaries and additions by participants at this event also highlighted how people experienced the same events differently (as well as providing the basis for some of our writing in this chapter).

As we moved into the third phase outlined earlier, methodological innovation gave way to a reporting structure as individual working group projects became more developed. The Forum meetings had served their purpose, which was to co-develop specific, achievable projects in the context of exposure to a wide range of research methods. In the next section, we turn to discuss the role that emotions, values, taste and standpoint played in the Forums and the challenges that we all faced in embodying the theories that inform our work, from Paolo Freire's (2001 [1972]) notion of 'restless, impatient, continuing, hopeful, critical inquiry' to John Law's (2004) advocacy of mess in social science research.

## Values, emotions, embodiedness and standpoints

The initial concept of the Forums recognised that decisions would be informed by opening up challenges rather than closing them down. Challenges often circulated around the strong values, emotions, embodiedness and standpoints that participants brought with them into the Forum setting. Despite the diverse collaborative methods that we employed and attempts to reflect productively on our diversity, it is difficult to identify what we might have done differently. We were clear from the outset that the Forums were going to be messy. Perhaps we needed to identify and acknowledge more directly from the outset the emotions that were both expressed in the room and simmered below the surface. Perhaps we needed to find more effective methods to manifest the Forums as a process of becoming rather than of knowing and to argue for why this was important.

In the first Forum, we were transparent about our ambitions from an emotions- and values-focused position. In an early planning meeting, we agreed to a process that would:

- model a welcoming, relaxing and non-intimidating environment;
- model both the need for structure and the organic nature of the journey ahead;
- model participatory group involvement and individual 'creative' dialogues;
- further empowerment, particularly for those voices that are less likely to be heard/given space, addressing barriers to participation;
- further emotional and intellectual knowledge and awareness of the challenges of group dynamics; and
- consider mixed-mode models of communication, the co-production of knowledge and the use of space, including institutional spaces.

To return to Foucault's sense of government, these ambitions aimed towards a different sense of ordering people's behaviour according to self-described positive values. Here, we imagined, was a space to co-create regulation *for* engagement rather than *for* control. To address those points, we agreed to run the first Forum in a university space in Bristol that was felt to be calm and welcoming, which would be followed by the second Forum in a community space in Wales that exemplified long-standing community–university collaboration and drew on an established infrastructure for the involvement of diverse community members.

The second Forum at Gurnos, Merthyr Tydfil, expressed what sociologist John Law (2003: 3), in his 'post-structuralist detour', describes as the need to not repress mess in the quest for total orderly representation. In both his article on mess (Law, 2003) and book, *After Method: Mess in Social Science Research* (Law, 2004), John Law argues for the need to embrace and account for messiness in our research practices, and we argue that the Forums nicely expressed the irrepressible and uncontainable mess of all encounters. Mess comes from our diverse emotions, values, experiences and standpoints. By the end of the second Forum, the messiness of community tensions came to the surface. We had intended to focus on the role of personal narrative and how that might mirror a theme for the day: the politics of data. Although we had agreed that the day would be hosted, curated and facilitated in a site-specific manner – in other words, that the hosting organisation would take ownership for both the form and content of the day by using their specific community development toolkits with the Productive Margins group – we did not anticipate the emotional journey that this might entail or the specific political contexts being experienced at that time in the community around the organisation and operation of Communities First. From the very outset, the physical journey from Cardiff to Gurnos through the ex-mining communities of the Rhonda Valley, Abercynon and Merthyr Tydfil meant that we revisited the loss of the miners' strike on the valley communities. We then stopped at Aberfan to visit the graves of the 116 children killed by the coal tip that buried their school in the 1966 disaster.

The collective mapping exercise that we had planned was both dialogic and emotional. We began by critiquing the politics of cartography and data, and then set to remapping South Wales and the South-West of England, using a range of hard-copy maps, cutting them up and remixing them to create narrative spaces that spoke to our individual and collective embodied experiences of place. Participants spoke of their personal stories relating to the maps, about their family heritage, displacement, love and loss. For us, this evoked Sue Cohen's (1998: 372) observation: 'I thought as I have in the past how spatially there can appear to be unity, in that space can fix us, but by opening up the fluid boundaries of space we begin to explore more dangerous, unsettling territory'. At the end of the exercise, and with Aberfan still in our minds, we felt unsettled by the politics and ethics of reworking space and place.

After the mapping exercise, we were introduced to a musical developed by Gurnos children, which responded to the politics of iron and steel in the valleys. The undercurrent of loss that began for us at Aberfan and was extended in the mapping exercise was echoed here and, later, in a discussion of how ghost stories hold the pain of bereavement. In a subsequent Forum, we discussed the impact of the miners' strike on present-day communities and considered how grief and 'failed' dissent do not go away, but remain beneath the surface, occasionally manifested. While the literature on the relationships between nostalgia, heritage and place is extensive and beyond the scope of this chapter, it is worth noting that our experiences of this Forum echoed Svetlana Boym's (2001) important work on nostalgia and place, which she highlights as a historical emotion tied explicitly to modern notions of the local and universal. That sense of nostalgia relies on narrative strategies such as storytelling, drama and the tales that tour guides tell us as they show us places. Geographer Mitch Rose (2008) has written specifically about the role of these kinds of performance narratives in the sense-making of place, arguing that those narratives are not separate from or imposed upon place, but are, instead, co-constitutive of place.

Tensions arose through a change of mood. Moving from the earlier part of the day's focus on loss, Bristol's Knowle West Media Centre presented *Whose Data?*, a promotional film about the work of five artists who were commissioned in 2011 to work with live, local data and how it can be used to resist and subvert the powers of the state (see: http://whosedata.net/). Lead artist Dane Watkins and commissioned artists Paul Hurley, Richard Layzell, Julie Myers and Susanne Stahl experimented with comparative weather data, data from the till receipts of local shops, energy consumption, fruit tree locations and ideas of surveillance. The stark differences between the aesthetic values and emotional registers of the children's musical and *Whose Data?* produced tensions in the room, which we filled with assumptions about how others made sense of the different works. However, those emotions were never surfaced explicitly in the Forum and we were left in the heaviness of polite silence. Certainly, there was a tangible restlessness among some of the community members by this stage.

Forum participants then raised the matter of funding and voiced frustration that it had not been addressed earlier. How were they expected to sustain their involvement in the programme without funding beyond support for time spent in meetings? People were tired as they had had to get up early to make the journey. There was friction and a splitting between community organisers and academics. The sum of £500 for seed funding for the initial community participation in developing research ideas was not felt to be adequate to achieve anything meaningful, despite the fact that community participants were remunerated for time spent on the Productive Margins programme. However, adding to the reception of the seed funding as too meagre was a negative reaction to the idea that the Forum would then collectively decide which research ideas should go forward.

Although the rationale was to generate a pool of project ideas from which the strongest could be taken further, this approach to democratic decision-making was seen to run the risk of cutting organisations adrift were their projects not chosen. There was a sense that Productive

Margins might go the way of many research projects: utilising community knowledge while leaving community organisations to flounder in the hostile environment of austerity. Moreover, in the context of politically motivated austerity, how were pressured partners to be expected to retain the staff and volunteers to deliver their part of this slow-moving programme? 'What do we get out of this?' 'What are your motives?' 'Just give us the money and let us get on with it.' The emotional responses of research partners evoked the complex workings of governmentality that constrained ambitions for experimentation.

The Forums might be described as having played out the 'forming, storming, norming and performing' patterns of group dynamics, with the second Forum resonating with the tensions of the 'storming' stage, when differences in power, status, working methods and so on start to surface (Tuckman, 1965). However, the lived experience of the Forums was messier than Tuckman's managerial model. John Law (2003) argues that social science methods tend not to lean towards different and inconsistent realities, but instead to look for clarity and precision, which represses the uncontainable of all social encounters. The idea that things in the world might be fluid, elusive, ambiguous, multiple or unthinkable is not given credence. Although our ambitions for the Forum were well formulated, our methods could not resolve a desire to remain open and experimental with a desire for smooth, non-conflictual collaboration. Law suggests that rather than everything being considered to be present and known, researchers must ask what is being repressed – but how were we to regulate the Forums more knowingly in order to make emotions, values and standpoints manifest productively? Whereas the funding body gave Productive Margins the rare opportunity to make manifest how regulation might be perceived on the margins with some licence to be 'messy', most funding is founded on repressing the mess: 'grant giving bodies all tend to buy into the full package of common sense realism. They don't much care for the vague, the imprecise, the multiple' (Law, 2003: 9). Law (2003: 11) argues for new disciplines of research that acknowledge 'that our methods are always more or less unruly assemblages'.

In the third Forum, Tehseen Noorani presented findings from his initial scoping studies (Noorani, 2013, 2014) and spoke to the question of unruliness. He asked us to anticipate and make use of serendipity – of not knowing what will emerge, seeing the journey as a combination of luck and sagacity, and receptively working together while leaving loose ends. It was at this Forum that the seed for the Alonely project emerged out of what was initially a small desultory group meeting at the end of the day to discuss possible research themes. Furthermore, while some co-investigators at the fourth Forum in Cardiff questioned the assumed need to involve artists in all projects (they were assured that they did not need to), Southville Community Development Association (SCDA) enthusiastically enmeshed theatre in the Alonely research project, which was pivotal to its ensuing success.

Indeed, not all co-investigators were negatively affected by the tensions in the Forum. Rather than feeling alienated by the messiness of the Forum, some people, especially those from the SRCDC in Cardiff, understood and embraced its ambitions. For some, the experimental nature of the Forum was one of the most inspiring aspects of Productive Margins. As Nathan Evans commented at the time: "The Forum creates a natural organic open space, a Petri dish – it's a laboratory for experimentation – multidisciplinary academics, community activists – inspirational – that space allowed for us to come together to start conversations – about children, families and poverty. An incubation space". The experimental nature of the Forums emerged through their repeated format of encouraging hosts to structure and facilitate the days by using their own organisational methods balanced against an open approach in order to encourage unexpected outcomes. While high-risk and highly emotional, the Forums demonstrated that frictions, discomfort and challenging critique can lead to productive work.

We return to Gibson-Graham's (2008: 16) argument that opened this chapter: to adopt an experimental approach in research is to commit to learning rather than judging and to remain open and alert to the possibilities of what we may learn in new and emergent situations. That openness extends to our own understandings of ourselves in the experimental space. We are all hybrids, with multiple identities and interests, and some of us have both research and activist backgrounds (Cohen et al, 2017). We frame things differently depending on the contexts from which we emerge and in which we act. Our hybrid roles, disciplines, standpoints, values, emotions and experiences all came together in the Forums as forms of praxis, in the sense that Nik Theodore (2015) invoked praxis in his University of Bristol seminar on the ethics of co-producing urban research: collective reflection and analysis that collapses the distance between the 'other' and re-imagines the space that divides us in order to suspend hierarchies in the process. On the crucial question of standpoint, which owes a debt to the feminist standpoint theory of scholars such as Sandra Harding (1992) and Nancy Hartsock (2004 [1983]), Theodore argued that we have to stretch and democratise methods by recognising that forgotten places and spaces are also forgotten sites of knowledge. Research ethics demand acknowledging the value of both disruption and *dissensus* while also recognising the ethical responsibilities and values embodied in other-than-academic standpoints (Rancière, 1999; Reed, 2012; Klassen, 2016).

## Conclusion

In this chapter, we have described sites and moments of intensity: fishbowl exercises, cultural appropriations in workshop settings, the group politics of self-regulating eyebrows and concealed frustrations with the ways in which other people work and the values they hold. These were also sites and moments of intense productivity, where new collaborative relationships emerged and stuckness shifted to produce the startlingly new. Over the course of the programme, the Forum changed and shifted. In part, the changes were the inevitable result of changes in personnel over the course of a five-year programme as people and organisations drifted in and out. However, the changes that took place were more than simply the result of the changes in who was present at any one given meeting. Changes emerged from an organic entity, a constant becoming, in the way that Gibson-Graham describes it at the start of this chapter. Most marked was the emergence of three core projects that were birthed out of the Forum, grew up within it and then assumed a dynamism of their own that re-energised the Forum as a site of experimentation with both co-production and regulation.

The Forum was not, however, a centre: it was a middle, a place in which to begin to act. Important questions around forms of expertise and the role of the academic were raised and debated at the heart of our meetings, and, crucially, in hushed tones and snatched chats in the corridors. We worked hard at working through what research is and might look and feel like in a context of universities and communities working together. We explored what was happening at the margins of power and at the margins of the Forum. The Forum was an assembling of actors, processes, emotions and messy non-human elements that, to return to Foucault's (2000 [1982]: 341) sense of governmentality, designate 'the way in which the conduct of individuals or of groups might be directed', and that control the possible fields of action of others. However, that is perhaps to impose an overly specific academic language on the Forum that its diverse participants would not recognise. Part of the challenge of reflecting on the praxis of the Forum is to do so in ways that speak to the lived experiences of its constituents. Perhaps one way of describing the Forum is suggested in Marisol de la Cadena's (2017: 2) work in the Peruvian Andes: 'our conversation became the *shared* site where our worlds also *diverged* as they emerged in/with their constitutive difference. A partial connection par excellence, "our conversation" was the complex site from where [we] felt and thought with [our] friends, even when [we were] doing it alone' (emphases in the original).

Our embrace of experimentation has entailed remaining open to learning, to possibility, to the unknown and to the challenging. The Forum was a site in which we struggled to come together to create a coherent approach to co-production. At the same time, the Forum powerfully reminded all of us that the urgency in our task was to work through questions of regulation collectively and in new ways – ways that could hold differences without the need to represent or resolve. Informing our understanding has been a commitment to the value of interdisciplinary praxis, where praxis has been understood and mobilised differently by all of us in the diverse contexts of Hannah Arendt's (1998) theory of action, a Gramscian sense of embodied, practised theory (Gramsci, 2005) and Paolo Freire's (2001 [1972]) sense outlined in his *Pedagogy of the Oppressed*. Praxis involves all the things that we bring with us into the room – our concepts, standpoints, values, emotions and our own embodiedness that regulate our co-production and produce the limits of our experimentation. While collaboration can be messy and anti-hierarchical, as Jo Freeman (1970) argued in her pioneering essay 'The tyranny of structurelessness', unless individuals and groups within collaborative settings seek to make visible the power structures – their privilege – that they bring into the room with them, then claims to democracy are naive at best. Making transparent the means by which collective responsibility can enable the productive exploration of differences is, therefore, necessary.

Yet, as public administration scholars Ann Marie Thomson and James L. Perry (2006) discuss, those processes of collaboration can be a Latourian 'black box'. When sociologist Bruno Latour writes of the black box in *Science in Action* (Latour, 1987) and *Pandora's Hope: Essays on the Reality of Science Studies* (Latour, 1999), he is referring to the ways in which work is made invisible through its performance. When collaboration and co-production are seen as inherently positive, democratic methods, without close description of the means by which they are undertaken, co-production becomes a black box and can mask the power structures that Freeman (1970) raises. Thomson and Perry draw on Donna Wood and Barbara Gray's synthesis (1991) of multidisciplinary approaches to collaboration in order to highlight the antecedents, processes and outcomes of successful collaboration.

# Co-production as experimentation

They agree that there remains a significant gap in understanding the interactive processes of collaboration (Wood and Gray, 1991: 21). They point to the ways in which high levels of interdependence, a need for resources, previous histories of collaboration and complex issues join with processes of mutuality, autonomy and organisational independence to enable self-governing collective action that achieves goals and embeds relationships. The antecedents, processes and outcomes that Thomson and Perry schematise echo our experiences in the Forums discussed in this chapter.

What would we do differently if we were to do all of this again? How might our findings be used to model a future project? There is no single answer to this, though we might suggest that co-production projects spend more, rather than less, time at the beginning in order to keep the spaces open for the different ways in which language is mobilised by individuals and organisations. Projects need to embed practical reflexive processes such as journaling that are shared back to the group. Collaborators need to build in strategies for holding difference without rushing towards mediation or amelioration. We also strongly suggest that first meetings involve values-mapping exercises so that a group understands what motivates its individuals to take part. Moreover, projects need the courage to not shy away from open discussions about money and power. Who holds the budgets? What are the regulatory constraints, and why? It is vital to not pretend to have a flat, structureless project when the budget-holding institutions are themselves hierarchical. The Forum process that we have discussed in this chapter highlights the considerable challenges of co-production. The power and politics at play in meeting spaces manifested the agency that community organisations always-already possess, which is an important corrective to notions of 'giving voice' to communities. While the Forum showed that agency is distributed in complex ways, it raised important questions about whose voices are really heard and listened to. In the chapters that follow in this volume, readers can begin to trace the diverse journeys that projects took and consider how these might be mapped back to the ways in which the Forum operated as a space of government, a site of experimentation and a shared space in which worlds diverged as they emerged in the collective work of difference.

INTERLUDE

# Community researchers and community researcher training

*Helen Thomas-Hughes*

## Background: community researchers in the Productive Margins programme

The role of community researchers within the projects of Productive Margins was envisaged at the earliest stages of programme development. This vision was driven, in part, by the expert experience of one of the partner organisations who had previously led a longitudinal qualitative research project in which the fieldwork was primarily conducted by community researchers. It was also informed by the programme's founding understanding: that people and communities have expertise, experience and creativity that can catalyse new spaces for engagement in and the redesign of regulatory regimes. This echoed a wider trend towards the inclusion of community or 'peer' researchers within co-produced research processes, recognising that community researchers are, in many ways, a practical example of co-production's attempt to radically redistribute power within the research process.

## Who are community researchers?

Community researchers are typically people without any prior recognised research training, with minimal knowledge or experience of research, and who are also 'peers' to a project's research participants, sharing at least one 'lived experience'. Community researchers tend to be community members, and they are distinct from the community partner organisations that are co-producing a project. The roles and responsibilities of community researchers within research projects shift substantially across contexts. Community researchers can be paid employees of an organisation or university, but most are community members who work on a voluntary basis, receiving some alternative form of remuneration for contributed time. In some cases, community researchers are partners in all facets of a research project and are members of the core research team. In the majority, however, they are instrumental in one or more specific aspects of fieldwork or recruitment, or in consulting/reviewing project design, data and findings in a more advisory capacity.

Community researchers' status as community members locates them in close personal proximity to people whom policymakers often characterise as 'hard to reach'. In the literature (see the 'Further reading' section), community researchers are said to: minimise power differentials between academic researchers and communities who have been marginalised or stigmatised by previous research; reduce 'blind spots' experienced by researchers who are at a distance from the realities that they are studying; and produce findings that are more applicable to community contexts. However, community researchers also often negotiate complex dualities whereby they are situated as advocates and representatives of the communities to which they are members as well as researchers. As such, they need to navigate complex moral and ethical dilemmas around their own identities and positionalities in relation to the communities that they are researching, for example: finding themselves wanting to present overtly positive images of communities that typically experience stigma; finding that their dual roles shape the scope and type of data obtained; and encountering community members reluctant to engage with them due to concerns about confidentiality and the risk of 'gossip'. Ultimately, the way in which community researchers negotiate their positionality within a research process can significantly impact on the quality, integrity and 'usefulness' of the data collected, and this means that attention needs to be paid to the support and training that is put in place for community researchers within co-produced research projects.

## Training and support for community researchers: reflections from the research programme

Community researchers played a significant role in three of the research projects in the Productive Margins programme. Furthermore, the support, training and development of community researchers was the focus of several spin-off research activities, including co-designing and delivering research training with a localised community research team as part of the Easton & Lawrence Hill Neighbourhood Partnership, and convening national conversations with community researchers from a range of research programmes.

Community researchers' roles within projects were generally oriented around carrying out an element of fieldwork, with community researchers recruited from community organisations' existing or target clientele and then offered training and support to take part as active on-the-ground researchers. This meant that training spaces were typically the primary site whereby community researchers could connect with the wider project and team. As such, training became an important site for co-production. Alongside receiving tailored methods-based training and support and guidance in conducting research, community researchers could draw on their experiential knowledge and expertise to collectively develop new perspectives on and ideas for the direction and activity of projects that could then be fed back to the project team through the researchers or community organisation.

In each project, research training was co-designed iteratively between an academic research 'trainer' and the organisation hosting the community researcher team. This meant that training was designed both to fit with the normative practices of the organisation, and to be responsive to the motivations, interests and expertise of the community researcher team. For example, the team of community researchers working on 'Who decides what's in my fridge?' (see Chapter 5) came together through a Somali Women's lunch club hosted at one of the partner organisations. Training was delivered in weekly three-hour workshops, followed by the lunch club's normal shared lunch. During shared lunches, the trainer would join the community researchers in a conversation space that aimed to reflect on and develop the content of training and hone the project's focus through the community researchers' experiential expertise. Practically, the training had been designed to accommodate the variable literacy and language skills across the team and so was discursive and interactive, with a focus on practical skills engaged with through role play.

Across projects, training aimed to create a space that would imbue community researchers with the confidence and expertise needed to conduct research activities, equipping them with the reflexive skills that would enable them to negotiate their unique positionality within the process and undertake research ethically while also foregrounding the epistemological value that community researchers' 'personal subject area expertise' brings to a research project. Training had to be situated carefully, recognising the inherent contradiction between co-production's aim to destabilise academia as the privileged site for the production and dissemination of knowledge through acknowledging differentiated experiences and expertise, and the delivery of training which demands that someone with a formal academic background teaches community members so that they can take part in research appropriately. There was a recognised risk that training could become a space that inscribed new forms of 'dominant power relations', exacerbating some of the paradoxes of power and representation that are known to arise in co-produced research.

The experience of co-producing training for community researchers within the Productive Margins programme led to the development of a guidance structure for future training packages (see Thomas-Hughes and Barke, 2018) which argues that training should be grounded in theories of co-production, in principles of andragogy and in reflexive practices. Andragogy principles advocate learning environments that draw on the life experience of adult learners, take a problem-solving approach and situate responsibility for learning in the hands of the adult learner. Reflexive practices extend the life-experience approach to examine the hybridity of community researchers' insider/outsider positions, and enable community researchers to consciously operationalise their perspectives, experiences and emotions within the research process and field.

Emerging from the work of Productive Margins, there is an aspiration that future training for community researchers might cultivate sites of mutual co-learning, where reflexive accounting is put to work through animating the everyday, professional and academic experiences of community researchers, research trainers and project-based researchers to shape the teaching of research-specific skills in ways that inform new intellectual perspectives and modes of research practice. In this way, training for community researchers has the potential to form part of an infrastructure that is flexible enough to create spaces for 'public learning' through which communities and civil society groups might develop the skills and knowledge to tell their own stories and share their own histories on a public stage. Such training might enable communities to reframe issues and concerns, and experiment with new solutions that can then be translated into other places, spaces and networks. Training for community researchers can be a tangible embodiment of a commitment to lifelong learning as a fundamental principle in the transformation of society. In this way, we hope that an increased focus on training for community researchers might open up access to established forms of education in ways that transform and re-imagine traditional university boundaries.

## Further reading

Barke, J. (2016) 'Isolation and loneliness of older people: coproducing research with community researchers', University of Bristol. Available at: www.productivemargins.ac.uk/files/2017/02/Alonely-Report. pdf

Barke, J. (2017) 'Community-based research and approaches to loneliness prevention', *Working with Older People*, 21(2): 115–23.

Bell, D.M. and Pahl, K. (2018) 'Co-production: towards a utopian approach', *International Journal of Social Research Methodology*, 21(1): 105–17.

Devotta, K., Woodhall-Melnik, J., Pedersen, C., Wendaferew, A., Dowbor, T.P., Guilcher, S.J. and Matheson, F.I. (2016) 'Enriching qualitative research by engaging peer interviewers: a case study', *Qualitative Research*, 16(6): 1–20.

Dwyer, S.C. and Buckle, J.L. (2009) 'The space between: on being an insider-outsider in qualitative research', *International Journal of Qualitative Methods*, 8: 54–63.

Easton & Lawrence Hill Neighbourhood Partnership (2017) 'Understanding wellbeing through community research in Easton and Lawrence Hill'. Available at: https://upourstreet.org.uk/sites/default/files/project/files/Understanding%20wellbeing%20through%20community%20research%20in%20Easton%20and%20Lawrence%20Hill%20-%20March%202017%20(web).pdf (accessed 11 June 2018).

Flicker, S., Roche, B. and Guta, A. (2010) *Peer Research in Action III: Ethical Issues*, Community Based Research Working Paper Series, Toronto, Ontario, Canada: Wellesley Institute.

Garnett, S.T., Crowley, G.M., Hunter-Xenie, H., Kozanayi, W., Sithole, B., Palmer, C., Southgate, R. and Zander, K.K. (2009) 'Transformative knowledge transfer through empowering and paying community researchers', *Biotropica*, 41(5): 571–7.

Mosavel, M., Ahmed, R., Daniels, D. and Simon, C. (2011) 'Community researchers conducting health disparities research: ethical and other insights from fieldwork journaling', *Social Science & Medicine*, 73: 145–52.

Ryan, L., Kofman, E. and Aaron, P. (2011) 'Insiders and outsiders: working with peer researchers in researching Muslim communities', *International Journal of Social Research Methodology*, 14(1): 49–60.

Sperlinger, T., McLellen, J. and Pettigrew, R. (2018) *Who are Universities For? Re-making Higher Education*, Bristol: Short Insights.

Thomas-Hughes, H. (2018a) *Critical Conversations with Community Researchers – Making Co-production Happen?*, Bristol: University of Bristol and AHRC Connected Communities. Available at: https://connected-communities.org/wp-content/uploads/2018/02/Critical-Conversations-Final.pdf

Thomas-Hughes, H. (2018b) 'Ethical "mess" in co-produced research: reflections from a UK-based case study', *International Journal of Social Research Methodology*, 21(2): 231–42.

Thomas-Hughes, H. and Barke, J. (2018) 'Community researchers and community researcher training: reflections from the UK's Productive Margin's: Regulating for Engagement programme', Bristol Law Research Paper Series, ISSN 2515-897X.

# 3

# Beyond Prevent: Muslim engagement in city governance

*Therese O'Toole*

## Introduction

This chapter examines the Prevent strand of the government's counterterrorism strategy as a form of regulation, exploring its evolving local reception and implementation over the period from the New Labour to the Conservative-led Coalition governments. Launched in 2007 by New Labour as a community engagement, 'hearts and minds' approach to countering violent extremism, Prevent set out to partner and engage with Muslim communities to address the causes of radicalisation. In its 2007 guise, this involved locally focused Muslim community engagement projects. That approach was widely criticised for the limited offer of engagement that it seemed to present and was beset by allegations that Prevent was a means by which the government sought to achieve the mass surveillance of British Muslims (Kundnani, 2009). A body of academic literature emerged analysing Prevent as an attempt to 'discipline' British Muslims through interventions in Muslim civil society and religious organisation (Heath-Kelly, 2013). It is possible, then, to see Prevent as exemplary of the more problematic aspects of regulation – as a top-down, coercive, disciplinary regime. In this chapter, I analyse what the offer of engagement to Muslim communities through Prevent entailed and how, once instituted, it played out at the local level through a presentation of findings from the Productive Margins project on Muslim civic engagement in Bristol.

I argue that it is important to consider the effects of regulation in ways that go beyond consideration of the aims and logics of regulatory systems, to analysing carefully the nature and implications of regulation in practice. This requires taking account of the contexts in which regulation is introduced and the agency of various actors who come into contact with regulatory systems. Taking this approach also reveals the pluralistic nature of regulatory landscapes in which regulatory systems do not always or necessarily form a cohesive regulatory regime.

I analyse the regulatory implications of Prevent through three phases of the research project. The first phase was based on a case study of the implementation body for Prevent in Bristol – Building the Bridge. Drawing on the data from this case study, I explore Bristol's approach to implementing Prevent in practice. I show that in Bristol, the top-down character of Prevent gave way to a more bottom-up approach that departed in significant ways from its original design. In so doing, it created a new political space for the articulation of Muslim interests in the city that had not hitherto existed (Lewicki et al, 2014). The case study contributes to findings that in its 2007–11 phase, the implementation of Prevent was subject to local variation and innovation (O'Toole et al, 2013, 2016).

The second phase of the research involved co-produced, participatory research with Muslim women involved in Building the Bridge and from across the city. Drawing on this work, I consider the focus on gender equality and empowering Muslim women, which were key objectives of much Prevent activity in its pre-2011 (and, to some extent, post-2011) phase. I analyse the ways in which Prevent sought to regulate the inclusion of Muslim women in local decision-making. While many women were critical of engagement through the rubric of Prevent, many nonetheless took up opportunities for 'empowerment' as a means of articulating their critique of the exclusion of Muslim women – in both secular civic and religious community spaces.

The third and final phase of the research examined the post-2011 direction of Prevent under the Conservative-led Coalition government, and its focus on mobilising public sector personnel to identify and report on signs of extremism, which became a statutory public sector duty with the passing of the Counter-Terrorism and Security Act 2015 (CTSA). Research in this phase comprised the analysis of documents on Prevent implementation and interviews with public sector personnel involved in the implementation of the Prevent duty. In contrast to the emphasis on partnering and engagement with Muslim communities (however problematic) that characterised Prevent in the period 2007–10, the post-2011 approach can be characterised as regulation without engagement. However, I suggest that this approach to Prevent poses regulatory difficulties in the ways in which its implementation as a statutory duty across a number of public sector institutions brings it into tension with other sets of regulatory and professional norms across those institutions.

## Regulating through Prevent

Prevent is one element of the UK government's evolving counterterrorism strategy (CONTEST) that was developed in 2003. Prevent was publicly relaunched under New Labour in 2007 with the publication of the policy document *Preventing Violent Extremism: Winning Hearts and Minds* (DCLG, 2007a). The 2007 policy set out a community engagement approach to preventing terrorism based on four key strands: 'promoting shared values, supporting local solutions, building civic capacity and leadership and strengthening the role of faith institutions and leaders' (DCLG, 2007a: 5). To achieve these objectives, it placed an emphasis on local authorities' role in implementing Prevent. Implementation at the local level was conducted through partnering with Muslim communities and typically coordinated through local strategic multi-agency partnerships.

Black (2002) points to the variety of ways in which states seek to achieve regulation that go beyond 'command and control'-style governing and formal legal instruments, and include the use of administrative mechanisms of 'standard setting, information-gathering and behaviour modification' (Black, 2002: 26). Deploying such formal legal and administrative mechanisms, through the Prevent agenda, the government sought to counter violent extremism through the regulation of Muslims *as a whole*.

For example, in determining where Prevent resources should be directed, the government designated areas with significant Muslim populations – initially specified as 5,000 or more – as Prevent Priority Areas. In so doing, it constituted Muslim presence itself as a security risk (see also Holmwood and O'Toole, 2017: ch 2). Under this logic, with an estimated population of 30,000 Muslims, Bristol was identified as a Prevent Priority Area. Prevent also involved regulatory interventions across Muslim religious and civic practices and organisation. For instance, the government sought to reconfigure forms of Muslim religious authority and organisation through its support for the establishment of the Mosques and Imams National Advisory Board (MINAB) in order to set standards for a UK-based system of mosque regulation. It attempted to promote 'moderate' forms of Islam, for example, by funding the Radical Middle Way project, a scholars' roadshow and set of resources promoting a theological alternative to al-Qaeda's account of Islam. There were also attempts to reconfigure Muslim civic representation, bypassing existing structures of Muslim representation, with the establishment by the government of the National Muslim Women's Advisory Group and

Young Muslims Advisory Group in 2008. Information gathering was a key administrative function imposed on local authorities by National Indicator 35 (NI35) – the government's performance management framework to monitor local authorities' progress in 'building resilience to violent extremism'. Significantly, NI35 monitored not just local authorities' 'knowledge and understanding of the drivers of violent extremism', but also their 'understanding of and engagement with Muslim communities' more generally. Ultimately, as the Department for Communities and Local Government's (DCLG's) Prevent guidance stated – and notwithstanding its acknowledgement that it was 'a tiny minority who oppose tolerance and diversity' (DCLG, 2007b: 1) – a 'key measure of [Prevent's] success will be demonstrable changes in attitudes among Muslims' (DCLG, 2007b: 7).

A body of critical academic literature subsequently emerged analysing Prevent as a form of disciplinary regime, highlighting the governing techniques that sought to know and regulate British Muslims in order to render terrorism pre-emptively governable. Heath-Kelly (2013) argues that this form of governance was enabled by constituting Muslims as both 'risky', that is, posing a security threat, and 'at risk', that is, vulnerable to radicalisation and requiring intervention (see also Mythen and Walklate, 2016). Under this logic, increasing areas of Muslim civil, cultural, social and religious life were brought within the parameters of security governance (Heath-Kelly, 2013; Martin, 2014).

Literatures on both regulation and governance from the early 2000s onwards highlight tendencies towards decentring and fragmentation which meant that states became increasingly dependent on a range of different agencies and actors to regulate or govern. Black (2001: 107), for instance, identifies a decentring of regulation that is driven by the complexity of social problems and the acknowledgement that 'no single actor has all the knowledge required to solve complex, diverse, and dynamic problems'. Consequently, the 'government does not have a monopoly on the exercise of power and control' (Black, 2001: 108) and is reliant on other actors and networks to achieve regulation. Similarly, Bevir's (2016) account of decentred governance highlights the emergence of networks of governance created through vertical and horizontal coordination between different agencies and actors for the purposes of policy development and implementation (see also Bang, 2003; Griggs et al, 2014) – particularly to address so-called 'wicked' policy problems. The implementation of Prevent – under the New Labour government – reflected these broader tendencies to govern through networks and partnerships, rather than to rely on bureaucratic expertise alone or vertically integrated 'command and control' forms of governing. This approach was broadly consonant with New Labour's Third Way communitarian approach to governing that sought to mobilise third sector actors into governing networks and partnerships (see Newman, 2001; O'Toole et al, 2012). In Bristol, such partnering and coordination were achieved through Building the Bridge – a multi-agency community forum comprising local authority, police and other personnel from local statutory agencies, along with Muslim participants. As I discuss later, the structure that the Prevent implementation body took in Bristol was distinctive relative to how it was configured elsewhere.

However, one consequence of the tendency to govern through networks is that while the state may aspire to regulate whole populations, this tends to be much less cohesive in practice – not least because it is conducted within a heterogeneous field of governance actors, domains and norms, and is subject to 'conflicting beliefs, competing traditions, and varied dilemmas [resulting] in diverse practices' (Bevir, 2016: 232). Consequently, Bevir (2016: 234) argues, governance becomes a site of struggle, 'not just between strategic elites, but between all kinds of actors with different views and ideals reached against the background of different traditions'. Similarly, Black (2001) points out, the reliance of governors on various actors, forms of expertise and networks means that regulation is subject to unintended consequences. As Bevir (2016: 227) makes clear, just as with other policy fields, this is also true of security governance, which reflects 'the many cultures and traditions through which civil servants, street-level bureaucrats, voluntary sector actors, and citizens interpret and resist joined-up security'. Taking this approach opens up the possibility that actors may comply with, adapt to, appropriate or resist policy agendas. Indeed, fairly soon after its inception, Prevent came to be widely criticised for its focus on Muslims and the limited and securitised nature of engagement conducted under the rubric of counterterrorism by Muslim civil society organisations – the putative partners in the implementation of Prevent. Consequently, many Muslim actors simply refused to participate in Prevent, limiting the achievement of its objectives in many areas (Birt, 2009; Khan, 2009; O'Toole et al, 2016).

O'Toole et al (2016) elsewhere argued that Prevent should be viewed as both state regulation *and* contested practice. In this chapter, I show that notwithstanding the limited nature of engagement through Prevent, the relative autonomy given to local actors in the 2007–10 phase enabled the creation of a new political opportunity structure in Bristol that had not hitherto existed. In that phase, the empowerment of Muslim women, while founded on a model of engagement that essentially sought to co-opt rather than empower women, gave women some leverage to enact autonomous political objectives. In the post-2011 phase, Prevent has shifted away from engagement with Muslim communities to mobilising front-line public sector personnel to regulate Muslims through forms of 'sous-veillance' (surveillance from below), reflecting a broader tendency towards more centralised forms of governing on the part of the Conservative-led Coalition government. However, this shift towards more centralised forms of monitoring and regulation has taken place in a context of overlapping regulatory systems and approaches, which has created tensions in the implementation of the Prevent duty.

## Study

The research on which this chapter is based was conducted within the Productive Margins programme of research, which set out to explore the impact of regulatory systems on communities' engagement with decision-making. This project set out to explore the local implementation of Prevent – as a form of regulation – in Bristol and its implications for Muslim civic engagement in the city. The study involved a team of three academic researchers (O'Toole, Modood and Lewicki) working collaboratively with Muslim participants of Building the Bridge to co-design the research, which evolved into three phases.

The first phase investigated the implementation of Prevent in Bristol, which was enacted through the creation of Building the Bridge, a civic forum comprising representatives from Bristol City Council, the Police, statutory and voluntary agencies, and Bristol's Muslim communities. Based on 22 qualitative interviews with key participants involved in Building the Bridge, the study explored how the forum developed, as well as its achievements, challenges and trajectories (see Lewicki et al, 2014).

The second phase of the research focused on Muslim women's engagement in decision-making in the city. The research team collaborated with a specially constituted steering group of 16 Muslim women participants drawn from the membership of Building the Bridge, and included community, faith and student activists concerned with Muslim women's inclusion in decision-making structures. This phase involved co-produced research investigating how spaces for Muslim women's engagement might be made more effective, including a launch event with four prominent Muslim women speakers,[1] eight workshops with 70 Muslim women from across the city, a co-produced short film (*What Do You See?*), a participatory arts project (*Paper City*), an exhibition (*Bristol Big Sisters*), a dissemination conference and a policy briefing co-authored by members of the steering group (Aabe et al, 2015).

The third phase was based on documentary research on the changes to Prevent following the publication of the revised 2011 Prevent strategy and its implications. With the introduction of Prevent as a public sector duty in 2015, this led to the proliferation of regulatory obligations and guidance issued across public sector domains to ensure compliance with the Prevent duty. Here, I explore the forms of hard and soft regulation that emerge from the corpus of guidelines, self-assessment, risk assessment, compliance checklists and reporting templates that are generated by government and private providers. I explore what the documents say and *do* (Prior, 2008) based on an analysis of this corpus and qualitative interviews with six public sector personnel charged with implementing the Prevent duty.

## Regulation through Prevent: Building the Bridge

In 2008, Bristol City Council and Avon and Somerset Police held a series of meetings and a community conference with local Muslims to discuss the implementation of Prevent in Bristol. Following the logics of Prevent in that period, the meetings set out to engage Muslims in Bristol in the local delivery of Prevent. Muslim participants were, however, critical of the terms of engagement of these meetings, pointing to the limited range of Muslim participants present at the meetings, the lack of opportunity for Muslim participants to shape the agenda, the negative connotations of the term 'Prevent' itself and the ways in which its city-wide implementation cast the Muslim community as a whole as prone to terrorism. As a senior police officer recalling one of those meetings told us in an interview, they encountered:

> 'a confident community, which is great, and lots of energy and people turning up, which was, for a community meeting, very, very unusual ... and there was a huge amount of sensitivity; I was really surprised about the sensitivity there was.... I was really quite taken aback at that meeting; I suppose there were a ballpark figure of 50 people in the audience, mostly from Muslim communities, and they gave us a really hard time.'

Subsequently, a number of changes were made to the approach to implementing Prevent in Bristol. These included renaming and reconstituting Prevent with the creation of 'Building the Bridge' as a hybrid multi-agency–community forum in order to distance it from the negative associations with Prevent and to reconfigure the structure to enable Muslim input into its aims and implementation. The latter was achieved through the creation of a Partnership Advisory Group (PAG) comprising a range of Muslim participants in order to include different Muslim voices in the forum and to enshrine the agenda-setting powers of Muslim members. The PAG advised, and set the agenda for, the Building the Bridge delivery board, which comprised personnel from Bristol City Council, Avon and Somerset Police, other agencies from the Local Strategic Partnership and Muslim representatives. The delivery board was furthermore headed by a Muslim chair and vice-chair, both of whom were elected by local Muslim communities and also sat on the PAG.[2] This structure was different to how Prevent was delivered elsewhere – notably, in the chairing and agenda-setting role of Muslim participants (see O'Toole et al, 2013). It was also a relatively new way of working for the statutory agencies involved, as one senior police officer told us:

> 'There was real nervousness from my own Special Branch, who were saying, "Hang on a sec; we can't be doing this. We can't let communities lead this work".… And you had nervousness from some of the leaders in the local authority, lots of them giving lots of support, but saying, "Well, no, you can't have groups like this being led by members of the community. What happens if it's the wrong member of the community who gets to lead it?"'

Nonetheless, he argued that if they wanted "this to be successful, then it's got to come from within the community", arguing that cooperation "can't be centrally government driven if communities don't feel like they've had a say in it", and that it needed to be based on "a partnership right from the beginning, as opposed to something that was being police-led". The importance of community buy-in to regulators exemplifies Black's (2001: 123) contention that analyses of regulation must attend to 'issues of complexity, the fragmentation and construction of knowledge, the fragmentation of the exercise of power and control, autonomy, and interactions and interdependencies'. The increasing emphasis on the co-production of regulation exemplifies these complexities and interdependencies.

As O'Toole et al's (2013, 2016) research shows, between 2007 and 2010, some local authorities reinterpreted or modified Prevent, using the funding that it released to pursue community engagement or cohesion objectives. In part, this was due to the relative openness of the policy guidance from central government, but it was also a result of local actors seeking either to mitigate the negative aspects of Prevent or to pursue more autonomous objectives or develop models that were more appropriate to local contexts. Importantly, many local authorities were mindful that engagement with Muslims for the purposes of Prevent could also have implications for their engagement with other policy agendas, such as community cohesion, which also relied on Muslim community engagement.

Once in place, Building the Bridge focused on a range of issues, some of which were driven by the Prevent agenda, such as creating community-led systems of reporting concerns about radicalisation and educational projects to 'challenge extremist ideology and support mainstream voices'. It also enabled a critical feedback loop on particular policing practices that affected Muslims, such as the operation of Schedule 7 policing powers, which had been introduced under the Terrorism Act 2000 and gave police the power to stop, question, detain or search a person in a border area – including ports and airports – if they consider that the person 'is or has been concerned in the commission, preparation or instigation of acts of terrorism'.[3] The use of Schedule 7 powers had been a source of grievance (Blackwood et al, 2012), with Muslim travellers complaining of being routinely subjected to prolonged and intrusive questioning and delays when arriving at Bristol airport, while the use of body-image scanners raised concerns for some about modesty. These issues were raised through Building the Bridge and resulted in a negotiation with the police over how Section 7 stops should be conducted at Bristol airport, including establishing the need to provide explanations to those being stopped, and that questions about reasons for travel and mosque attendance were inappropriate. At times, Building the Bridge's agenda also went beyond narrowly Prevent concerns to address other issues affecting Muslims in the city, such as the effect of marches by the English Defence League (EDL) on local communities, the lack of provision for Muslim burial in the city and the policing of traffic around mosques during Friday prayers.

The deputy chair characterised the role of Muslim representatives in the following way:

'I think the council was just providing support and advice really – not making decisions about anything in the board. We set the agenda, we set the priorities, we set the activities, we worked with community organisations to develop their own projects, so I think we were in charge in that period.'

In a context where there were relatively few existing mechanisms for black and minority ethnic representation in the city (Bousetta, 2001), the creation of Building the Bridge created a new political opportunity structure that had not hitherto existed and enabled the organisation and articulation of specifically Muslim concerns. In part, this achievement was due to the dependence of policymakers charged with implementing Prevent on harnessing Muslim community structures and knowledges. Nonetheless, it echoes Cornwall and Coelho's (2007) account of participatory decision-making, which sees it as occurring in 'invited spaces' (that is, marked by deeply asymmetric power relations) that nonetheless have the potentiality to become 'spaces for change'. Due to the dependence on local agencies and Muslim communities for the implementation of Prevent, local actors in Bristol (and in other areas) were able to rewrite the terms of engagement to a certain extent, shifting what could have been (and, indeed, was elsewhere) a top-down mode of regulation into something somewhat more responsive.

## Regulation for engagement: empowering Muslim women?

There were several issues that participants conceded had been begun but not progressed sufficiently through Building the Bridge, particularly the engagement of women – despite this being a key Prevent objective. As one woman member of Building the Bridge told us:

> 'From the first few community Prevent meetings I went to, it became clear that the definition of the 'Muslim community' in reality meant 'Muslim men'. I found that these men were often self-appointed community leaders who began to be the face of the Prevent agenda – women and young people had little or hardly any representation. It was interesting because women and young people were at a double disadvantage where both Muslim men and the local authority failed to encourage them to shape the Prevent agenda. So, it was quite refreshing when, at the insistence of the female Prevent lead, there was a real emphasis on creating separate groups for young people and Muslim women. There were definitely continuing attempts by the community to keep the agenda male-dominated, but it was great that Building the Bridge supported this work. The

> Prevent agenda did eventually encourage young people and women to be actively involved, but this was a while in coming and, arguably, did not go far enough.'

The focus on empowering Muslim women was a key element of the 2007 Prevent policy generally, and elsewhere. In 2008, the DCLG had established the National Muslim Women's Advisory Group (although this was later denounced as ornamental and co-opting by one of its resigning members; see Gohir, 2010), while, locally, Prevent projects were encouraged to engage with Muslim women. However, this focus on 'empowering Muslim women' through Prevent tended to position women as 'peacemakers' and viewed their inclusion instrumentally as a mechanism for 'domesticating out of control Muslim men' (Brown, 2008), or as a moderating force on Muslim theological interpretation and practice (Allen and Guru, 2012). This perspective reflected long-standing assumptions about Muslim women. Burlet and Reid (1998), for instance, found that in the aftermath of the Bradford riots of the 1990s, the local authority consulted with women on the assumption that they would exert a moderating influence on rioting young men. It was also a view of Muslim women that was reflected in then Prime Minister David Cameron's introduction in 2016 of an English language fund for Muslim women, which he proposed as a mechanism for tackling the radicalisation of young Muslim men (Cameron, 2016b). This approach and such assumptions were evident in Bristol, with Building the Bridge running a project on 'Women as Peace-makers' with Prevent funding. Brown (2008) argues that this approach disregarded Muslim women as citizens, or even political radicals, in their own right.

Despite these limitations, Wadia (2015: 86) notes that Prevent 'brought a significant number of women into civic and political life'. In the process, she argues, it enabled women to challenge both 'the political strictures imposed by male community leaders' and their exclusion from mainstream institutions; consequently, many 'took up the state's offer to be "empowered" through the Prevent programme' (Wadia, 2015: 97–8). Similarly, our research found that many women decided to accept the offer of 'empowerment' through Prevent and push for changes beyond the remit of Prevent – particularly to the terms of their inclusion within statutory, community and religious spaces. As one woman member of Building the Bridge recalled:

> 'I was really pleased that Muslim women were given a space to develop and to shape the agenda; we held conferences,

we had workshops, we invited prominent speakers to talk about women's rights. We spoke about women in Islam and what authority we have to govern ourselves and others. I remember speaking to [another woman participant] at the time that I was quite sad that we needed Prevent to create safe spaces to have these discussions; these conversations were already happening in small clusters but lacked real coordination. You know, we have a number of really powerful Muslim women in our community, but our voices were just not breaking through into the mainstream.'

While partial and bound up in some problematic perceptions about Muslim women's roles within their communities and in governing agendas, the focus on women's empowerment that was set out in the Prevent agenda nonetheless created a political opening for some women, who found that their new role in civic and statutory structures credentialised their status in speaking on a range of issues (see also Jones et al, 2014). This included speaking out about the constraints on Muslim women's involvement in religious and community structures of decision-making. Women's routine exclusion from mosques and mosque governance emerged as a key issue in the course of our research. This centred on the lack of adequate provision for women's attendance at mosques, women's lack of representation in systems of mosque governance and the broader (and more contentious) issue of women's role in theological leadership and interpretation.

In relation to the first issue – concerning the lack, or inadequacy, of provision for women's attendance at mosques – most mosques in Bristol, as elsewhere (Gale, 2005), had been established in converted buildings by a first wave of male migrants, such that many had no provision for women worshippers, or women were assigned to small kitchens or the back of the house behind curtains – arrangements that many women found unsatisfactory or disrespectful. Many women related this to the routine exclusion of women from the systems of mosque governance in the city. At the time of the research, of the 17 mosque councils in Bristol, none had any women representatives. Our research found resistance from male members of mosque organisations in the city to the prospect of the greater involvement of women in mosque governance. As one respondent, a member of the Bristol Council of Mosques, insisted, since women's husbands sit on mosque committees, women did not need to be directly involved, claiming: "At the end of the day, it's their husbands and families which are funding the mosques so the wife may not directly be voicing her opinion in the mosque but through her husband, we manage to hear all her concerns."

In several of the workshops, though, women discussed their aspirations to play a more central role in mosque governance, and set out alternative visions of mosque life. The latter entailed creative suggestions to reconcile claims of modesty with possibilities of more direct participation through innovative mosque design, and discussions of how mosques could become multifunctional spaces to pray, study and celebrate, but also of welfare or refuge, providing advice, counselling and support to community members. There was also discussion of the ways in which they could function as spaces for women to discuss theological guidance on living and practising as a Muslim woman in the UK, such as in relation to Islamic teaching and in vitro fertilisation (IVF) (see Aabe et al, 2015). For some participants in our study, involvement in forums like Building the Bridge was seen to support women's efforts to influence mosque governance because of the ways in which it credentialised their status and voices as community representatives on these issues.

This issue developed into broader discussions about the role of women in providing theological leadership or interpretation. This was contentious within the research, and there were divisions within the project's steering group and workshops over what kind of theological role women should play. Some women were advocates of the right of women to provide theological leadership in mixed congregations. Some participants in our study were involved in more radical initiatives to promote women's involvement in mosque life, such as the Inclusive Mosque Initiative (IMI). Founded and organised by women, the IMI organises pop-up mosques where anyone, regardless of gender, sexuality or theology, can worship in mixed congregations, and promotes an openness to women playing a role in religious leadership (see IMI, 2013, 2015; Lewicki and O'Toole, 2016). However, this approach was deeply opposed by others, as one steering group member asserted: "If I was to enter a room and noticed a woman leading a mixed congregation in prayer, I would simply walk straight out and never come back again." Such differences were also reflected in intense debates within the project meetings over the relevance of feminism to the project's concerns with Muslim women's equality. Some members of the group were self-described feminists, who read their commitments through a feminist lens, while others in the group objected to what they saw as the secular and ethnocentric biases of feminism. While this was a source of ongoing tension throughout the research, the concept of 'gender equality' provided a far more consensual master-frame for women's activism and the research.

Subsequently, following the reforms to Prevent after 2011 discussed later, gender politics in the city and nationally became increasingly entangled in the complex politics of the counter-extremism agenda. This agenda draws heavily on claims about gender equality and empowering Muslim women but does so in ways that tend to cast Muslims *generally* as mal-integrated and holding values that are incommensurable with 'fundamental British values' – as specified in the 2011 *Prevent Strategy* (Home Office, 2011). As Grillo (2015) shows, gender-equality activists and right-wing commentators alike frame gender attitudes among Muslims as a barometer of extremism in lobbying for state intervention in Muslim community structures and practices. However, there are tensions between these agendas. This can perhaps be exemplified by the issue of female genital mutilation (FGM). At the time of the research, FGM was, and remains, a salient issue in Bristol, not least because of the activism of several prominent local Muslim women activists and organisations, such as Nimko Ali, Daughters of Eve and Integrate Bristol, in calling for greater governmental and community awareness of, and action against, FGM. Their activism had been very successful in raising the profile of the issue locally and nationally, particularly among education and health professionals, and had given rise to the 'Bristol model' of FGM prevention based on the more proactive involvement of front-line professionals in identifying and intervening in cases of those potentially at risk of experiencing FGM. On the one hand, the prominence of the FGM issue exemplified the success of Muslim women activists in driving the agenda and securing statutory support and regulatory action. On the other, our study found that the Bristol model of FGM awareness was divisive because of the way in which it was seen to position some Muslim communities as mal-integrated, and to subject women and families in those communities to intensive forms of (intimate) surveillance (see Lewicki and O'Toole, 2016).

## Regulation without engagement: Prevent post-2011

When the Coalition government came to power in 2010, it immediately announced a review of Prevent, and in 2011, it released its revised *Prevent Strategy* (Home Office, 2011). The revised strategy contained several changes, including a more centralised approach to implementing Prevent in place of locally driven community engagement approaches, and a shift in focus to mobilising front-line personnel in public institutions to spot and report on signs of radicalisation (see O'Toole, 2015). With the passing of the CTSA, Prevent was placed on a statutory footing, *requiring* local authorities and several public sector institutions to implement the Prevent duty. In the process, Prevent became a more top-down and centralised system of regulation.

This had several implications for local authorities previously charged with the implementation of Prevent. In the first place, the identification of Prevent Priority Areas was to be based on intelligence rather than Muslim presence. While this did not greatly alter the list of Prevent Priority Areas, some areas were no longer a priority on this basis. Following the revised strategy in 2011, Bristol was no longer designated a Prevent Priority Area, with the consequence that central government funding for Building the Bridge ceased. This did not lead to the immediate collapse of Building the Bridge as local agencies signalled their desire for its continued existence, albeit with certain reforms, including a greater emphasis on gender parity in its governance. Second, Prevent became much more centralised, with the Home Office taking a much more directive role in determining how Prevent was to be implemented. Third, and consequently, local authorities became charged with delivering Prevent awareness training under the guidance of the Home Office, rather than engaging in civic capacity building with Muslim communities. This was accompanied by the dismantling of the mechanisms for state–Muslim engagement that had been established under the New Labour government (see O'Toole et al, 2016; Warsi, 2017).

In the place of community engagement, then, what developed from 2011 and particularly following the passing of the CTSA was what might be termed 'regulation without engagement', with the transfer of the implementation of Prevent passing to public sector institutions and focused largely on radicalisation awareness training and the monitoring and reporting of signs of radicalisation. Subsequently, statutory guidance issued by the Home Office (and other government departments) extended the requirements of the CTSA to demand the regulation of extremism very broadly conceived, including non-violent extremism, rather than primarily or only terrorism.

Accompanying this conceptual expansion has been the evolution of a Prevent compliance industry, with an array of mechanisms of regulation that are enacted by a variety of agencies, including government departments, statutory bodies, charities and non-statutory agencies. This has entailed statutory and quasi-autonomous agencies becoming providers of Prevent compliance self-assessment tools, risk-assessment tools, compliance and monitoring services, and micro-guidance for use by public sector institutions to enable their compliance with the Prevent duty. The tools generated by these providers often exceed what is formally required by the Prevent duty or even the Prevent duty guidance, in effect promoting forms of hyper-compliance with Prevent. In so doing, these tools advance a view, and provide an infrastructure for ensuring, that vigilance towards extremism – very broadly conceived – should be a normalised aspect of public sector professional practice. In effect, this has created a more expansive regulatory system based on a complex infrastructure of sous-veillance, with a highly specific and detailed delineation of tasks underpinned by a very broad definition of risky behaviours.

Nonetheless, there are tensions involved in such regulatory expansion. As Prevent has been rolled out as a statutory duty across public sector institutions, becoming a feature of the everyday professional practice of front-line personnel, it has come into contact, and tension, with other regulatory systems in these sectors. For instance, in the fields of education and health, the implementation of Prevent has been positioned as an extension of existing safeguarding duties in these sectors, being embedded within the range of existing monitoring and reporting safeguarding mechanisms. However, the characterisation of Prevent as an extension of schools' existing safeguarding duties has been challenged by teaching professionals. The National Union of Teachers (NUT, 2016) passed a motion at its annual conference in 2016 calling for the reform of Prevent, arguing that Prevent was *not* compatible with the understanding of safeguarding among teaching professionals, which emphasises the need to create safe spaces for children to express views or discuss difficult issues. Similarly, an Open Society Justice Initiative report on Prevent was concerned with the ways in which the safeguarding duty in schools was in tension with the requirements of the Prevent duty, stating:

> Although the government describes Prevent as a form of 'safeguarding' … the two sets of obligations have materially different aims, particularly with respect to children. In contrast to the Prevent strategy, for which the primary objective is preventing terrorism, the primary objective of the duty to safeguard children under domestic legislation is the welfare of the child. (Open Society Justice Initiative, 2016: 17)

In the field of health, Heath-Kelly and Strausz's (2018: 3) research reported that the 'positioning of the Prevent Duty as a safeguarding measure is ambiguous. Safeguarding professionals alerted us that they are operating in a "grey area" with Prevent, and that significant differences exist between Prevent Duty safeguarding and normal safeguarding'. In higher education, there has been an ongoing debate about the tensions between the requirements of the Prevent duty to report those expressing extremist ideas (that is, ideas that are in opposition to the Home Office's definition of 'fundamental British values') and bar extremist speakers from speaking at campus-hosted events, and universities' statutory duty (enshrined in the Education Act 1997) to defend freedom of expression (see Scott-Baumann, 2017).

Such tensions across these sectors reveal that regulatory systems frequently operate in a heterogeneous landscape of regulatory systems. As the preceding examples suggest, these do not necessarily form a cohesive regulatory regime. The functioning of Prevent as a form of regulation in its current, more expansive form means that it is likely to encounter diverse actors and agencies with not just divergent or resistant views about Prevent, but also pre-existing and not necessarily compatible commitments and obligations to other regulatory systems.

## Conclusion

In this chapter, I have traced the evolving Prevent agenda and its implementation as a form of regulation. Much of the literature on Prevent has characterised it as a pervasive and discriminatory form of regulation. Indeed, with the passing of the CTSA, it has become highly embedded in and ubiquitous across public sector institutions. Nevertheless, I maintain here that, in practice, paying attention to its operation as a regulatory system requires consideration of what happens when it meets the constellations of civil society or public sector actors who are its targets or who are mobilised for the purposes of its implementation.

### Notes

[1] These included: Baroness Sayeeda Warsi, the first Muslim woman to sit in cabinet; Sughra Ahmed, President of the Islamic Society Britain and the first women to be elected president of a national Islamic organisation; Fahma Mohammed, a Bristol-based student and female genital mutilation (FGM) activist; and Shagufta K, a performance poet.

[2] A local lawyer and imam, Zaheer Shabir, was elected chair, and a local health manager, Mohammed Elsharif, was elected vice-chair.

[3] Section 41(b) Prevention of Terrorism Act 2000.

# 4

# Regulating for 'care-ful' knowledge production: researching older people, isolation and loneliness

*Helen Manchester, Jenny Barke and*
*the Productive Margins Collective*

## Introduction

Collaborative, co-produced research is positioned as increasingly essential to the university in delivering public good and in finding answers to the increasingly 'wicked' problems that we face as social researchers (Facer and Enright, 2016). Important questions need to be asked concerning how far current regulatory norms and practices around research maximise insights and the realisation of transformative change. In the UK at least, despite the prominence of 'co-production' in higher education research funding strategies, the balance in research funding remains weighted towards research in which problems and interests are identified from within the academic community. This chapter tells the story of a research project that aimed to develop more equitable and inclusive 'regulatory systems' around the production of knowledge concerning the isolation and loneliness of older people. As such, this is a chapter about regulation in, and of, research programmes that is intended to highlight the way in which 'top-down' regulation, embedded in university ethical processes, funder requirements and forms of accountability around research, create particular relations between universities and publics. This article draws attention to alternative regulatory systems for knowledge production emerging from our co-produced research process that draw particularly on feminist concerns centred on an ethic of care. We call this 'care-ful' research.

In order to explore these alternative regulatory systems, the chapter examines how we 'care-fully' co-produced regulatory structures during our research with older people around an increasingly 'publicly' discussed issue of the loneliness of older people. Research into isolation and loneliness tends to focus on the psychological and medical causes or consequences of loneliness (Schirmer and Michailakis, 2015). In our work, we wanted to understand how the loneliness of older people is framed and understood across society and, particularly, by older people themselves. In this chapter, we consider how adopting an ethic of care, founded on accounts in feminist thinking (Beasley and Bacchi, 2007; Code, 2015; Bellacasa, 2017; Sörensson and Kalman, 2017), supported us to practically co-create and sustain a particular set of regulatory systems and processes around our research. The model involved us taking seriously values such as 'attentiveness, responsibility, nurturance, compassion, and meeting others' needs', and we worked with an understanding of care as a contested term that goes beyond the self to embrace our interdependencies, and involves some kind of action or material doing (caring for, caring about, caregiving/receiving), but is also often associated with burden and/or labour (Tronto, 2009 [1993]: 102). We draw on a long tradition in feminist scholarship that foregrounds the examination of knowledge hierarchies and the need to recognise and challenge asymmetrical power relations between researcher and researched, acknowledging that unequal power relations and knowledge hierarchies are often written into existing regulations around research (hooks, 2004; Caretta and Riaño, 2016; Sörensson and Kalman, 2017). Challenging these knowledge hierarchies requires different notions of value in research processes and an alternative approach to research outputs.

We draw on the experience of community partners and academics, across two settings, in order to explore the processes and practices through which knowledge (of all kinds) was created, contested and transformed in this partnership (McFarlane, 2011), as well as the different 'attentions' required in this process. In the following sections, we discuss how our co-produced, 'care-ful' regulation of knowledge production emerged in these two very different locations. We explore more closely how an ethic of care helped us interrogate 'just how the "co-mingling" of scientific practices and their various publics takes place' (Barry and Born, 2013: 247). We consider how new regulatory frameworks, based on our co-produced methodologies and an ethic of care, were built through examining in detail the situated, material, affective and ethico-political involvement of ourselves as researchers and the people we worked alongside to co-construct knowledge, and the plurality of public legacies and outputs that this led to. Our concerns are related to the regulation of older people's engagement in public knowledge production – we want to raise questions relating to *what* knowledge counts, but also *whose* knowledge counts and *how* this knowledge might be produced and exchanged more equitably.

## Attending to specificities of lived experience and materialities

Our project took place in two locations, involving community workers, academics, arts practitioners and community members in the Bedminster area of Bristol in England and in Merthyr Tydfil in Wales. Our aim was to understand more about older people's experiences of loneliness within two hyper-local contexts, and to consider how the two communities could design social action projects or other initiatives to support older people who experience loneliness. The research was co-produced in each location between a community-based research associate and the local community. The project was supervised by a central working group comprised of academics from Bristol (RS) and Cardiff Universities (EW), the research associates (JB in Bedminster and CB and then RND in Merthyr), leaders of the two community organisations (SDH in Bedminster and LD in Merthyr), and an academic lead (HM).

Situating knowledge production through acknowledging that this involves both the social and material worlds in which the research occurs is a key theme in feminist standpoint research that was a starting point in this project (Beasley and Bacchi, 2007; Bellacasa, 2017; see also Chapter 2, this volume). Before we began our research, we met as a working group in each site and walked the area with a local, knowledgeable guide. We discussed the history of the areas generally and the history of community development and participation specifically. We considered the impact of geographical location on the everyday, embodied experience of older people. There were interesting differences and similarities between the sites that underlined the importance of understanding loneliness and social isolation within a situated context. We considered the relevance of hilly topography, transport provision, participation in political movements (for example, the National Union of Mineworkers in Merthyr), dispersed communities, deprivation and gentrification (for example, in Greater Bedminster), which all impact across different communities, both personally and collectively. Our guides told us stories of loss (for instance, of industry and public space) and of resilience (in community action projects). This built our understanding of the need to explore the isolation and loneliness of older people in each location in relation to economics, histories and politics, but also to landscapes, materialities and embodied lived experiences (see Figure 4.1 for some initial work

**Figure 4.1:** Mapping memories, friendships and connections in Southville and Bedminster

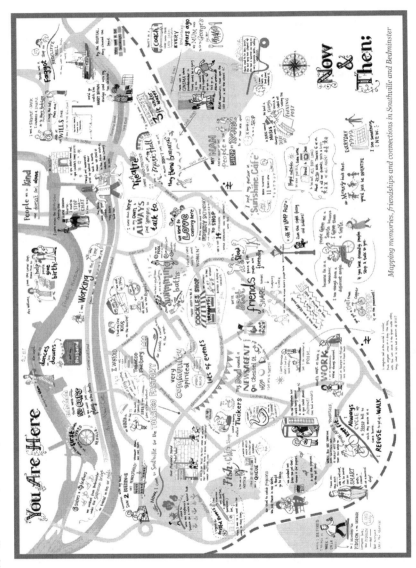

Source: 'Now and Then' funded by AHRC Connected Communities Festival, 2015

with an artist to become familiar with the Greater Bedminster area). Engagement with these real-world experiences and histories was a necessary requirement in our research as we felt that this allowed us to move beyond knowing things 'in general' and to engage more fully, and in a more responsible and responsive way, to the knowledges held in the community (Code, 2015).

The original project brief had suggested that the two sites would work with and train older peer researchers in order to research isolation and loneliness in their communities. However, we found that this model was not applicable in a straightforward way in either site and research design emerged from the messy realities that we encountered in the areas. In Bedminster, drawing on strong links already established by the community organisation around working with older people, the research associate identified and brought together a group of (mainly) older people to co-produce research with. Collaboration was between the research associate and a peer research group, and initial activity involved developing research plans and questions collaboratively. In Merthyr, building on our experiences through our walking and talking methodologies and following further discussion with local community development teams in the area, it became apparent that there was an element of research fatigue. The research associate felt very wary about using the term 'research' as she felt that in the local context it "provokes feelings of mistrust in a community that was used to having research done to it". The research associate therefore worked ethnographically with a carefully selected local poet, storyteller and photographer in order to build relations with key gatekeepers in the community and to begin to explore and make visible (verbally and visually) the stories of older people that had hitherto been largely below the radar.

Through our initial co-produced methodologies with those working in the area, we identified that our research needed to be regulated in response to the specificities and lived experiences of older people in the two communities, including attending to the landscapes, topographies, histories of participation and other affective concerns. As researchers, this meant that we had to adapt and move fluidly between different approaches and that similar methods could not necessarily be adopted in our different contexts. Relationally, the research process became a collective, negotiated process imbued with the various materialities, interests and understandings of the human and non-human actors involved. Regulatory regimes that 'care' are necessary for this kind of research, including funding regimes and ethical processes that allow for the relational labour, time and effort involved in building trust in order for communities to feel confident to express their subjectivities. This can be particularly challenging when working with non-dominant and potentially vulnerable communities (Hill Collins, 2000), where research conducted in the past may have been governed by top-down regulatory systems and relations designed by researchers interested in rational knowledge production, objectivity and detachedness.

## Attending to ethics and affect

In the previous section, we suggested that methods and practices in 'care-ful' co-produced knowledge production are relational and materially situated rather than being governed only by individual or normative institutional regulatory regimes. This produces the need for regulatory regimes that recognise ethical principles of care, friendship, intimacy, solidarity and empathy, which involve practical enactments of responsibility towards 'others-in-relation' (Whatmore, 1996). Ellis (2007: 4) proposes that 'this type of ethical thinking requires researchers to act from our hearts and minds, to acknowledge our interpersonal bonds to others'. In this section, therefore, we explore the role of emotion and affect and the possible alternative ethical regulations required in attending to these elements in 'care-ful' research.

As we started to develop projects and collaborate with older people and artists, it became apparent that many of our collaborators were motivated to engage with the research due to their own, or close friends' and relatives', experiences of loneliness. While our research was not developed in any way as a psychological intervention, it became necessary to recognise that, in and of itself, there is a socialisation effect in gathering a group of older people that may produce positive change (Martinson and Minkler, 2006; Masi et al, 2011). Researcher reflexivity is a key element that contributes to the quality of co-produced research (Caretta and Riaño, 2016). In this project, everyone involved, including the working group, the artists that we worked with and the older people, were encouraged to reflect on their own lived experiences of isolation and loneliness. We considered how they impacted on the research process, as well as how the research process might impact on experiences of loneliness. This necessitated careful consideration of ethical relations and a recognition of the emotions associated with the research process. Responding to the way in which community researchers and artists on the projects gave a great deal of themselves when working on this project, the community lead in Merthyr (LD) observed that this meant having to be more open personally than may be usual within a research project and felt that it was important to "bring the personal" into the project rather than "sitting with our work hats on, hiding behind our titles". The emotional labours associated with this work in building 'care-ful' knowledge production required different ethical regulatory systems and processes. Here, care is understood not simply as a moral obligation or as part of the 'work' associated with participatory research, but also as a challenge to the foregrounding of rational decision-making and the lack of attention given to unruly bodies and emotions in research relationships (Beasley and Bacchi, 2007; Mol et al, 2010). For instance, we instigated a buddy system for our researchers (both the peer researchers and the university researchers) – someone on the team with whom they could go to (not their line manager) in order to discuss any emotional concerns that they had. The research associates also had to design systems to ensure the safety of peer researchers in the field, including providing emotional support following difficult interviews.

Questions of caring for, caring about and being cared for are also inherent within our research topic. Older people are often perceived as vulnerable and in dependent, precarious relations with others (Mol et al, 2010). This discourse, and its effects, became clear in our initial work. In Merthyr, we began our work by exploring individual narratives around loneliness and isolation, and varied outputs were produced, including stories, poems, songs and photographs. The research associate and artists considered the themes, words and ideas that ran across the diverse stories in order to start to develop a picture of lived experiences of loneliness across the community. Through this work, they came to focus beyond the person in isolation and looked wider, for instance: at the impact of natural and urban landscapes on a community's sense of its own isolation and loneliness; at the regulatory nature of certain internal and external spaces in the community; and at the disconnections between different generations in the area. This initial exploratory work highlighted the need to avoid the words 'loneliness' and 'isolation', which carried both a stigma and a focus on individual blame and self-help with them that were found to be unhelpful in relation to the project. Drawing on feminist conceptions of care as an interdependent, collective process, rather than an individualistic one, our findings began to raise concerns for us around how social and welfare systems purporting to 'care' often do the opposite through an increasing focus on individualism and personalisation.

Added to the initial work that suggested the importance of the socio-material situatedness of the research, these concerns led to us to considering how we might investigate mutuality and interdependence, both with natural and built environments and with others, in relation to tackling isolation and loneliness. In collaboration with youth and community workers in the area, we therefore designed a set of intergenerational activities that explored the possibilities of and difficulties in building intergenerational connections and solidarity, and the impact of natural landscapes and topographies on loneliness. Working with a photographer, participants were asked to take photos of the local area and then use these as a prompt for discussing issues around connections in the local community. The photographs focused on the natural and non-natural spaces in the area where participants of different ages felt 'at home' or 'out of place'. The ensuing discussion illustrated the physical and 'felt' segregation of different ages in the community, where younger and older people inhabited very different spaces. The activities marked a continued shift towards the 'disconnections and connections' felt within the communities in which they live and work, rather than a focus on isolation and loneliness. This helped to build a common and public language around which artists, research associates, local community members across generations and formal and informal community organisers felt able to move beyond the individual blame and stigma attached to loneliness in the community. The focus on connection and disconnection drew attention to the 'person in relation' (with the environment, with services and with each other) rather than the 'person in isolation'. Regulatory regimes specific to researching loneliness and isolation tend to follow disciplinary or field conventions that encourage researchers to classify and bound research participants by generation and/or age. Our research suggested that it was important to widen the participants that we worked with to encompass others in the communities in order to draw attention to mutuality in relations of care that might better counter social isolation and loneliness. In this way, we were also able to avoid paternalistic notions of care that conceive older people as vulnerable and 'carers' as generous helpers. This challenges the regulatory model of the bounded 'sampling' of research populations often required by funders, by disciplinary regimes and in academic outputs, and suggests the importance of accounting for interdependence between different communities and groups in research design.

Across the sites, those involved felt that ethical frameworks gave them clarity, protection and permissions, and that this helped to 'hold' their anxieties around engaging in the research process. For instance, ethical issues around conducting the research were discussed in more detail with the artists working in Merthyr in relation to their own practice and materials (for example, what does it mean to take a camera into a care home for older people?). However, our ethical framework was also negotiated relationally and situated in each of our sites as the research progressed. This is illustrated well in relation to the Bedminster group, who were keen to get involved in a more traditional qualitative research experience. This meant that we needed to build sufficient common knowledge around the regulations associated with research in order for it to adhere to particular conventions, including ethical practices and robustness in relation to the production of research. We spent some time introducing key methods and processes to the community researchers. However, our focus was not simply on teaching the older people to be social scientists 'just like us'. Rather, we needed to provide room within the process for them to bring their own lived experiences, tacit knowledges and other professional understandings to the project as we felt that this would both value their knowledge and expertise and potentially enable new kinds of knowledge to emerge. The process of building common knowledge was understood as involving the construction of 'inter-'spaces where all in the group felt able to bring different kinds of cognitive and emotional knowledge and expertise, and where all involved were committed to learning from each other and to teaching what they know (Edwards, 2005). It was clear from the outset that the peer researchers involved had a huge range of expertise, skills and experience that they brought to the researcher role. This was related to their previous professional roles, but also to their age and their diverse experiences of the world and the local area, all of which we acknowledged as equally valuable. We discovered that adopting this approach required us to take on different roles and methods as researchers, and challenged traditional knowledge hierarchies, where rational, academic knowledge is seen as more valuable than tacit knowledge and expertise.

Our peer researchers' experiences impacted on our methods in various ways. In discussing interview schedules and questions, we were able to draw on different ways of eliciting information from counselling, social work and broadcasting backgrounds. The 14 interviews between the peer researchers and the older people that they interviewed became very conversational, and the previous professions of the researchers made a difference to how the interviews developed. For instance, Dave's past experience as a volunteer with people with mental health issues and his past histories of mental ill health were brought into the field as resources. His interviews involved him sharing personal narratives with interviewees, which often created more intimate moments. Another peer researcher had been a social worker and her ability to listen and create a safe space for the interviewee to speak was clear in her interview style. The research associate felt that the researchers asked more probing questions than she would have felt comfortable to ask and noticed the attentiveness of the researchers, who were able to connect, notice and pick up on shared experiences, perhaps because of their generational and place-based shared experiences. Interviews were empathetic and conversational, and in the process, they reduced the traditional hierarchies between interviewer and interviewee.

While a similarity in age with interviewees might support empathetic research, the research associate was also very aware that it could lead to emotional concerns. A few researchers explicitly stated that the interviews they had undertaken made them wonder "Could that be me?" The open and intimate discussion of these issues was a vital part of the research process that led us to develop an understanding of isolation and loneliness grounded in emotional, affective concerns and relations. Bias is often seen as something to avoid in research interviews; however, the group discussed the impossibility of removing yourself and your own stories and emotions from the interview situation, as well as the usefulness of not doing so. The traditional model of research often involves a single researcher, who brings their own academic knowledge and understanding to the field, often reproducing dominant discourses in the field (Sörensson and Kalman, 2017). In contrast, the peer researchers brought many and varied experiences and emotions into this discussion. Our co-productive approach, working alongside older people as researchers, and acknowledging and discussing their own affective concerns, allowed the academic researchers to access an insider view of isolation and loneliness. This enabled us as a team to move across the boundaries between insider and outsider research and to both build new knowledge and challenge traditional knowledge hierarchies and approaches. One example of this would be our increasing focus on the importance of intergenerational encounters in tackling issues of isolation and loneliness.

So, what have we learnt in relation to the 'care-ful' regulation of research? Attending to specificities of experience, emotion and affect requires us to spend time building trust and collaborative processes where knowledge hierarchies can be challenged. Different settings require different approaches, and regulatory regimes need to be open enough to allow for this. This might require funders to recognise that it is not always possible to spell out methods, approaches and timelines in detail in advance, and a recognition that building new knowledge with non-dominant communities requires their intimate involvement in the research – not as bystanders or 'subjects', but as agentic collaborators throughout the research process. Different ethical regimes are also necessary for this kind of work. Here, ethical relations go way beyond 'frameworks' to encompass the negotiated process of developing shared languages, methods and spaces in which different knowledge, lived experiences and expertise might be considered more equally (Brydon-Miller et al, 2015). Regulatory regimes such as ethics committees and ethical guidance in research institutions often struggle with collaborative research, and, indeed, relational ethical frames. An openness to the negotiated, ongoing relationality in ethical encounters in the field within these regulatory structures could enable more ethically strong collaborative research to emerge.

In the previous section, we looked at how a 'care-ful' approach can affect the kinds of relations and knowledge that emerge from the research process. In the following section, we explore how these different regulatory regimes may also lead to the production of diverse outcomes, outputs and legacies, and the need to account for, and encourage, these emergent legacies in the regulatory structures governing knowledge exchange and dissemination.

## Regulating for knowledge exchange and diverse legacies

Spaces generally created for knowledge production and exchange favour certain kinds of 'public' knowledge. They are often spaces where the embodied and experiential knowledge generated through everyday practices are devalued (Jupp, 2007). Fraser's work suggests that a single 'public sphere' is neither desirable nor possible as groups at the margins will often find it difficult to find the right words or 'voice' to express their concerns. She suggests that multiple public spheres or counter-publics, where groups at the margins feel able to express their views in a variety of modes, are necessary (Fraser, 1990). However, current regulatory regimes around the legacies of research tend to foreground a singular measure of value or impact, often defined in quantitative terms or in relation to passive 'audiences' (Facer and Enright, 2016), and often occurring at the end of the project life cycle.

Recognising that these regulatory regimes undermine efforts to hear the voices of groups at the margins involved in participatory research, we worked together with our community collaborators to co-create multiple spaces and encounters for knowledge exchange, including those that could be characterised as counter-publics, throughout the project life cycle. For instance, following the narrative work and the intergenerational photo activities in Merthyr, a series of smaller community-based exhibitions and a larger exhibition of the material gathered to date were planned. This was conceived as an experiment in opening up space for more mutual and collective community dialogue around isolation and loneliness, away from formalised processes connected with social and welfare systems that foreground personalisation (though, importantly, those running these kinds of services were invited to come along). The thinking behind the exhibitions was to recover some of what had been rendered 'non-credible' or non-existent in wider conversations around loneliness in the area (de Sousa Santos, 2004). The work that the artists carried out on the project to both capture the stories of the older people and to render credible the informal roles that many community members (from the local cafe owner, to the walking group coordinator, to the bingo group organiser) took on in relation to combating loneliness and isolation were highlighted. The importance of recognising these roles and building alliances and relationship between formal and informal carers in the community were key findings of the research. The exhibition helped those running statutory services and the informal carers represented in the exhibition to begin to build common knowledge and a shared language around the issue of social isolation and loneliness. This was vital to the process of engaging older people and other members of the community in the project. However, the flatness of the image, for instance, photographs of individual older people in a care-home setting, or of the landscape surrounding the area, also failed in some ways to express the embodied and felt realities of older people's experiences of isolation and loneliness, as well as their connections with others. The artists and curator therefore designed a series of site exchanges in order to move beyond the formality of an exhibition space. The narratives, stories, songs and photographs collected at each of the sites that the artists had spent time in were shared with community members at other sites. For example, creative outputs from artistic work at a care home were shared with a bingo group. The juxtapositions, similarities and differences between the sites became visible in these encounters, leading to reflections concerning isolation and loneliness that embraced the materiality of different spaces and the emotional concerns of the different communities, as well as the range of actors implicated in thinking about isolation and loneliness.

In Bedminster, the peer researchers were keen from the start to ensure that research findings were applied and led to tangible legacies. For some, this project had been an opportunity to explore the concept of loneliness and develop spaces in which it could be discussed, both for themselves and for others. Others had more activist motivations, wanting to 'do something' about loneliness, and saw the research as a way of understanding which social action projects in the local community might help to prevent or combat loneliness. Allowing for outputs that met both individual and institutional desires was critical in ensuring that people felt valued, competent and heard in line with the ethic of care that we were adopting. The peer researchers in Bedminster together decided to prioritise three outputs or legacies: first, the researchers wanted to find a way to bring in their own individual experiences and address the stigma around loneliness by creating spaces in which people could talk about the issue; second, as the data highlighted the possible role of technology in preventing loneliness, the researchers wanted to explore that further; and third, the group wanted to explore preventive interventions, including a local community-led retirement course.

The first objective was met through co-writing a theatre piece/monologues with local dramaturge Adam Peck, based on the data but also allowing our collaborators' individual experiences to emerge. Alison, for instance, wrote a monologue about walking as comments made by interviewees had chimed with her own initial embodied practice of walking to feel at home/find 'home'. This creative process allowed the peer researchers to hold onto something individual alongside the production of collective themes for a more formal report, reflecting the importance of multiple outputs in a co-produced research project. As a team, this process again illustrated the value in bringing in our own lived experiences and acknowledging and embracing our 'affective intensities' with the work and the data, rather than approaching it from the 'cold' perspective of the detached researcher. Here, the community researchers were moving between insider and outsider positions as they wrote their monologues, building on their own experiences but also attending to the data that they had collected in interviews. There was a desire to create a public space in which to discuss loneliness and this was produced through performing the monologues created in the form of a theatrical piece conceived and directed by Bristol-based performer/director Lucy Tuck. The theatrical piece was able to draw attention to the embodied experience of isolation and loneliness (for example, sitting alone in your house talking to yourself), and the care often 'handed out' to older people (for example, the patronising hand on the shoulder). The intention was to highlight these felt and embodied aspects of loneliness and isolation often ignored in the literature and to de-stigmatise the issue through holding intergenerational conversations with a broader community. The first performance at a local theatre concluded with an informal question-and-answer (Q&A) session, which has been replicated at performances since. These intimate spaces, held by the peer researchers, provided people with the opportunity to share their own, and others', experiences in order to consider potential ways of preventing and alleviating loneliness, and to think about loneliness as a life-course concern (see Figures 4.2 and 4.3).

Across both of our sites, artists and community partners played a key role in working alongside the research team to share emergent knowledges in accessible and diverse forms that helped to make tangible the lived experiences, and to materialise the affective concerns, of those whose voices are often not being heard or listened to. This is complex relational work that must be recognised in regulatory regimes of research – including by funders and university finance and contracts departments. Artists and other external collaborators must be seen as project partners, and properly paid and embedded in the project life cycle, in order to build trust, dialogue and understanding, particularly of those in non-dominant community groups.

The ethic of care that we adopted in our approach to knowledge production was also visible in the events held and managed by the peer researcher group. For instance, a sense emerged of the interdependence

**Figure 4.2:** Performance of *Alonely* at the Connected Communities Utopias festival, London (2016)

Source: Barney Heywood, 2016

## Regulating for 'care-ful' knowledge production

between people across generations and the need for caring and care-ful spaces where the individualised view of social isolation and loneliness and the stigma associated with it could be challenged. Through these connections, a policy event at Westminster, 'Loneliness and Isolation across the Lifecourse', was designed to highlight the need to build solidarity and conviviality in communities and among generational groups. In addition, funders were invited to consider the need for slower and more care-ful approaches to research and community development around social isolation and loneliness, as well as some of the different regulatory regimes needed for these approaches to flourish.

We characterise our approach to knowledge exchange and the legacies of this project as an activist stance, where we made a commitment as a team to opening up new possibilities and encounters beyond the academic community throughout the project life cycle. We wanted to make a contribution to building more equitable practices and ways of living in the world (Gibson-Graham, 2008). We did this through co-creating and pluralising different spaces and opportunities for communities whose knowledge and expertise are often devalued in knowledge hierarchies to be heard and listened to. We view this as part

**Figure 4.3:** 'Loneliness is ...' wall at the Connected Communities Utopias festival, London (2016)

Source: Barney Heywood, 2016

of our 'care-ful' regulation of knowledge production and exchange, not as a paternalistic moral obligation, but as a political commitment to rendering credible less heard voices and practices around countering social isolation and loneliness, and challenging knowledge hierarchies.

We make a case for pluralising outputs from research, for understanding that outputs occur throughout the project life cycle and, more generally, for rethinking what counts as a 'valuable' output or 'useful knowledge' in collaborative research (Facer and Enright, 2016). Our outputs from this research are many and diverse. They include a series of exhibitions, reports for community organisations and service providers, academic papers, and performances of monologues at national festivals and local community events. We have also written and secured funding to enable the development of our Tech and Talk Cafe and to pilot a hyper-local pre-retirement course. Embodied legacies for community members and service providers include an increased confidence to tackle issues related to loneliness in their local community. Institutionally, our university, the community organisations involved and others working in the areas have been able to negotiate and consider new collaborative and intergenerational approaches to tackling loneliness and isolation. Regulatory regimes around research tend to produce sites of knowledge exchange (or knowledge transfer) that favour decontextualised academic knowledge and therefore often devalue voices at the margins. New regulatory regimes would need to recognise the value in multiple sites for knowledge exchange that represent and nurture diverse forms of knowledge.

Often, those forms of accountability that are most valued in academic circles are less easy to produce in these kinds of intensive collaborative projects (Facer and Enright, 2016). Our research has suggested that a more diverse range of knowledge outputs and legacies needs to be recognised within academic accountability structures (going beyond current conceptions of 'impact' and 'public engagement'), as well as the need to reframe writing and other knowledge-exchange techniques as part of the mode of inquiry, embedded through the entire life cycle of a project. We also call for changes to be made to ensure that community partners can actively contribute across all stages of the process of research.

## Conclusion

Academic articles that explore participatory research largely ignore the processes of doing the work in favour of accounts of the academic knowledge produced. In this chapter, we have deliberately explored the process of the research in two different sites. Focusing in on the process has enabled us to highlight how an ethic of care enhanced the participation of the community members and researchers. In exploring the process, we have also been able to shed light on alternative regulatory regimes around knowledge production that might yield richer and more diverse understandings and greater public benefit. This regulatory regime draws on many established practices in qualitative research but brings them together around the lens of an 'ethic of care' to draw attention to 'care-ful' research as being a collective endeavour imbued with the various materialities, interests and passions of the human and non-human actors involved.

The diverse opportunities for knowledge exchange and the varied legacies that emerged, which drew attention to the relational and interdependent nature of isolation and loneliness in communities, challenged regulatory systems in the social care and welfare systems that tend to portray social isolation and loneliness as an individual problem that individuals must solve themselves. This creates a stigma around loneliness that can inhibit finding solutions. A more 'care-ful' approach to social isolation and loneliness emerged during this project that drew attention to the mutuality inherent in any solutions to isolation and loneliness. The diverse legacies produced met the needs of everyone involved, including the community organisation, the individual older people and the university researchers.

### Box 4.1: 'Care-ful' knowledge production

This chapter has suggested that the following ten elements come to the fore when taking a 'care-ful', co-produced approach to knowledge production:

1. Taking values and doings such as 'attentiveness, responsibility, nurturance, compassion and meeting others' needs' seriously in research relations and regulations.
2. Situating knowledge production and acknowledging that this involves the social, emotional and material worlds in which the research occurs – research should respond to the specificities and lived experiences of those involved in the research.
3. Involving non-dominant communities as agentic collaborators, not bystanders or subjects.
4. Viewing research as a collective, negotiated process that takes time, for example, allowing for the relational labour, time and effort involved in building trust.

5. Including relational ethical principles that recognise care, friendship, intimacy, solidarity and empathy as components of research design.
6. Seeing researcher (and co-researcher) reflexivity as key to knowledge production.
7. Recognising the emotional labours associated with this kind of research – recognition of the unruly bodies and emotion in research relations.
8. Challenging traditional knowledge hierarchies in order to foreground tacit knowledge and expertise, as well as academic knowledge.
9. Co-creating multiple spaces and encounters for knowledge exchange, including counter-public spaces, which represent and nurture diverse forms of knowledge.
10. Taking an activist stance, for example, adopting a commitment to opening up new possibilities and encounters beyond the academic community and rendering credible less heard voices and less visible practices.

There is a great deal of emotional labour involved in 'holding' this kind of collaboration, including work in building personal connections, friendship and mutual understanding with people who might not share your view on life, politics or faith. We recognise that while this kind of knowledge production and research with community members can greatly enhance the research process and the value of findings within the local community, it is also a process highly fraught with tensions, raising questions around the synthesis of different ways of knowing the world, around power relations and around social action/activism. However, the effort involved is also pleasurable and has led to many social occasions, new alliances and stronger networks for our research, community and policy work.

We encourage others involved in co-produced research, and, indeed, those involved in designing policy and regulations for the welfare and social care system, to consider adopting an ethic of care in order to think beyond current personalisation agendas, and to be attentive to and acknowledge interdependencies and situated materialities, histories and affect in their work. 'Care-ful' research involves taking seriously the ethico-political, affective and material practices of our research encounters, and, in doing so, points out the rather different regulatory regimes and practices that might need to be designed in the situated realities of the project sites.

# 5

# Who gets to decide what's in my fridge? Principles for transforming the 'invisible rules' shaping the regulation of food habits in urban spaces

*Naomi Millner, Sue Cohen, Tim Cole, Kitty Webster,
Heidi Andrews, Makala Cheung, Penny Evans,
Annie Oliver and the Food Working Group,
as part of the Productive Margins programme*

## Introduction

This chapter focuses on the forms of regulation that shape food habits in ways that we are often unaware of. Invisible rules comprise the forms of regulation that influence food production and consumption at levels that we may be unable to control, such as globalising economic processes, labour processes, dynamics of supply and demand, advertising, and marketing. However, they also comprise the 'cultural' rules that – often in implicit ways – dictate who can use which spaces, how it is appropriate to shop or cook, and who may associate with whom. The invisibility of both sets of rules within urban spaces lead many people to answer, in the first instance, that they are the ones who get to decide what is in their fridge. However, through collective reflection, we unearthed the ways in which: labelling misleads us; work and life rhythms combine with street design to influence where we shop; and advertising affects what our children want us to buy. Consequently, the agenda to transform the invisible rules that shape urban food spaces is strongly grounded in the need to render these rules more visible as part of a 're-regulation' (as opposed to a deregulation) of the forces that overdetermine and enclose our food habits, driven by the experience of people whose concerns have been marginalised.

Here, we present some of the results of our co-produced research project that explored how people experience the regulation of food habits in their communities. We draw on multiple sources produced through the project (audio recordings, visual mapping, photography, workshop notes, focus groups and interviews with participants) to explore three key ideas. We begin by exploring the notion of food justice, which seeks to embed discussion of food regulation in attention to the spatial dimensions of food access. Here, we point to the ways in which the project sought to make visible invisible rules and to develop processes of 'commoning' in order to address the spatial inequalities of urban food spaces. In the second section, we challenge notions of 'cheapness' and instead present ideas of food *affordability*, following Michael Carolan's (2013) argument that cheap food is part of the problem of unequal food access.

Working through the data produced through our participatory project, we emphasise food in terms of its social dimensions, arguing that food habits are shaped and regulated at multiple scales. Further, we suggest that food justice cannot be achieved without engaging with *what food affords us*. This leads us to present ten principles of designing for sharing 'from the garden to the city' that acknowledge food as always more-than-food: as contexts, socialities and spaces. In the final section, we establish the building blocks for 'more-than-food policy' by demonstrating the importance of working with assets rather than deficits. Here, we argue that unleashing alternative histories and geographies within communities has the potential to reshape the present and re-imagine the future.

## Food justice is a spatial issue: commoning as a means to transform food spaces

Our starting premise – and one shared by the Productive Margins programme as a whole – was that to tackle issues of unequal access to food, we needed to bring the expertise and experience of diverse groups together around a common table. Dividing the world into the 'food poor' and 'food rich' ignores underlying principles of regulation that inform knowledge production and render some as experts and others as the passive poor to be helped. We choose to use the term 'food justice' rather than 'food poverty' throughout the project and this chapter in order to acknowledge how broader structural conditions shape access to food, as well as the need to address how responsibility and blame are apportioned to the household scale. Food *in*justice is linked with the progressive 'decontextualisation' of food and the concealment of the environmental and social costs that occur in the mass production of 'cheap food'. Food justice means changing broader structural conditions to ensure access to affordable and nutritious food *and* creating fairer forms of regulation (Gottlieb and Joshi, 2010: 6). Across the project, we sought to develop approaches that connected, and spanned, the scales of the global and the individual in both making visible, and engaging with, questions of regulation and food justice.

In the development of the participatory activities that took place within each community context, we therefore sought to collaboratively connect everyday forms of expertise relating to food and food spaces. This builds on a shared acknowledgement that unwritten rules surrounding who is a 'knower' regarding food issues are a central part of the problem, reflecting a pervasive knowledge politics that keeps privilege in place by making the views and experience of those marginalised in the system appear illegitimate or irrelevant (Rancière, 1999). This position leans upon earlier feminist and post-colonial scholarship, which, in different ways, emphasises the agencies and perspectives of 'others' systematically excluded from political visibility or speech (Millner, 2017). However, the terrain of environmental expertise leads us to an expanded notion of food justice in which not only human rights, but also the qualities of inter-species and inter-systemic relations, are at stake (Ferguson and Northern Rivers Landed Histories Research Group, 2016). To address this field of misperception, our activities focused on the question 'Who decides what's in my fridge?', with the intention of building from initial observations on our food choices, through collective reflection on food habits and constraints on choice, to articulate the ways in which changes in global markets, urban spaces and advertising cultures inform collective food habits in ways that are subtle and difficult to locate.

The project was a collaboration between the University of Bristol and three community organisations in Bristol: Coexist in Stokes Croft; the Knowle West Media Centre (KWMC) in Knowle West; and the Single Parent Action Network (SPAN) in Easton. A working group comprised of representatives of each organisation co-designed the aims and methodology of the project, including participatory workshops in the two main neighbourhoods that KWMC and SPAN work in (Knowle West and Easton), as well as a series of knowledge-exchange activities. In Knowle West, research activities focused on gathering quantitative and qualitative data through surveying the local community and organising events, building collective capacity in the process. A mobile 'fridge' installation was designed by Junior Digital Producers (JDPs) at KWMC to survey attitudes to food habits in the neighbourhood, and findings were later incorporated into visual displays. In Easton, a group of local Somali women at SPAN took part in peer research training, including participatory mapping and peer interviewing, as part of a broader action research process. Coexist, based in the inner city, played a key role in facilitating knowledge exchange between groups and enabling food-based conversations, especially through their Community Kitchen. For example, they hosted a performative workshop in February 2016, and a 'Food Utopias' event at the end of the project, including a meal that showcased our collective findings (see Figure 5.1). Participants tended to evaluate learning more about the perspectives and cultures of others as among the highest benefits of participating in the project. In feedback from activities in Knowle West, one participant reported that "the best thing was finding out what different communities had in common and talking to other people' (Coexist workshop, 24 February 2016). This was echoed in a KWMC focus group, where Yasmin reflected on her journey with the project by pointing out how dialogue with other people enabled her to reflect differently on "the diversity of people and how they shop" (KWMC focus group, 13 June 2016).

In the second half of the project, we also worked with an artist, Anne-Marie Culhane, who facilitated a series of 'pop-up' events and installations to widen public engagement with our findings, working closely with the groups and individuals who had been most involved in the project activities. This contributed to the eventual design of

Figure 5.1: The Food Utopia feast

Source: Photograph by Kitty Webster, 2016

the Somali Kitchen concept, a pop-up event involving all five senses, including the tasting of Somali cuisine, outdoor music and DIY spice-mix making. Dialogue between the communities highlighted shared concerns with the spatial regulation of food habits (for example, via street design) and the *lack of regulation* surrounding the aggressive marketing of high-fat, high-sugar foods at a global scale. It became clear that both groups were interested in further exploring how local environments and neighbourhoods work to influence the decisions that we make about food, and how to create change.

The methods we adopted focused on experiential knowledge exchange and were influenced by the pedagogical principles established by the Brazilian popular educator Paulo Freire (2001 [1972]). Although the language of praxis has been developed in many contexts, we were inspired by the definition established through the educational movement that Freire instigated in Brazil in the 1960s to create meaningful change. He combined literacy programmes with practices that enabled oppressed groups to 'read' invisible rules and collectively name unequal power relationships. We mobilise the terminology of praxis to articulate the collective capacity and know-how that are cultivated through cycles of theory, application and evaluation in order to take action against oppression. Throughout the life of the project, it was consistently the moments in which collective reflection made it possible to notice and name broader patterns in society that felt the most energetic and significant. For example, in a focus group, Aisha noted that "if you know the connections, you can raise the issues" (SPAN focus group, 16 February 2016). What is meant here is not that Aisha had no prior knowledge, but that until exchanging perspectives with others, the common threads through experience may be invisible and are therefore extremely difficult to contest. In the same focus group, this point was picked up by another participant, Sahra, with emphasis on the need to collectively decode rules that are essential to the claiming of rights: "There are a lot of barriers. And I noticed that in this country, if you don't know the law … you do not get your rights" (SPAN focus group, 16 February 2016). Through the process of moving from focus groups and discussions to collective framings of the issues, we noted the importance of, first, the creation of collective names for situations that are difficult to articulate, and, second, processes that allow for the translation of these names into the language of law and legal entitlements in order that they may be claimed as rights. This identifies different scales of regulation affecting food habits, some of which are easier to transform through 'bottom-up' action than others.

## Commoning as a means to transform invisible rules

To acknowledge the importance of this process of collective naming within the process of actualising food justice in the city and the way in which it works to transform invisible rules, we use the idea of 'commoning'. Commoning reaches towards the idea of collective empowerment and the material transformation that becomes possible through the development of collective literacy. The idea picks up on a recent turn to focus on the everyday practices of sharing, exchange and communication across difference through which alternative social fabrics can be built, social fabrics that resist the enclosure of life according to logics of profit and accumulation (Bresnihan and Byrne, 2014). Commoning also emphasises the *processual* and reiterative way in which common life is established in relation to shifts in the regulation of economic spaces, the remaking of urban fabrics and new forms of social alienation (Kirwan et al, 2015). In this chapter, commoning is both the methodology through which a different vision of the city is established, and the experience of collective naming that takes place when this methodology succeeds – in small, often fragile, moments – in forging new connections, as well as a sense of conviviality between social groups who do not ordinarily associate.

In practice, this language of commoning is particularly helpful for describing the surges of positive feeling and energy that resulted from very different groups coming together to share knowledge. Participants from Knowle West were mainly white and British-born; participants from Easton were mainly black, from a Somali background, although some families had lived in different European Union (EU) countries before coming to Britain. Coexist, acting as facilitators in this exchange, were mainly white, middle-class social entrepreneurs and artists seeking to engage with their more diverse neighbourhoods. In a visit to Feed Bristol, a food-growing project run by Avon & Bristol Wildlife Trust, Ann from Knowle West remarked that in relation to the Somali women's group, she had come to notice that:

> 'We're not that different. Although sometimes life makes you think you're different. But they're not that different. They still laugh and have a joke.... That's another thing you learn when you go to these projects. People are not different. They've still got their lives; they've got their children; they're worrying about meals for their husbands, and things like that. All part of life, isn't it?... You have to meet them, not just think about them.... Everybody's

got the same problems. I'm older, but they've got their children; they're worrying about their children buying fast food and things like that. They have to care about them. They've probably got husbands coming home wanting a meal at a certain time. Basically the same, just dressed different, and a different culture, isn't it?' (Feed Bristol visit, 16 June 2015)

Throughout this process, we have come to see food as a 'boundary object': an object that may have very different kinds of significance in different cultural contexts but which creates overlap between those contexts by being shared between them. McSherry (2001: 69) suggests that a boundary object 'holds different meanings in different social worlds yet is imbued with enough shared meaning to facilitate its translation across those worlds', while Strathern (2007: 46) emphasises that boundary objects 'do not imply bounded objects – they are entities on the borders of discourses'. In an interview, Mary, from Knowle West, echoed this sentiment, suggesting that:

'It was just different to meet somebody with a different fight, but on the same level, if you know what I mean.... The fight was about trying to put your stamp on what you want. Theirs was around fast food – they didn't want their kids to eat junk food – and ours was around access to supermarkets. We ain't got a supermarket and we ain't got the luxury of choosing all those shops that they've got up there, and their fast-food outlets. And it's not only a supermarket. I keep saying it. It's not just a supermarket; it's the whole kit and caboodle that goes with it, that's going to make this community thrive.' (Mary, KWMC, 18 August 2016)

Here, Mary summarises the key themes that emerged in each group process: the problem of 'too many takeaways' in Easton and the way in which this influences children's unhealthy eating habits; and the lack of food-buying options in Knowle West altogether. While these issues reflect different spatial histories and social struggles, the common theme of disenfranchisement from processes of spatial planning united the two groups and led to a building of common feeling and common language over time. Such moments are particularly striking in a historical period where ethnic and cultural groups are increasingly polarised in the UK and beyond.

Through the course of the workshops and events that made up this project, it became increasingly clear that food justice issues cannot be separated from what some call 'spatial justice', which centres not on the right to have food, but on the *right to know* (Millner, 2017). Building on Henri Lefebvre's influential spatial thinking, spatial justice in Edward Soja's (2013) account emphasises that social injustices are configured, in part, through the ways in which societies are spatially organised, including infrastructures of access, networks of distribution and the unevenness of processes of regeneration. An analysis of spatial regulation (and not just social regulation) is therefore necessary to tackle issues surrounding food production and food habits. As Safiya noted in a SPAN focus group: "different areas make us different" (SPAN focus group, 19 February 2017). Where we live and work is influenced by factors of affordability, class and housing; where we live and work means that we are exposed to different risks and choices, eat different foods, and (re)compose our bodies differently. Sabiha noted that even moving from Easton to Horfield had had an impact on her children's eating habits: when she lived in Easton, her children would eat takeaways every day, whereas "now they don't because we've moved to Horfield" (SPAN workshop, 27 November 2016).

In workshops, participants supported this spatial dimension to food justice, reporting the importance of their surrounding environments in influencing what they eat and buy. In Knowle West, for example, it was felt that there were few healthy eating options:

'and sometimes you forget your lunch or whatever and you think: "What am I going to have?" And the only option around you is a fish and chip shop.... It makes you realise that something needs to be done here. There's not enough options for people to get fresh, healthy food at a decent price. That's a negative impact on your health if you keep doing it.' (George, KWMC, 22 August 2016)

Thus, as we developed questions of 'Who (or what) gets to decide what's in my fridge?', we increasingly understood the way in which spatial regulation is enmeshed with other forms of economic and social regulation. This brought us to interrogate: systems for food production, but also the built environment, green spaces and cultural atmospheres surrounding food; other systems of formal rules (regulation), such as city planning (Who decides, and how is it decided, whether a company can open a takeaway or a supermarket, and how can this be challenged?); food advertising and labelling; and food supply chains and their relationship with demand. All communities suffer the impact of the deregulation of markets, but sometimes in different ways. For example, in spite of long-term campaigning by many in Knowle West, no supermarket had located to the outer estate because of perceived insufficient economic return, while those in Easton suffered from the uncontrolled proliferation of unhealthy fast-food takeaways in the inner city.

Within this nexus, it remained vital that food habits are transformed at the individual level in ways that arise from personal and collective reflection. For example, in a SPAN workshop, Muna excitedly noted the changes that her son had made to his eating habits. As a result of her involvement in this project, she had suggested to her son how much he might save if he did not go to takeaways so regularly. Her son began to cut out takeaway food and saved enough money in a short time, which he planned to put towards joining the gym (SPAN workshop, 11 December 2016). What is crucial here is neither to overplay individual decisions in the shaping of food habits, nor to reinforce particular cultures of 'healthy eating' that often have moralising and class-based undertones. Rather, we want to underline the importance of spaces for collective reflection in the project and in the city for exchanging and translating personal experience from the context of time-pressured decision-making to collective knowledge and claims. It is not a case of the project working group educating others, but a case of opening time-spaces that allow for reflection on decision-making processes that are often rushed or strained, and made to seem smoother by marketing or labelling that sell us quick fixes. This is a challenge because time poverty limits space for collective reflection. Meanwhile, through the project, we learnt to focus on narratives of change, noting what makes processes of individual and community transformation possible, and what the factors are that allow people to see, name or affect their own food habits, alongside identifying the structural conditions that are much harder to shift. These reflections shape the remainder of this chapter and inform the principles that we offer in the next section.

## From cheapness to affordability

As a city, Bristol is widely regarded for its thriving local food scene, with many organisations and groups working to reconnect urban residents with a more localised food system, often growing organic food and distributing it through independent and alternative outlets (for an overview and examples, see Carey, 2013; Moragues-Faus and Morgan, 2015). However, these interventions can be out of reach for low-income groups and time-poor residents. More affluent consumers and/or those with more time are increasingly able to pursue, and pay for, nutritious, locally produced and more sustainable food. At the same time, austerity, the benefit cap and stagnating wages have meant that for many others, accessing decent, healthy food is increasingly difficult. Bristol is a divided city, with high levels of wealth sitting uneasily in a city where one in every four children live in poverty and food-bank use has risen by 28 per cent in the last three years. Sixteen official food banks are operating in the city, with use continuing to rise. Food is a powerful marker of social exclusion, both for individuals and communities (McGlone et al, 1999). The lived realities of this were highlighted in the SPAN workshops, where participants talked of living "hand to mouth" and the pressing "need to feed our kids" (SPAN workshop, 6 November 2016).

The food inequalities seen in Bristol are replicated on the global scale. Global hunger is a distributional problem, linked with economic, political and social inequalities. Abstracting food makes it possible to think of something like food security – ensuring that people have enough nourishing food to eat – without looking at broader historical questions surrounding what led to this poverty, or political questions concerning who decides what should be grown and how. This has led to a concentration on the large-scale export-oriented industrial production of single crops destined for Europe and the US, which suits the free-market system of exchange that these colonial nations have set into place because it conveniently removes colonial histories from the picture of how and why countries are in debt. Subsidies have made certain food staples (especially corn) cheap and abundant, thereby providing incentives for their use as substitutes for more expensive commodities, leading to new foodstuffs like high-fructose corn syrup. The global food industry creates high levels of cheap and abundant industrial products derived primarily from a handful of subsidised staples. Subsidies make processed foods extremely profitable – at least significantly more profitable than whole, unprocessed food. This profitability creates deep pockets to fund expensive advertising campaigns. In one study, preschool children reported that food in McDonald's wrappers tasted better than food in plain wrappers even though the same food item was consumed (Robinson et al, 2007).

The marketing of such food was a theme that participants picked up on, especially vis-a-vis place-specific social and cultural ways of knowing. Bob, from Knowle West, noted how "they lay out the store to make you look up, buy certain things, catch your eyes. They change it, all sorts" (KWMC workshop, 11 March 2016). This was a particular concern for Somali mothers in Easton, who felt that their homes were bombarded with advertising leaflets posted by fast-food takeaways and that their children were targeted on their walk to and from school. As Aisha explained:

> 'eating junk and unhealthy takeaways has become part of the culture of this community. It's so accessible, it's cheap, it's available. It's always round the schools, primaries and secondaries. So it's become a part of the culture, but it's not something we are used to in this community because as a community, we come from Somalia. So we are not used to eating this kind of food. So we think that as Somali people, as Somali families, we think that we are eating British food, but this is not British food. It is very unhealthy. And it is damaging the health of our youngsters.' (SPAN focus group, 27 May)

The appeal of highly processed foodstuffs to children in particular was a recurring theme in conversations among Somali women in Easton. One asked, "Why do children love takeaways so much? What do they put in it? They put magic in it!", and others chimed in: "They put something in it. They put magic in it? Magic!" and "They put something addictive in it" (SPAN workshop, 30 October 2016). Our conversations linked this observation to the new 'science' of value adding: the modification of supermarket food products through the addition of sugars, fats and mildly addictive derivatives such as peptides in order to increase 'repeat sales value' (see, for example, Hughes, 2009).

As these comments suggest, project participants distinguished between 'cheap' food and 'affordable' food. Food needs to be inexpensive but the proliferation of cheap, processed food is part of the problem. While cheap, processed food may satisfy hunger quickly, it is often low in quality and abstracted from the context of its production. Evidence links 'cheap' food policies, which tend to focus on calories and costs rather than more holistic indicators, to 'misnourishment' (Carolan, 2013). Thus, it makes sense to include many of the health-care expenditures associated with the obesity pandemic in calculations of the 'cost' of the dominant food system. Projections suggest that the continuing rise in obesity could cost the National Health Service (NHS) an additional £5.5 billion by 2050 (Kopelman et al, 2007). Rather than obesity being a problem of too much food, in many cases, it is linked to the proliferation of policies and subsidies that support the production of cheap, processed foods. Less than 10 per cent of EU food subsidies, for example, support vegetable and fruit production, while among the top five beneficiaries are large multinational companies like Tate and Lyle and Campina, who market products heavily based on processed sugar and corn starch (Carolan, 2013). Cheap food might, seemingly, cost little, but it is extremely expensive, both in terms of economics, when the whole system is looked at, and in terms of other costs that do not reduce to the measurement of pounds or dollars: food crises, widening inequalities and environmental devastation (Wise, 2013).

In contrast to a continuing driver to produce 'cheap' food, the project sought to uncover a set of key principles that focus on 'affordable' food within our wider thinking about commoning and sharing. The ten principles presented in Figure 5.2 engage with spatial regulation at a variety of scales by articulating how the commoning of time and the commoning of space might be folded into community-led urban design processes.

## From deficits to assets

Across the interviews, individuals drew on a rich range of examples of both time and space. These alternative geographies and histories afforded experiential access to other food cultures. Rather than thinking about communities in terms of deficits, there are rich assets, in particular, found among those whose expertise and knowledge is less frequently drawn on: older people and recent immigrants. Older residents in Knowle West drew on a wealth of food memories from childhood and as young adults, while Somali women drew on a wider network of global food memories. These were not simply the binaries of familial home (Somalia) and present home (Bristol), but also included a series of intermediary places along a journey of immigration with their own distinct food cultures. This afforded global awareness of different influences on food and health, and participants benchmarked their experiences against the ways in which the food environment is managed elsewhere, as well as shaped their own hybrid food cultures. As one SPAN participant explained, lived experiences of other food cultures continued to shape daily practices in Bristol: "We don't eat takeaways very often. We lived in Holland for 17 years and have kept those European habits. I was born there. We are wary of the hygiene too. In the Netherlands, it is better controlled" (SPAN workshop, 27 November 2016). Rather than reading these reflections of other food cultures as nostalgic longings for lost worlds, we see them as alternative histories and geographies that can, and are, drawn upon; they shape present food habits and can also be operationalised as means of re-imagining the future.

Who gets to decide what's in my fridge?

**Figure 5.2:** From the garden to the city: ten principles for community-led design of urban food systems

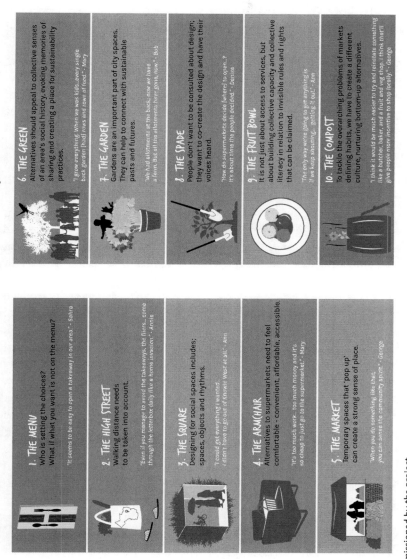

Source: Artist commissioned by the project

This is not to say that participants were naive as to the changing material and structural contexts in which they now lived. In Knowle West, in particular, there was keen awareness of the changes that had taken place over the last half-century. Yasmin drew on the closure of a traditional bakery and its replacement by a convenience shop as critical in shaping both purchasing and eating patterns (KWMC focus group, 13 June 2006). Meanwhile, Fran was convinced that the time of shopping in small local shops – an oft-repeated memory from older residents from Knowle West – was well and truly over (KWMC workshop, 11 March 2016). However, while she was well aware of the broader structural changes that had taken place, Fran did not see history simply as a lost past – as ideas of nostalgia would suggest – but rather saw history a mine to be drawn upon to re-imagine the future, reflecting that "we can use natural foods, because we used to, but now everything is cheap and processed. But it must be possible again – because we used to" (KWMC workshop, 11 March 2016).

Given their experience of other food cultures of the past, older residents from Knowle West placed emphasis on buying food – and not just eating food – as social experience. The loss of local shops was mentioned by many – the sense of creativity, connection and grounding of food in social exchange was associated with a richness surrounding food cultures that has been lost. Some participants suggested the need to have a sense of a 'local centre', a sense of the place having its own sense of value that is not primarily defined by being outside or distant from the city centre (Ann, KWMC, 22 August 2016). The importance of the high street is both its walkability from home and its sociality (see Figure 5.2). Memories of bumping into people were picked up by older residents, for example, Bob commented that "when there were shops, people walking around continuously, we were always talking to people, communicating, you had places to go" (KWMC Fridge Raiders event, 22 January 2016). Shops are not just about buying things, they are also to do with where the community goes (together) so as to build more sense of connection (George, KWMC, 22 August 2016).

Embodied historical memory of past food cultures was also drawn upon by older residents to imagine and enact change. Knowle West resident Bob reflected that they stopped growing vegetables because everyone else did (embodying principle 7 in Figure 5.2). Now that he is older and has more time, he has a different perspective and feels that it is perhaps time to "Maybe go back to the old things we used to do" (Bob, KWMC, 1 September 2016).

This sense of a rich storehouse of historical (and geographical) possibilities is something that we discovered through the process of working with communities with a rich set of food assets in both Knowle West and Easton. Principle 6 in Figure 5.2, *the Green*, emphasises that food alternatives work best when they appeal to collective senses of social history, evoking memories of sharing and creating a place for sustainability practices. Older residents in Knowle West and Somali women in Easton were conscious that they held threatened food knowledge and felt a responsibility for generational transmission, to the extent that the latter group of women are setting up the Somali Kitchen as a community interest company with some support from Coexist and Anne-Marie Culhane, not just a food business, but a social enterprise that furthers participation in food and cultural exchanges.

Individuals across both communities feared the loss of distinctive time- and place-based food cultures by the market, in particular, by a homogeneous and homogenising fast-food culture. As Mary from Knowle West explained:

> 'It's just so sad that we've lost that way of life, and we need to do some more around education to get that back into kids' minds, that they can get out there, they can eat, it is fresh, it is nice. You can eat grass, you can eat berries. You can eat practically everything. But a lot of it is they don't need to. They've got a McDonald's down the road, haven't they?' (Mary, KWMC, 18 May 2016)

These concerns with fast-food culture were voiced with particular emphasis by many of the participants from Easton, who highlighted that eating "junk and unhealthy takeaways" was a key issue as it had become part of the 'culture' of the community (SPAN focus group, 27 May 2016). One of the most significant elements of the research project in this regard were self-conscious attempts to draw on, celebrate and disseminate shared place-based histories through enacting alternative histories and geographies in the here and now. In Knowle West, this built on a range of pre-existing initiatives, for example, a Bread Group that, as one participant explained, operated through intergenerational "networks" that tapped into the food knowledge held by "grandfathers and fathers of families" who were "passing that on", which he now, in turn, was passing on to his own children (KWMC focus group, 13 June 2016). Building on the success of these venues for sharing indigenous knowledge, we held a foraging event in Knowle West. During this, talk turned to past experiences of picking apples, blackberries, damsons, gooseberries and sloes, and a reassertion of place-based histories of Knowle West as a site of foraging and domestic and commercial (Ribena) drink manufacture.

Pop-up events were one way of summoning these auras of past time-spaces and associations with affects tied to distant locations. This shared focus led us to commission artist Anne-Marie Culhane, who proposed bringing a 'shed on wheels' to Bristol to act as a hub for food-based activities and workshops. Anne-Marie designed and curated the Taste of Knowle West and Somali Kitchen events at the Shed on Wheels with the support of the Community Kitchen at Coexist, working with the partner organisations and community participants in Knowle West and Easton. The Taste of Knowle West events focused on celebrating foods that have been grown, foraged and conserved in the area for many decades, which was an important part of resisting the idea that the area is a 'food desert', despite the fact that there was still perceived to be an inadequate access to a wide range of food options. The pop-up 'Somali Kitchen' installation at Junction 3 in Easton attracted more than 600 visitors and has given rise to a spin-out social enterprise continuing beyond the life of the project. This was recalled as a highlight by many. Sahra, for example, commented that:

> 'It made me proud. This is very important for me to share my culture, and also my potential, to my area. It was fantastic. I didn't expect that. And also now we are more popular, and everyone is saying "What are you going to do?" and "that was a great idea". The idea worked. The smell of the city, and everybody came to it. The spices. I still love it and thinking about it." (SPAN focus group, 9 September 2016)

At Junction 3, Somali women reclaimed and reinvented a space originally designed for 'inside/outside community events' that had been appropriated by market forces after the financial crash (Cohen and McDermont, 2016). This pop-up kitchen was seen as an opportunity to 'share the space [and] the culture' (Somali Kitchen fieldnotes, 18 July 2016). This is a good example of principle 5 in Figure 5.2, *the Market*, where the place-making that the pop-up created included the opportunity for intergenerational sharing that was seen as so important among participants from both communities. Furthermore, rather than being a one-off intervention in space, the experience resulted in a desire to replicate this experiment through the creation of a community interest company, which is underway at the time of writing (see Figure 5.3).

Such experiments in the fabric of urban life also engage with the enclosure of time and space associated with neoliberal capitalism. In particular, the deregulation of working time is particularly marked in the UK, especially among those forced into casual labour and the gig economy. This makes regular eating times problematic compared to countries like Italy and France, where a break in the day is part of the quality of life, although that itself is changing under changing work patterns. The pop-up concept disrupts the usual commuter flows, creating an opportunity for fresh encounters. This is important as many people experience alienation in relation to their daily habits. The differences in regulation between Britain and elsewhere in Europe were drawn upon by those who had experienced other national contexts prior to arriving in Britain. As Susu remarked: "I found out when I came here it was very difficult for me because there wasn't a table time. Some people they don't even have tables in their house! So it's kind of a different way of living. So it was difficult for me" (SPAN focus group, 19 February 2016). 'Table time' was a concept created in this same focus group that took on considerable valency among participants. This is a good example of principle 3 in Figure 5.2, *the Square*, in action, which encourages us to recognise that shared rhythms and spaces need to be taken into account within questions of food

**Figure 5.3:** The Somali Kitchen in Easton

Source: Photograph by Ibolya Feher, 2016

regulation, not just individual needs and choices. The experiences of many of the Somali women of living in other European locations, including the Netherlands and Denmark, helped them to observe that the spatial unevenness of Bristol's food landscape is not inevitable. Drawing on past experiences elsewhere, Susu reflected on the way in which *the Square* was manifested by her experience in Italy:

> 'We don't have a timetable for the food. I think Italians have a good timetable for food. They eat breakfast and then they plan a good lunch. They'll close the office. Even the people that work, they'll leave the work and they'll come home to eat with the families, at the table. And they eat dinners with the families. Here, we don't value the quality of the families and the quality of the food.' (SPAN focus group, 19 February 2016)

Both table time and pop-up events give us a sense of what alternatives might look and feel like. The Food Project helped to develop a Freirian transitional space for people to act on, as well as reflect on, the world, with a view to creating such alternatives (see principle 9 in Figure 5.2, *the Fruit Bowl*).

Some of the conversations in both Knowle West and Easton reflected on the impact of the free market and the lack of regulatory controls in disadvantaged areas (see principle 1 in Figure 5.2, *the Menu*). This means, for example, that a proliferation of fast-food takeaways dominates street culture, while market spaces and historically important social places have been eroded. Reflecting on these issues led to using the principles to lobby Bristol City Council to make Stapleton Road, Easton's principal high street, a cumulative impact area (CIA), favouring small and diverse individual enterprises. With the support of Policy Bristol, we also produced a policy briefing called 'Too many Takeaways' and collaborated with the Bristol neighbourhood organisation 'Up Our Street' to advocate for a change in the way in which permissions are given for new takeaways in Bristol at the level of city planning.

## Conclusion: principles for transforming the rules that shape urban food spaces

The evidence presented in this chapter points towards the need for community planning frameworks that allow more 'bottom-up' input (see principle 10 in Figure 5.2, *the Compost*) into the design of urban spaces for well-being and sharing, which foreground community-based processes of learning and inquiry. This is important as the notion of designing healthy spaces has a contested history in Britain, where campaigns for 'improving' the conditions of the working classes emerged primarily from reformist agendas that carried out quite moralising behaviour-modification agendas under the guise of improving health and sanitation. From the beginning, our project has sought to destabilise the divide between the 'food poor' and the 'food rich' and to encourage the recognition that expertise is everywhere. As the wider Productive Margins programme insists, people with direct experience of poverty and social exclusion are experts-by-experience. If co-production or collaborative research is to work, clearer framing is needed for inquiries that connect experts-by-experience with missing knowledge, and by being clear about what questions are at stake (see principle 8 in Figure 5.2, *the Spade*).

Rather than try to recreate the past or distant homelands, we have built on the emphasis on spatial justice and community-led empowerment processes to create ten principles for informing urban design. Each principle captures a different aspect of the way in which dimensions of the city or 'community spirit' intersect with the regulation of food habits. Paying attention to the power of food memories, we considered how the spaces of feeling and 'auras' associated with the past in these principles might animate a future-oriented approach to policy redesign. We have also developed the language of invisible rules and commoning to talk about social and economic inequality and regulation in a way that opens up possibilities for change.

As a boundary object, food is a crucial connector of worlds that enables those present around the table to interrelate socially, spatially and environmentally in ways that trigger the sharing of past memories, present conviviality and future possibilities. For these reasons, we suggest that food provides a vital route into thinking 'more-than-food policies' – forms of re-regulation that address the way in which inequality in food access and food choices comes to materialise, while pointing to pervasive social and economic issues that reach far beyond food.

# 6

# *Life Chances*: thinking with art to generate new understandings of low-income situations

*Debbie Watson, Sue Cohen, Nathan Evans, Marilyn Howard, Moestak Hussein, Sophie Mellor, Angela Piccini and Simon Poulter*

## Introduction

In what ways do regulatory regimes enact, delimit and inhibit the progress of families on low incomes across England and Wales? Although they may not explicitly interact, diverse regimes are affectively experienced, including immigration status (including from European Union [EU] countries), employment assessments and activation, mental health, child protection, structural and overt racism, and the non-portability of professional qualifications across national systems. In this chapter, we explore how contemporary social practice art materialises these intersections and enables disruptions of regulatory regimes in ways not possible using traditional social science approaches. We focus on a research team that included artists Close and Remote, and explain how the team co-produced, with community members and academics, a socially engaged artwork – *Life Chances* – that aimed to generate new knowledges about the regulatory regimes that low-income families with children experience. Aiming towards what sociologist Yasmin Gunaratnam (2012) describes as a form of improvisational empathy, *Life Chances* worked with Thomas More's (1516) *Utopia* and Ruth Levitas's (2013) *Utopia as Method* as 'a form of speculative sociology of the future' (Levitas, 2013: 85). By staging and troubling contradictory notions of 'life chances' through art, we specifically ask how the regulatory services that families encounter in two urban settings – the Easton area of Bristol and Butetown, Riverside and Grangetown in Cardiff – shape, constrain and enable the life chances of individual families and communities, or what Pierre Bourdieu (1977) refers to as *doxa*, and how these services might be 'otherwise'.

*Life Chances* was co-designed by academics from Bristol and Cardiff Universities, artists Close and Remote, and two community organisations: the Single Parent Action Network (SPAN) in Bristol and South Riverside Community Development Centre (SRCDC) in Cardiff. From the outset, there was an intention to work with social practice art. In addition to its emphasis on collaborative working closely reflecting the principles of co-production, we wanted to work with the everyday materials that families on low incomes encounter. Moreover, we were interested in working with a creative practice that would manifest the distributed, entangled and durational relationships across diverse regulatory regimes. For the purposes of this chapter, a definition of socially engaged art practice might follow Mikkel Bolt Rasmussen's (2017, n.p.) sense of 'Art that leaves the art institution and performs different kinds of interventions or artistic social work, often intended to create some kind of dialogue in conflict-ridden urban space'.

Contemporary participatory, socially engaged art has been inspired by a range of European and North American art movements, including: the readymade tradition of Dada; the focus on the everyday and the spectacle found in Guy Debord's Situationist International movement (Plant, 1990); Fluxus conceptual art events; and performance artworks such as Allan Kaprow's *Happenings* of the 1950s and 1960s, and Miriam Schapiro and Judy Chicago's 1970s *Womanhouse*. In other words, social practice takes up the materials of consumer culture and seeks to recuperate it – making art with, rather than simply for, communities. In socially engaged art, the social, everyday encounter forms the material, the process and the aesthetics of the work (see Box 6.1).

Vibrant debate concerning the role of art in community-involved projects has focused on the relationships between the aesthetic value of the artwork and what art historian Grant Kester terms a dialogic aesthetic that emerges as part of the process in socially engaged art: 'In a dialogical aesthetic ... subjectivity is formed through discourse and inter-subjective exchange itself. Discourse is not simply a tool to be used to communicate an a priori "content" with other already formed subjects, but is itself intended to model subjectivity' (Kester, 2005: 5; see also Douglas, 2018; Pool, 2018). Central to this dialogic aesthetic is 'empathetic identification', which Kester suggests can be achieved along a series of counter-hegemonic axes: the rapport between artists and collaborators; within the collaborators themselves, where a form of solidarity can emerge; and across the collaborators and other communities. In contrast, art historian Claire Bishop argues that the ways in which 'the intersubjective space created through these projects becomes the focus – and medium – of artistic investigation' leads 'to a situation in which such collaborative practices are automatically perceived to be equally important artistic gestures of resistance: there can be no failed, unsuccessful, unresolved, or boring works of collaborative art because all are equally essential to the task of strengthening the social bond' (Bishop, 2006: 179–80).

In *Life Chances*, we aimed to address equally the artistic significance, aesthetics and rigour of the multiple elements of the work and the quality of the collaborative relationships and processes that were at the heart of its production. Between December 2015 and July 2016, 22 workshops were undertaken separately in Bristol and Cardiff and with both groups together twice in Chepstow. The workshops involved jewellery-making, field trips, novel-writing, game design and writing and performing music and poetry. Most workshop participants ($n$ = 17) were mothers of dependent children in receipt of asylum support, or benefits and/or tax credits. Two of the original participants were male, the rest were female; most were from a black or minority ethnic background, including of Black British (Jamaican), Asian or African heritage. Five had arrived in the UK from another EU country, having left countries in Africa and Asia; four of these had been asylum seekers when they arrived in that EU country.

The workshop methods (see Box 6.1) were geared towards producing what we describe as a work of sociological fiction (see Leavy, 2015). We deliberately adopted this term to evoke sociology's contested aim of producing broad-based change through society-level engagement with justice agendas. Sociological fiction, documentary fiction and creative non-fiction methodologically resonate with the production of verbatim and documentary theatre (Forsyth and Megson, 2009), experimental performative and reflexive documentary (Minh-Ha, 1990; Renov, 2004), and the ethnographic and fictional turns in contemporary art more broadly (Rutten et al, 2013). Fictionalised accounts of real events aspire to present people's lives in ways that offer aspects of identity protection, enable ethical encounters with people's testimonies and aim to present testimony and experience in order to critique and transform structures of power. These accounts have a long history that stretches to the late 19th century with Étienne Lantier's journey in Emile Zola's (2004 [1885]) novel *Germinal*, which fictionalises conversations that Zola had with Turgenev. In film, Robert Flaherty's (1922) *Nanook of the North*, Georges Rouquier's (1946) *Farrebique* and Jean Rouch's (1967) participatory ethnographic fiction *Jaguar* all use fiction and participation in order to evoke the drama of everyday life, challenge structures of power and critically frame the ethical and creative relationship between artist and collaborator. In anthropology, a turn towards fiction was initially driven by an acknowledgement of the 'literariness' of ethnography (Clifford and Marcus, 1986: 4). While art historian Hal Foster (1995: 303–4) critiqued the 'realist assumption ... in quasi-anthropological art, in particular with its siting of political truth in a projected alterity', our specific mix of sociological fiction, making workshops and game design plays in the spaces of entrepreneurial ideology and critical art practice to trouble any stable siting of political truth in a projected alterity.

## 'Life chances' as a concept

'Life chances' is a widely used phrase, adopted by UK governments to headline their policies on children, families and poverty but with different ideological foci depending on which political party has championed the concept. In particular, the use of the concept by the UK's Coalition and Conservative governments (2010–16) placed responsibility on individuals to explain their claims of denigration of 'society', rather than on the state. The ideological work of the use of this concept has been to emphasise the role of individuals in 'actualising' their life chances through, for example, some form of entrepreneurial economic activity to lift them out of poverty – an agenda that we were keen to avoid replicating in the making and selling of jewellery that the project encouraged.

However, this is not the only use of the concept as several governments and think tanks (New Labour, Coalition and Conservative governments, the Centre for Social Justice, the Fabian Society) have used the term 'life chances' performatively to produce different effects. The Conservative government's life chances strategy did not define the concept of life chances, but linked it to tackling poverty and disadvantage and making opportunities more equal, emphasising the 'family' and parenting strategies and capabilities (Lister, 2016). This located successful life chances in the two-parent heterosexual family, the cornerstone of a strategy aiming to ensure that parents stay together. Announcing this strategy, former Prime Minister David Cameron (2016a) stated that:

> Families are the best anti-poverty measure ever invented. They are a welfare, education and counselling system all wrapped up into one. Children in families that break apart are more than twice as likely to experience poverty as those

whose families stay together. That's why strengthening families is at the heart of our agenda.

The very notion of life chances can, however, be traced back to the sociologist Max Weber (1978), who first framed the concept when expanding on Marx's analysis of the social/economic factors that inhibit/enable the advancement of different class-based groups. Weber believed that people's life chances were conditioned by economic and structural determinants, and that members of a class (where there is a shared likelihood of obtaining goods and a position in society) shared common life chances. Some believe that Weber's concepts have been mistranslated (Abel and Cockerham, 1993), with *Lebensführung* (life conduct) and *Lebensstil* (lifestyles) conflated into 'lifestyles', emphasising choice. Arguably, Weber saw lifestyles as, in part, economically conditioned. In a commentary on Weber's ideas, Dahrendorf (1979) explains that life chances are the (logical) probabilities of certain events happening, which, in turn, depend on structural conditions such as income, property, norms and rights – not the attributes of individuals.

Weber's concept of lifestyles draws together structural conditions (life chances) and personal choices (life conduct) as its basic determinants. *Lebensführung* and *Lebenschancen* are the two components of *Lebensstil*. *Lebensführung* refers to the choices that people have in the lifestyles they wish to adopt, but the potential for realising these choices is influenced by their *Lebenschancen* (Abel and Cockerham, 1993: 554). This interaction of lifestyle choice (conduct) and potential for influencing choice (chances) is essential to appreciate in the way in which we chose to utilise the concept, where the inherent irony in this inversion from Weber's original concept by the UK Conservative government is unravelled in this co-produced research project. The project name operates as a reification of the concept, exploring individual and collective agency and participatory resistance to regulatory injustices and controls on low-income families from the perspectives of those families involved in the research and through a deep understanding of life chances in the Weberian sense, rather than with a focus on individual conduct or lifestyle choices.

## The semiotics of political propaganda

In workshops with participants, artists Close and Remote focused on the government's *Life Chances* posters that were tweeted and circulated in social media as part of their *Life Chances* agenda. These posters presented heteronormative, mostly white, family groups with no more than two children accompanied by slogans outlining the government's pledges to improve life chances through the provision of relationship support, mental health services, careers advice, housing regeneration and investment in health. The imagery was idealised and lacked any sense of diversity apropos family structures. Close and Remote used these posters in workshops and invited people to participate in a semiotic – specifically, a Barthesian – analysis of the rhetoric of the image.

Drawing on the linguistic analyses of Ferdinand de Saussure, Roland Barthes attempted to wrestle with the problem of whether images were semiotic in a linguistic sense. His sense of the total meaning of the image relied on a mix of the fascination with story and diegesis with the intelligibility of 'culture' as a series of symbols (Barthes, 1977). One of the *Life Chances* posters showed a family of three – a white mother, father and child – hand-in-hand in the foreground, walking towards the viewer. They are standing on a horizontal band of white. Behind them in the mid-ground is a band of light green. In the background, constituting the landscape up to the horizon line is a band of darker green. There are a few trees, simply rendered as blocks of either white or green. On the horizon line stand two tower blocks, side-by-side. The sky is a plain, pale blue. The workshops explored these images as graphic components, as a narrative of a white, heteronormative family realising their 'life chances', and as a series of signs: the tower block in the background signifies the family's socio-economic status; the blue sky signifies hope; and the green grass signifies nature. With these individual components identified, workshop participants replaced visual elements with alternatives to explore how the poster's rhetorical force could be transformed. The white family was alternately replaced with a black family (see Figure 6.1), with a Muslim woman in hijab with a child (see Figure 6.2), with a single father and his children, and other similar images. The landscape was transformed by replacing the tower blocks and green grass with a sandy desert, mosque and olive tree. Importantly, the people in these images are faceless. It is perhaps an unintended outcome of the mannerisms of illustration trends, but this suggests a uniformity and anonymity of despair as the people remain part of a 'faceless society'. Close and Remote introduced participants to a reflexive visual literacy that enabled them to rethink and rework the rhetorics of the political image into powerful and effective counter-propaganda images.

The poster workshops led into further discussion of participants' experiences as families on low incomes. The women who participated in the workshops had a range of craft skills, specifically jewellery-

*Life Chances*

**Figure 6.1:** Reconfiguring 'family' in *Life Chances* imagery

Source: Image by Close and Remote

making. Engaging in skills and cultural technique shared through jewellery-making produced a series of pieces that combined motifs from home countries in Asia and North Africa. Close and Remote had introduced a design of concentric circles made from copper strips in initial workshops (see Figure 6.3), which developed repeatedly in a range of jewellery shapes (see Figure 6.4) and was eventually used to structure the process of the *Life Chances* game (see later), which was based on characters developed out of the stories told in the workshops, separated into constituent parts, fictionalised and combined into new narratives.

Overall, the semiotic analyses that drove new poster designs and the jewellery workshops evidence a conceptual and aesthetic rigour as each element informed the development of subsequent aspects. Sharing methods of image deconstruction with the research volunteers was an important moment in the workshops as the methods enabled

Imagining Regulation Differently

**Figure 6.2:** Changing the landscape

Source: Image by Close and Remote

a move out from critique towards creative production and was a new process and experience for the artists themselves. Specifically, using the same aesthetic palette as the original *Life Chances* poster ensured that critique in the form of new posters and jewellery would be recognisable to participants. French philosopher Jacques Rancière (2004: 63) usefully discusses the relationships between visibility, aesthetics and politics:

**Figure 6.3:** The *Life Chances* logo and jewellery material

Source: Image by Close and Remote

> [A]n aesthetic politics always defines itself by a certain recasting of the distribution of the sensible, a reconfiguration of the given perceptual forms. The dream of a suitable political work of art is in fact the dream of disrupting the relationship between the visible, the sayable, and the thinkable without having to use the terms of a message as a vehicle.... Suitable political art would ... [produce] a double effect: the readability of a political signification and a sensible or perceptual shock caused, conversely, by the uncanny, by that which resists signification.

The workshops acknowledged the necessity of the double effect of the readability of political signification and the shock of the new offered through the remixing of visual elements.

## The 'game' of *Life Chances*: *Lebenschancen*

The initial workshops produced new posters and jewellery, and were used to workshop hybrid characters to be used in the collaborative writing of a novel. Moreover, this work generated the necessary

**Figure 6.4:** Examples of jewellery made in workshops

Source: Image by Close and Remote

elements of the *Life Chances* game, the aim of which was to enable people to experience character stories as both an embodied experience and as a dynamic, performance-based art. Designed for the Arts and Humanities Research Council's (AHRC's) Connected Communities Community Utopias festival in 2016 (to coincide with the 500-year anniversary of *Utopia* [More, 1516]), the game was designed to disrupt everyday knowledge of life on low incomes from the perspective of interrogating what life chances meant in the context of welfare reform, punitive regulatory measures and, in particular, the intersectional experiences of nationality, citizenship, education and access to capital and resources in all their forms (see Figure 6.5).

In the game, players quickly find that some characters have greater access to capital and are physically more mobile on the board than others. For example, Mona Ali, a non-EU asylum seeker from Somalia with a secondary school education (see Figure 6.6) is unable to move from the starting position in most scenarios played, while other characters have greater economic capital to draw upon, or the ability to increase earnings as they have the right to work in the UK (a right denied to asylum seekers such as Mona).

**Figure 6.5:** The original *Life Chances* game mat

Source: Image by Close and Remote

Here, it is possible to see multiple regulatory impacts on Mona and her daughter, which start with her asylum status but are then experienced through an inability to work and better her situation, and asylum housing processes that move her from Bristol, where she has family support, to substandard housing in Cardiff, where she feels completely isolated, which exacerbates her already poor mental health.

While we started with the language of transactions between people who have different 'starting points' in the game, it became evident as the game developed that there were alternative analyses that could be used to understand what was happening. Transactions are not solely at individual levels or purely concerned with economic capital, but reliant on the regulatory systems and societal structures within which people transact. To understand what the gameplay was enabling in respect of understanding the nuanced interactions of people in different regulatory regimes, we have utilised concepts

# Imagining Regulation Differently

**Figure 6.6:** Example of one of the *Life Chances* game cards

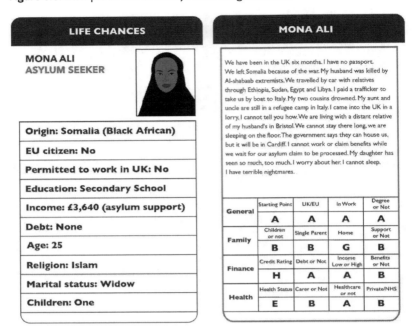

Source: Image by Close and Remote

from Pierre Bourdieu. The game mechanics operate across a 'field', that is, a 'Configuration of relations between positions objectively defined, in their existence and in the determinations they impose upon the occupants, agents or institutions' (Bourdieu, 1992: 72–3). For players in the *Life Chances* field, the 'Medium of these relations, these determinations, is capital, which is hence both product and process within a field. All capital– economic, social and cultural – is symbolic, and the prevailing configurations of it shape social practice' (Grenfell and James, 2004: 510).

This is illustrated as players experience the nuances of *Life Chances*: some have little income; others have substantial income and wealth. However, in some cases, income is offset by possible debt as in some contexts, the poorest characters can progress (albeit fleetingly) as they do not have the means to borrow money in the first place, while those with high income potential are limited by poor health and the experience of Department of Work and Pensions (DWP) work assessments, or by caring responsibilities and the burden of childcare costs. Other characters illustrate the challenge of being highly skilled and educated in one country only to find that the capital (economic, social and cultural) that they understood that they had in one national context is either not recognised or cannot be exchanged in a new regulatory state when people migrate to the UK.

Bourdieu's theories have significantly informed our understandings of how the *Life Chances* game has operated in the project and has similarly deepened our understanding of life chances as a concept when lived stories are played out in the game field. *Habitus* operates as the organising structure within which individual actions and dispositions reside and is the 'power of adaptation. It constantly performs an adaptation to the outside world which only occasionally takes the form of radical conversion' (Bourdieu, 1993: 88). Some of the characters in the game experience *Hysterisis*, that is, Bourdieu's concept of being like a 'fish out of water' (Bourdieu and Passeron, 1979), where the structures of their habitus and dispositions remain the same but conflict with the environment in which they find themselves: 'Innocence is the privilege of those who move in their field of activity like fish in water' (Bourdieu, 1986: 257). This is particularly the case for recently migrated characters such as Nadjma Murabit, the qualified doctor from North Africa, who finds herself unable to practise medicine in the UK as she cannot afford £700 to take her English-language tests, or for Asha Silano, whose teaching qualifications from Somalia are not recognised in the UK. They are both qualified professionals but are in new national regulatory systems where they become 'fish out of water' and dependent on state financial assistance. The intersectional experiences of regulation and the impacts of multiple systems on individuals are also revealed. For example, Asha, unable to work in the UK as a teacher and reliant on benefits and her husband's minimal income as a bus driver, experiences further hardship as the novel outlines the impact of the Universal Credit system roll-out, where they had to wait for six weeks for their first payment. The result of this error is played out in the fiction as Asha is forced to access a food bank and is unable to pay for her youngest two children to attend a school trip. She is also worried about Brexit as she and her family claimed asylum in the Netherlands, resulting in some of her family having Dutch passports and some having UK passports.

For other characters, the taken-for-granted power, the ability to progress their life chances and their potential for capital accumulation also become visible in the game as they progress exponentially, while observing others that remain fixed in (literal) positions on the floor mat. This is exemplified by fictional characters such as Barry Hamilton, the chief executive of the fictional security firm G4N, which develops and manages the roll-out of the Universal Credit system in the novel, as well as Sir Newton Abbotsley, the owner of the *Daily Saliva* newspaper

– both of whose social, cultural and economic capital enable them to navigate regulatory systems and avoid financial ruin and political scandal. This is what Bourdieu describes as an experience of *doxa*, where 'The systems of classification imposed by the group to which an individual belongs, and the power relations within the group – is taken for granted and experienced as natural' (Dumenden and English, 2013: 1080).

Observing the game in action, it is interesting to note that even when embodying other people's characters and life narratives, players start to associate with 'people like me' (in the game world), and those who advance socially and economically start to compare income, education, career and family. Bourdieu (1977: 82) claims that dispositions, habits and behaviours mark out people as belonging in certain groups and located in certain habitus: 'It is each individual's habitus that determines the true nature of the interaction – that is, the habitus defines the social distance between social agents brought together in physical space because each individual carries with him/her forms of dispositions that are markers of his/her social position within social space'. This relates to Rancière's (2004) ideas of what is 'sensible' to some, and it is exactly this 'social distance' that engenders the 'insensible' that the game challenges. People can play different characters from different walks of life and physically stand in the same small space and together experience the injustices of an unequal society. Players are confronted in intense ways with questions of institutional racism, paternalism, social networks that enable progression in life chances and the role of the state in wealth redistribution.

## Box 6.1: Social practice methods

We used co-production methods throughout the *Life Chances* project. In its initial stages, we worked with project participants to co-write a call for artists to join the project and participate in the research. We considered art as knowledge-producing in itself (see Allegue et al, 2009), rather than as a way to communicate research, as a way to engage different publics in research or as an instrument of well-being (Matarasso, 1997). The call for artists was initially drafted by working group members with experience of producing art. It was then circulated to the wider working group and core participants for comment. We then co-designed the shortlisting and selection process to ensure that community participants felt that they owned the process and criteria. This mixed an initial pitch and trial-run workshop with community participants from Cardiff and Bristol with an interview with the core working group team. As part of their pitch, Close and Remote stated that the aim of art should be to make work that is of long-standing value, where value is understood as involving, but not be limited to, social benefit and is expressed through both process and outcome (see Simoniti, 2018).

Key social practice methods were:

- *Semiotic analysis*: in Saussurian semiotics (as opposed to Peircian), the sign is composed of a signifier (the form that the sign takes) and a signified (the concept it represents). Roland Barthes (1977) applied this to analysing images in order to argue that they work to 'naturalise' cultural forms. The goal in semiotic analysis is to establish underlying conventions by identifying significant differences and oppositions in an attempt to model a system of categories, relations, connotations, distinctions and rules of combination. By analysing the constituent elements of the government's *Life Chances* posters (colour, setting and representations of family, race, sexuality, ability), participants developed an understanding of the creation of their affective experiences of regulation vis-a-vis cultural signs.
- *Stimulus-response and devising*: through repeated performative signposting by the lead artists, participants and researchers were 'located' in the novel during the sessions: 'We are now in the jewellery business inside the novel – what happens next?'. This created a fictional and playful space in which participants could explore what running a business might mean outside of the apparent confines of everyday regulated experience. Workshop encounters created a setting in which to begin imagining a fictional narrative where people came together to participate in jewellery-making workshops and to share their experiences of living on low incomes. Actual participants first shared their lived experiences and then extracted aspects of these to begin devising characters comprised of disparate elements of testimonies from multiple people. This method of 'making and talking' (Watson et al, 2016) acted as a prompt for people from very different experiences and cultural heritages to collaborate.
- *Developing fictional characters*: the group used their analytical and conversational encounters to begin developing their fictional characters. They used drawing and writing on flip charts and using Google Docs to support a collaborative process. Sessions enabled co-authoring by bringing together participant experiences of regulation through characterisation and narrative. Participants amended and edited aspects of their characters and plotlines all the way through the writing process. Remixing aspects of different people's experiences allowed us to create hybrid collective-individuals and to re-imagine systems in ways that participants believed would better support their families in contexts of state intervention. Later in the process, the collaborative writing was supported by a scriptwriter, who sought to ensure that the fiction followed narrative conventions in terms of setting, character, conflict and resolution.

- *Transactional analysis*: drawing loosely on transactional analysis, we designed an approach derived from the therapeutic work of Berne (1958) and ideas from psychoanalysts such as Sigmund Freud in order to understand and map the transactions and ego states between adults and children in family therapy. We did not have any intention to adopt this approach in its technical, disciplinary sense. Rather, we adapted the approach to focus on the content of transactions between people in a physical interactive space, trying to expose and explore the transactions that are implicit in life systems (that is, benefits). This enabled participants to take characters from the book and develop them into playable actors in the floor-based game, where, depending on the detail of your character, you can move to different parts of the *Life Chances* mat denoted by points on interlocking circles modelled on the project logo and jewellery motif.

Key to the successful use of mixed methods in a social practice artwork was the aesthetic and conceptual rigour with which they were employed as intersecting. Each method, encounter and outcome was in a conversation with the other and was focused on the goal of creating a coherent, if distributed, artwork.

## Exploring regulatory terrain: social work

In the course of the workshops in Bristol, four participants spoke about their different experiences of social work, especially in children's services. One workshop included developing a fictional social work character, which raised questions such as: 'Who tells a social worker what to do?'; 'Do social workers get training about parents from a range of ethnic and cultural backgrounds?'; and 'How do you complain about a social worker?' To develop a better understanding of the children's services field while providing a backdrop to the novel's storylines, a social work academic with a long history as a practising social worker, together with a family lawyer, were invited to a workshop to answer participants' questions and to discuss problems and solutions. From this, we gained some understanding of social workers' *habitus*, their prime concern being the child, in some cases, infused with a different idea of parenting than that of the participants. The *doxa*, or 'rules of the game', in children's services were not obvious to participants. These included what is legally possible concerning looking after someone else's child (such as private adoption, parental responsibility) and giving up the care of one child to another family member (subsequently, the lawyer sent in information about delegating parental responsibility). Significantly, there was concern about not knowing the 'rules of the game' in relation to childcare procedures. Parents felt that there was a lack of transparency about what was happening and why, and what their role was or could be.

There was a lack of clarity identified in the group about whether a parent could obtain or query minutes of case conference meetings – the workshop experts advised that while minutes cannot be changed, a parent could send in a correction and ask for this to be circulated. Discussion in the workshop particularly focused on an incident reported to the group by one mother who was being audio-recorded in an interview with a social worker but was told that she could not make her own recording. This led to several participants endorsing that they had also experienced this and the social worker expressed her concern that this should not happen, but that she was not aware of any practice or legal guidance that would indicate to social workers that it was acceptable for parents to make their own recording.

The lawyer subsequently sent a report from the Transparency Project[1] outlining when this can be done to equip parents with the knowledge to challenge practitioners if this situation arose again for individuals (Transparency Project, 2016). This report emphasises the lack of research on this issue and maps why, and in what circumstances, parents may want to have their own audio record of meetings with social workers. Interestingly, the report notes that it is unusual for courts to consider recordings from parents and that there are accounts of recordings presented by parents to courts that are of very poor audibility and deemed inadmissible. The report authors do, however, cite legal cases where parental recordings were considered, though only in one case presented did this influence the court outcome:

> In Medway Council v A & Ors (Learning Disability; Foster Placement) [2015] EWFC B66 a mother made covert recordings of the abusive and racially insensitive foster carer who she was living with along with her baby, and until the recordings were played she had been disbelieved. The court relied on the recordings and made findings against the foster carer who was clearly heard verbally abusing the mother. (Transparency Project, 2016: 6)

The Transparency Project report pre-dates the introduction of the General Data Protection Regulation (GDPR) of 2018, but it clearly explains to parents and practitioners the legal situation in respect of the Data Protection Act 1998 and how parental recordings can be considered in the light of this legislation. At the time of the workshop, this guidance was valid and provided assurance to workshop participants that it was legal and possible to ask to record meetings with social workers, and, indeed, court proceedings, as long as permission was sought in advance. However, in the case of court recordings, the report notes that 'A court is unlikely to give permission unless it is clear that the recording is both relevant and reliable' (Transparency Project, 2016: 14).

The development of storylines in the novel highlights tensions between presenting a sufficiently realistic scenario of social work intervention and giving participants a voice in shaping the narrative. Two issues from the workshop with the lawyer and social worker that were used in the published novel included the right of parents to audio-record social work interviews and the legalities of parental responsibility. In both instances, scenarios were 'negotiated' between participants whose 'characters' embodied these issues and with those with knowledge of the system in order to keep the integrity of characters and narratives while also being realistic. This representation of emotionally difficult experiences was made possible through the fictionalisation processes and through real-life negotiations between participants who had devised the characters concerned, including the social work student (developed by one of the community development workers) who is seen to challenge the practising social worker, Debra, in one scene in the novel:

> *[The Scene] Debra (social worker) is visiting the home of Shireen, mother of Marlon who she claims is being racially bullied at school. Debra is accompanied by Secnach (visiting social work student from the fictional island of Zantonica, off the coast of Somalia). SHE, Shireen's friend is also present. Debra has sat down and put her digi-recorder on the table ready to record the discussion when ...*
>
> 'Hang on,' Shireen takes her phone out of her pocket, presses record and puts the phone on the table. 'I'm sorry but you can't really do that ...' Debra reaches over for the phone.
>
> 'Yes she can,' replies SHE.
>
> 'This is a confidential meeting about a child's welfare so I'm afraid due to data protection, I must ask you ...' SHE interrupts Debra. 'Shireen can record this meeting, it's within her legal rights.'
>
> 'This is true,' Secnach agrees, 'I was reading about this subject in preparation for this meeting. A parent can record a social work meeting if it is for their personal use.'

'Yes, well, thank you Seeknatch. I was about to say, before the interruption, that if you are recording the meeting, I must ask you to keep the recording for your personal use only. No sharing on Facebook or whatever,' Debra frowns at Secnach and reaches for a biscuit.

'Why would you think Shireen would post personal information about Marlon and her family on social media for all the world to see?' SHE narrows her eyes and shakes her head at Debra. Debra takes off her glasses and smiles. 'Yes. Sorry. I meant no offence. Shall we start again?'

'I suggest we do' says SHE.

'Have a seat, please,' Debra gestures towards the sofa.

'Thank you for offering me a seat in my own yard,' SHE sits down on the edge of the sofa.

Secnach catches SHE murmuring, this woman is a real eediat. Secnach looks over at Debra and can see by the tightness of her lips that she heard it too. (Poulter et al, 2016: 73–4)

The scene then moves to a discussion of parental responsibility for Marlon as Debra mistakenly assumes that Shireen and SHE are in a same-sex relationship and co-parent the child. This illustrates the lack of sensitivity and knowledge that the social worker has in engaging with the friends who support each other with the care of their children. When Debra realises her mistake, she then tries to remove SHE from the discussion as she cannot understand the relevance of her being there if she does not have parental responsibility.

As a piece of fictional writing, this provided a space for participants to make public the real situations that they felt were discriminatory, with practitioners who were ill-informed of their situation. Leavy (2015) suggests that empathy is created in fictional writing through *interiority*, which allows readers to access the inner lives and emotions of the characters, and through a process of *interpretive gaps*, that is, writing in such a way that 'readers have to use their imaginations to fill in gaps that can sensitise them to emotional complexity' (Leavy, 2015: 57). She claims that these processes are not dissimilar to social science research practice as both are in the pursuit of verisimilitude: the 'creation of a realistic, authentic and lifelike portrayal' (Leavy, 2015: 57). Debra is characterised as a white, middle-class, middle-aged social worker who lives in a cottage with a cat. It is this characterisation that prompted us to organise for a black Jamaican social worker to talk to workshop participants, and this felt important at the time to challenge the stereotype portrayed. Yet, the embodiment of Debra is symbolic of the white oppression, lack of cultural sensitivity and institutional racism perpetrated by regulatory workers towards them and their families that participants were determined to convey throughout the project process. It was unnecessary to tell the reader how participants *felt* about their experiences of social workers – Debra embodies these experiences and Secnach provides a foil, as well as an alternative reality within the realm of social work regulation.

Yet, in writing the novel, we also leave many things unsaid. These are the '*interpretive gaps*' that Leavy (2015) describes and that are possible in a speculative fiction such as this. We had no privileged access to any form of 'truth' and these gaps allowed honesty about this and the incorporation of hesitancy and uncertainty about what was known of people's stories, including those of the fictional Debra, who we discover is distracted by her own health concerns and caring for her mother who has dementia. The focus on producing a novel provides opportunities for readers 'to explore meanings rather than truth, existence as opposed to reality' (Tierney, 2004: 162). This is particularly the approach taken as we point to the layering of regulatory systems that impact individuals and the cumulative impact of injustices. In the scene outlined earlier, SHE is seen challenging social work practices and supporting her friend Shireen. Yet, the novel also reveals her own challenges with racism in the workplace and the ways in which she attempts to address this – ultimately resulting in her resignation and increased concern for her family's economic stability.

## Conclusion

In this chapter, we have argued that a social practice arts approach can enable examination of what are often a dizzying and alienating range of regulations and regulators. *Life Chances* has created a number of obvious tensions and lived contradictions. By supporting an engagement with 'the means of production', we manifested and materialised the agency that collaborators already had but were perhaps not facilitated to act out. Fictional spaces were complemented by real-world spaces in which a creative and critical use of the reified materials and languages of *Life Chances* as government ideology were reflexively enacted through the creative production of empowered, economically active individuals engaged in creative-entrepreneurial endeavours. This was never intended to represent the neoliberal antidote to poverty. Rather, it was a playful exploration of the means of production that confronted the political ideologies embedded in notions of entrepreneurialism. Making and selling jewellery became possible for participants but was never going to be a means out of low income, and we discussed this conflict throughout the project. Ironically, the entrepreneurial agenda has continued in unplanned ways as participants have set up a community interest company focused on supporting young people in impoverished black communities to develop economic skills through the vehicle of socially engaged art. This focus defies government agendas of entrepreneurial art as a means of income generation and continues our reification of *Life Chances* through participants' motivations to enable young people at the margins to access knowledge and skills in order to support their economic growth.

The project provides a novel perspective on the role of fiction, in that fiction of this kind can link real people and their lives to the power system and therefore create commentary. While the 'characters' presented have been utilised to illustrate the impact of individual regulatory regimes – asylum processes (Mona), the portability of qualifications (Nadjma and Asha) and child protection social work processes (Shireen and SHE) – the socially engaged arts methods have also created important insights on the intersectionality of people's experiences and the spiralling impact of multiple and often punitive regulatory systems on individual families. These insights are essential to social science understandings of the lived realities of regulation and became possible through the methodological approach adopted.

Overall, *Life Chances* has created autonomous artworks that disrupt and force the spectator to question the status quo, using utopian thinking to re-imagine the welfare regulatory systems that currently delimit people's lives. This socio–political art practice has resulted in both *objects* of arts practice identified as art and tentative, and as yet precarious, *processes* of empowerment, education, participation and democratisation. Importantly, *Life Chances* also has unmet potential to affect *spectators*, and it is this potential that continues to be tested in new contexts and with new audiences through engagement with regulators, policymakers and politicians as we explore the potential of the artwork to develop societal capacities to understand the experiences of families in low-income situations in more socially just ways.

## Note
[1]   The Transparency Project is a registered charity: 'We explain and discuss family law and family courts in England & Wales, and signpost to useful resources to help people understand the system and the law better' (see: www.transparencyproject. org.uk/).

7

# The Making, Mapping and Mobilising in Merthyr project: young people, research and arts activisms in a post-industrial place

*Emma Renold, Gabrielle Ivinson,
Gareth Thomas and Eva Elliott*

## Introduction

This chapter tells the story of a research-engagement project called Making, Mapping and Mobilising in Merthyr (otherwise known as the 4Ms project). The project explored young people's sense of place and well-being while growing up in Merthyr Tydfil (hereafter referred to as Merthyr), a small post-industrial ex-mining and steel-making town of roughly 58,000 people in the South Wales Valleys. Once a hub of industrial activity and innovation, along with other geographically close regions, Merthyr has experienced a deep social rupture in recent years owing to deindustrialisation and the closure of ironworks, coal mines and manufacturing industries that had served as cultural links underpinning the rhythms and rituals of Valleys life (Walkerdine and Jimenez, 2011; Ivinson, 2014). Our project took place predominantly in a housing estate based on a design reputed to have been inspired in the 1950s by romantic Italian hilltop villages. The estate expanded in the 1970s, and by the 2000s, had become dilapidated and a place with high levels of unemployment. In a context of tightening austerity, this housing estate and the people living there have been subject to stigmatising media accounts fuelled by television's 'poverty porn' industry (Tyler, 2015) and, at times, by local residents themselves (Byrne et al, 2016; Thomas, 2016). The 'realities' of poverty tend to be portrayed in popular media through no-hope narratives of despair (Thomas, 2016; Thomas et al, 2018).

In contrast to other projects in the Productive Margins programme, the 4Ms project did not set out to investigate a specific element of regulation. Rather, we approached regulation as it occurred through the everyday experiences of living in a place that is in many ways at the margins, in terms of the explicit as well as the hidden effects and affects of poverty. The initial aim of the project was thus to attune to young people's knowledge as experts of living in this post-industrial place and to co-create research methods and encounters in order to find out how a range of regulatory regimes mediate and impact on their everyday lives.

The 4Ms project took shape across a series of three overlapping phases. We began by exploring the affective contours of the young people's neighbourhoods (Thomas, 2016). During this first phase, activities were designed to enable young people to speak back to geographic information system (GIS) mapping technologies used by police to detect crimes in specific neighbourhoods (Innes, 2014). The following two phases were informed by research-activist scholarship[1] as each had an activist dimension that drew upon arts-based methodologies to source the expertise, experience and creativity of young people, and to distinguish how this expertise and knowing can be politically productive. The second phase invited young people to participate in more explicitly activist activities using arts-based methodologies (see the Zebra-crossings and Relationship Matters projects later). The third phase involved co-producing workshops with artists[2] to explore young people's sense of place. Each of these phases drew upon and extended the research findings from the GIS mapping tool.

In the following sections, we give a sense of the twists and turns of the research creations and activisms that unfolded across each phase. We show how research questions and methods, as well as the process of making research matter (Barad, 2007), evolved in ways that were unplanned and unanticipated. The next section briefly outlines the theories and speculative processes of attuning to dynamic and non-linear processes of pARTicipatory[3] research (Renold, 2018).

## Participating in place: finding our way

Throughout the project, we became increasingly inspired by Erin Manning's (2016: 47) processual notion of art as a way of learning and acting 'as a bridge toward new processes, new pathways'. Drawing on a medieval notion of art as 'the way', she defines art as a process, not something to behold. Manning argues that to conceive of art as the manner of *how* we engage helps us glimpse 'a feeling forth of new potential'. Our approach became a 'philosophically informed making and thinking about making which unfolds with a focus on invention and evaluation' (Hickey-Moody, 2015: 169). Inspired by feminist New Materialism methodologies (Barad, 2007), we came to pay attention to the role(s) of matter, artefacts and creative methodologies in the humanities and social sciences (Van der Tuin, 2016; Coleman and Ringrose, 2013; Taylor and Ivinson, 2013; Geerts, 2016; Ringrose et al, 2018). Moreover, we came to embrace the unpredictable nature of how 'chance, change, dissent and disagreement' are at the core of arts-based research approaches (Hickey-Moody, 2016: 172; see also Chapters 2 and 6, this volume). Indeed, working with Manning's notion of art as 'the way' has enabled us to take up Barad's call to take 'responsibility for the fact that our research practices matter' (see also Meissner, 2014) and allowed us to connect to the iterative opening of responsiveness in our pARTicipatory work with young people – in both school and youth centre settings – and the wider network of teachers, youth workers, artists and community organisers.

Throughout the 4Ms project, the team expanded across the 12-month period, and at various times included young people from a local youth centre and a range of schools, youth workers, teachers, artists, community members, and academics from Cardiff University and Manchester Metropolitan University. We worked with digital technologies (GIS mapping) and arts-based methods to enable forms of expression that went beyond seated interviews and the spoken word (Leavy, 2017; Wang et al, 2017; Gallagher, 2018). At various times, our pARTicipative approach included the use of still and moving images, walking tours, filmmaking, dance, soundscapes, and visual arts, all of which were made possible through our long-term collaborations with musicians, a choreographer, visual and sound artists, and a professional filmmaker. Our arts-informed approach aimed to connect to the embodied (Springgay, 2008; Ellingson, 2017) and multi-sensory (Pink, 2007) dimensions of being-ness in place, and to offer up alternate modes of expression in order to enable young people to express what was important to them. The following sections describe our evolving process, how it productively regulated *for* engaging with what came to matter and how we collectively responded to what unfolded.

## Regulating for 'response-ability' with 'art-ful' research-activisms

The first project phase involved reworking a GIS tool designed for police use. Research has demonstrated that when adults are interviewed by local police using the GIS tool to identify neighbourhoods and crimes associated with them, young people emerged as antisocial and as the perpetrators of crime. We found that because the survey questions were designed to detect crime, the tool was heavily biased. We attempted to modify the GIS tool to enable young people to speak back to findings that pathologised them and to counteract the regulating effects of the technology (Thomas et al, 2018).

As part of this, we sought help from the technicians who train the police to use the GIS tool.[4] The trainers helped us to address some of our concerns, as well as those of the young people. To mitigate against bias, we used the GIS tool – which included the survey element – within a broader and more open-ended narrative interview approach. As part of this, we included additional questions that enabled young people to identify the positive as well as negative features of places, such as where they felt safe (as well as unsafe). Instead of only relying on quantitative data generated by the GIS questionnaire, we audio-recorded the broader interviews and transcribed them in full. We used the interview transcripts, together with the GIS mapping data and the quantitative data from the GIS modified questionnaire, in research reports. Even so, the GIS tool regulated what young people felt they could discuss. In the course of the research, a number of young people observed that the tool could further stigmatise their town and distort their everyday experiences, and that it ignored positive perceptions of living in an ex-industrial place (Thomas et al, 2018).

The use of the GIS tool and our broader interview schedule was further regulated by issues of access. Two schools and the youth facility agreed to participate; however, teachers controlled which students to put forward. Teachers identified specific students who they believed were representative of both the year group and the school as a whole (that is, a mix of people with different genders, ethnicities and educational statuses). They told us that they also chose students who they considered would benefit from taking part, and/or who they felt 'could cope with missing a class'. A total of 56 young people took part, and despite several challenges, including the prevailing inappropriate wording of many of the GIS survey questions, the interviews and more open questions enabled us to identify several new and interesting topics to pursue. These focused on spaces associated with social problems in their town, such as instances of assault, drug/alcohol use and domestic abuse, and environmental issues, such as vandalism, litter and graffiti. All were perceived to impact on their sense of well-being or, at least, were cited as irritants or grievances (Thomas, 2016; Thomas et al, 2018). In the next section, we describe how we took these issues

## The Zebra-crossings project

Following the school-based interviews, we organised a further seven sessions in one school that was willing to continue working with us on an activist research project. The other school was keen to continue but eventually declined due to fears of young people missing lessons during an inspection period by Her Majesty's Inspectorate for Education and Training in Wales (Estyn).[5] However, this school agreed to a series of lunch-club meetings to address the issue of sexual harassment and violence (see later).

The activist project, 'Zebra-crossings', was a collaborative endeavour between the young people, the research team and Citizens UK, an organisation building diverse alliances of communities to 'organise for power, social justice, and the common good'.[6] A total of 11 young people volunteered to participate. Some had been interviewed in the first phase and others, who were part of a citizenship group in the school, were also invited to participate. As collaborators, Citizens UK worked with the young people and research team to explore issues informed by the earlier interviews.

Over a period of around three months, we ran various sessions both inside and outside the school, including local walking tours, focus group interviews and art-based activities. Although the concerns that emerged in these sessions were similar to those identified in the earlier interviews (for example, worries over drug and alcohol use, litter, and dark spaces without street lights), several were notably absent (for example, domestic abuse and sexual violence). A range of further issues were identified that centred on unemployment and specific areas of the neighbourhood. One such area was a popular location near the local hospital and youth centre. Young people expressed concerns over dim/broken street lights on a well-used path connecting different parts of the neighbourhood and an underpass that was clogged up with litter and drug paraphernalia. Another concern was the lack of a safe road crossing outside the youth centre. In the fifth session, some young people decided that they wanted to lead a public campaign around three concerns: poor street lighting on a path near the hospital; closing the underpass; and installing a zebra crossing outside the youth centre.

The group decided to involve other young people at a local youth centre in the campaign. In the final session, they invited local politicians and senior police officers to take a tour of the area in which they would outline their three-point plan. During the tour, young people dressed as zebras to draw attention to the request for a zebra crossing. The group explained to their guests how they felt when navigating these spaces, particularly at night. This creative approach attracted press interest, and the positive media coverage in local and national newspapers contributed to further meetings with local politicians, planners and the police. The local council advised the young people that if they obtained matched-funding, they would be able to implement their three-point plan. They did this and, three months later, the underpass was blocked off, a zebra crossing was installed and repairs to street lights started.

While some scholars may take the view that the young people's concerns about navigating dark public spaces simply indicate a fear of crime (for example, Nair et al, 1993; Welsh and Farrington, 2008; Peña-García et al, 2015), we found that their activism enabled them to reclaim *their* space, (re)gaining a sense of connectivity and belonging that had been 'lost in the dark' (Thomas et al, 2018). The campaign represented one effort to recover feelings of sociability and connectivity, and to strengthen counter-narratives of place-based stigma perpetuated by local and national media. In short, their campaign went some way to combat material abandonment and stigmatising narratives through representing *their* town as a place of civility and togetherness (see Thomas et al, 2018).

### *The Relationships Matter lunch club and the ruler HeART activisms*

Interviews in the first project phase alerted us to issues around harassment and violence. Young people spoke about forms of verbal, physical and digital experiences of sexual violence in peer-group cultures and in the wider community. Girls, in particular, spoke of the beeping of van horns accompanied by verbal or gestural sexual propositions. Domestic violence was signalled through descriptions of hearing sounds of violence through bedroom walls. Interestingly, none of these issues were raised in the semi-public forums of the Citizens UK group sessions.

Early in the 4Ms project, one deputy head teacher disclosed fears of how to cope with what he saw as an unprecedented rise in girls' self-harming behaviour and hints of relationship abuse. In response, one of the team, Emma, made a follow-up visit to the schools and offered to work with a group of girls in a lunch club. She invited three of 'the girls' (as they often referred to themselves) who signalled their willingness to 'do something' about the concerns they raised from the first phase. They had talked at length about witnessing gender-based and sexual violence on the streets, online and in school. All three of the girls were keen to return to this more participatory activist phase of the research, which they called the 'Relationship Matters' lunch club. This was an unforeseen, unplanned and only partially funded spin-off project from the more formally organised programme of change-making with Citizens UK. The girls were invited to expand the group if they wished, which they did. In the first meetings, they decided to explore the interview 'data' from the first phase of the project on gendered and sexual violence (including their own). Coincidentally, the Violence Against Women, Domestic Abuse and Sexual Violence Bill was progressing through the Welsh Assembly at the time. They started to align ideas about school-based, micro-violence with the wider national debate. This became one of those rare moments when research 'findings', change-making desires, national policy developments and researcher expertise coalesced.

Over the following weeks, Emma and the girls experimented with what the interview data on gender-based and sexual violence could do when explored with arts-informed practices (Renold, 2018). At this point, they improvised together rather than working with professional artists. This enabled them to attune to the art-fullness of proto-political possibilities of ideas and feelings as they rolled, flowed and came to matter. They had not planned on 'making' anything. The idea to create a ruler-skirt arose from a throwaway comment by one of the girls, who said: "Boys lift up girls' skirts with rulers". As soon as the words were voiced into the space, another girl scribbled in bold black capital letters, 'RULER TOUCHING', and an explosion of ruler-talk erupted about how rulers are used to sexually assault (for example, upskirting) and shame girls (for example, measuring skirt length), how experiences of sexual violence are often ruled out (for example, normalised and silenced), and how gender norms are used to regulate who you can be and what you can do ('rule her, RULE HER, rule her with your ruler'). Soon, they had created four 'd/artafacts': a runway of disrespect; the shame chain; the ruler-skirt; and the tagged heart (Renold, 2018).

Across two further lunchtime sessions, the girls began, as they suggested, 'rewriting the rules' through what we called 'outing practices' that sexually shame girls by marking comments on paper rulers. These paper rulers were turned into paper 'shame chains' to communicate how different aspects of sexual violence are interlinked and how sexual violence restrains them. They then graffitied comments of shame on over 30 bendy acrylic rulers with similar messages about hurt and abuse. They interspersed these with messages for change (for example, 'respect us'). The idea of assembling the rulers to create a wearable piece of fashion activism came into full swing, and the proposal for a ruler-skirt struck a chord. Each graffitied ruler was clipped to a belt, and the skirt took shape.

The ruler-skirt has inspired and informed a piece of direct action to change the school culture. The girls invited 300 students during their school assembly to take part in a piece of direct political action by completing the sentence 'We need a healthy relationships education because ...' on paper rulers. This evolved into political action when Emma shared this activity with other secondary schools, in turn, collecting over 1,000 annotated paper rulers. This evolved into a plan to push the affective buttons of policymakers in a last-ditch attempt to turn around a national Bill that was failing to respond to the voices and experiences of young people.

With the help of Citizens Cymru, they invited 40 other young people from urban and rural South Wales to join their 'Relationship Matters' campaign and Valentine Card HeART activism (Renold, 2018). Valentine's Day cards were hand-delivered to all 60 Welsh Assembly Members (AMs) with three ruler-strips pasted inside. This had an overwhelming effect and the AMs, many quite moved to have received a personal Valentine's Day card, united to support the inclusion of young people's needs and a new practitioner guide and mandatory healthy relationships training in the Violence Against Women, Domestic Abuse and Sexual Violence (Wales) Bill.[7]

Since the passing of the Act, the girls have shared their story and 'd/artafacts' in different ways as and when different opportunities have become available. Their ruler skirt continues to be worn at youth-led, practitioner, academic and policymaker events. Together, we have written up their project as a case study in the new practitioner guidance for Whole Education approaches to 'healthy relationships' (Welsh Government, 2015) and submitted this case study to the Women and Equalities Select Committee's Inquiry into Sexual Harassment of Women and Girls in Public Places[8] as evidence for the importance of creative approaches to sex and relationships education. Some of the girls became key participants in the new bilingual Welsh government online toolkit, *A Young People's Guide for Making Positive Relationships Matter* (Renold, 2016; see also Renold, forthcoming), and we co-authored their story as a book chapter (Libby et al, 2018) so that they can share their reflections in their own words for an academic and practitioner audience.

At the time of writing, it is three years since the young people's Valentine's Day card research-activism. Some rules were changed (new practitioner guidance and training) but their call for mandatory sex and relationships education was shelved and slotted into future developments for the new Welsh curriculum. However, in March 2017, Emma was invited to chair a panel of experts to examine the current and future status of the sex and relationships education curriculum in Wales. This can be viewed as impact: the ripple effect of the activist campaign. Our co-produced research-activism informs the report, and the 'da(r)ta' generated in the original ruler HeART assemblies is carefully placed alongside other published international research on youth voice, a minor gesture (Manning, 2016) of making young people's voices matter in a process given limited capacity to meaningfully consult with children and young people. Indeed, the Valentine's Day card activism takes centre stage as the image for the title page of the panel's vision for the future of a new relationships and sexuality education curriculum for Wales (Renold and McGeeney, 2017a, 2017b). A footnote in the document registers the legacy of a project that started out as a piece of speculative, inventive co-produced research-activism in a small room overlooking the South Wales Valleys in a place alive with revolutionary possibility.

The ruler-skirt has been activating and making ripples and waves in and across policy, practice and public spaces in ways that none of us could have predicted three years ago.[9] It has been touched and read, and its clatter heard, by hundreds of people of all ages from all walks of life: along school corridors, in the street, up escalators, on trains, in teacher conferences, on protests, in the Welsh government and at the United Nations Headquarters in New York (see Renold, 2019). In addition, the ruler-skirt has featured in films that we have made with professional artists, such as *Body Swing* and *Graphic Moves*,[10] to which we turn next.

## Making *Graphic Moves* with art as our *way*

In parallel with the GIS mapping research, we designed a series of arts-based workshops to facilitate other ways to express feelings of belonging, place and safety. The following sections dwell on some of the details of the art-making processes to provide insights into the 'feeling-forth', when intuition in acts of making opened the future to new imaginaries (Manning, 2016).

The workshops generated artworks that grew into the film and exhibition *Graphic Moves*. We worked closely with artists Seth

Oliver, Rowan Talbot and Heloise Godfrey-Talbot to co-produce the workshops, which drew upon expertise, techniques and resources that we, as academics, did not have. We built on our already-existing working relationships of trust and met often to bounce ideas off each other. This process of collective co-creation set the ground for the artists to design their specific workshops. Workshops were designed to enable a wide range of expression and enable 'anything' to happen. We were aware that details are important; the affordances of the rooms where the workshops took place, how many people could fit into a room, the amount of light, the furniture and equipment (such as ink, paint and water), and even the size of the paintbrushes all create potentials and curtail possibilities. These materialities both regulated and facilitated what might emerge. All these elements, and how the areas are taken up in the process of making, have some agency (Bennett, 2010) that becomes part of the creative process. The workshops were titled: 'Mashing up the land', 'The projection workshop' and 'Found sounds and community beats'.

We advertised the workshops, giving details of dates when the artists would be in the youth centre and brief descriptions of the activities. As the date arrived and an artist prepared their equipment, we could only hope that something generative would happen. We planned so that at least one of the academics from the research team participated in each workshop. Some workshops worked well and some worked less well. Some worked first time and others had to be changed and adjusted throughout. In some, the peer-group dynamics suggested that everyone was having fun. In others, the peer-group dynamics became unproductive and worked *against* rather than *for* inclusion, and we had to intervene or ask for support from the youth workers. We had to be vigilant, flexible and use our knowledge of working with vulnerable young people to support them and the artists. The following sections describe incidents from the workshops to give a taste of the importance of the process of making. It was in the making that micro-political moments of possibility emerged.

Shortly after we offered the workshops, the third season of the Channel 4 reality television series *Skint* – a 'poverty porn' (Tyler, 2015) series claiming to tell 'intimate stories of people living with the devastating effects of long-term unemployment' – focused on Merthyr (Season 1 looked at Scunthorpe and Season 2 at Grimsby) and was broadcast on three consecutive Mondays in April 2015. The young people's reactions to the pathologising representations of their place were more than we could have imagined. In workshops, they wrote: 'I feel betrayed'; 'I am dreading seeing the next episode'; 'I really regret taking part'; and 'I am not a bum'. Suddenly, the workshops took on a new urgency and became spaces where young people experimented with ways to speak back to *Skint*. The local morning papers were full of stories reporting interpretations of *Skint* from many angles, though many reinforced negative stereotypes of the place, perpetuating a long-running media trope that describes the town as 'a desperate place' of 'confusion' and 'bleak nihilism' that is 'full of crime' and 'where hard work has been replaced by hard drugs and crime' (see Thomas, 2016). We used such newspaper reports as part of the workshop.

### Mashing up the land workshop

As part of the 'Mashing up the land' workshop, artist Seth Oliver brought newspapers, such as the ones just described, to the workshops. He invited participants to rip the newspapers to shreds as the first stage of a creative paper-making activity. The activity involved soaking the ripped-up newspapers reporting the *Skint* documentary in buckets of water overnight to create mulch. A range of beautiful ink colours was provided and used to colour the water and to dye the mulch. A few days later, the mulch was removed from the buckets and passed through a wire sieve, rolled onto boards and left to dry. The results were new paper parchments. Negative media images of place, dissipated widely through Twitter feeds and encoded in newspapers, were physically ripped to shreds, destroying the very words and pictures that illuminated the place as a bad place.

In one of the mash-up collages, a juxtaposition of images provides some ironic insights into post-industrialisation. The collage[11] includes multiple references, such as The Smiths album cover that reads 'BARBARISM BEGINS AT HOME'. The workshops ignited corporeal acts of annihilation that generated intelligent, witty and contradicting images on new paper. The collages hold affective traces of pride, a 'feeling-forth' sensitive to the past of mining traditions, tinged in the present with the pain and shame of stigma, as well as a forward-looking gaze of future potentiality. Young people literally burst into song as they ripped, plunged and stuck materials together. The singing both evoked and recreated a deep-seated sense of communal belonging that has coursed through so many of our experiences with young people in South Wales Valleys communities.

## Imagining Regulation Differently

### The projection workshop

A group of girls that we had worked with previously in the youth centre unexpectedly turned up to 'The projection workshop' in the school. Up until then, they had distanced themselves from the school-based workshops. They were driven by a desire to 'do something' after watching the first Merthyr episode of *Skint*. Visual artist Heloise Godfrey-Talbot instructed the girls on how to compose a camera shot, how to adjust the focus and how to produce minute images, such as the way in which the wind rippled through a patch of daffodils on a grass verge in the playground. The girls told us that they wanted to photograph Morlais Mountain, which is sometimes visible from the school grounds. It was only years later that we came to understand the significance of the mountain to the local community and to them (Renold and Ivinson, 2019). The girls moved around the school grounds taking panoramic shots of the valleys spread out beneath. They took some intimate shots of back gardens where clothes lines hung, adorned with fluttering garments. These shots became sections of the film *Graphic Moves*, which turned into the vehicle for speaking back to *Skint*.

While the girls were filming, the camera pointed outward to the horizon, capturing the lush, green valley moorland and distant rolling mountains that surround their housing estate, a group of boys came towards us up the steps near the school entrance that was just behind us. The girls had to stop filming to avoid getting the boys in shot. We suddenly decided to ask the boys for their responses to *Skint*. Leanne (pseudonym) tentatively approached one boy, Barry (pseudonym).

Leanne:       'So, what did you make of *Skint*?'
Barry:        'My street was in it.'
Leanne:       'What street was that?'
Barry:        'Orchard Street.[12] It's not a bad street at all, I really like it, everyone is really friendly.'
[We knew from the GIS mapping tool findings that this street had a particularly bad reputation even on the estate, so we wanted to get his positive feelings on record.]
Gabrielle:    'Hang on a minute, would you say that again so we can audio-record it?'
[We grab an audio recorder and direct it towards Barry.]
Gabrielle:    'So, what did you say about Orchard Street?'
Barry:        'It's crap.'

Barry ran off and we were left bemused. It seemed that while Barry spontaneously counteracted the representation of his street that had appeared on *Skint*, when he was given a chance to 'go on record', a more dominant representation territorialised the occasion and Barry reproduced the dominant representation "crap" for a potentially public audience.

## *Reframing* Skint *with* Graphic Moves

When research team watched *Skint*, we noted that it did not include many shots of the mountains, greenery and valleys that can be seen from the estate. Instead, shots usually pointed downward to tarmac roads in need of repair, concrete walls, boarded-up windows and drab shop fronts. The shots actively created desolate images of the estate. When the countryside was filmed, it was through wide-angle scenes that created the backdrop mainly when people were being filmed as drunk, as if to exacerbate a sense of wildness.

*Skint* composed pathologising representations by combining elements such as a young man, flesh, wine bottle, water and the wild to create a message of the unruly. Some of the footage, for example, shows an image of the same water hole (at Pontsticill reservoir) that we used to advertise one of the workshops, and that also appears in sequences in *Graphic Moves* depicting the water flowing into the hole (view the film, Graphic Moves, here: https://vimeo.com/233439593).

In contrast to *Skint*, we created shots that would disrupt and confound the building of 'a' message. For example, *Graphic Moves* includes images of a girl's head that could be read as absurd and yet also beautiful.

The idea for this image emerged when young people projected video footage of outdoor shots taken from around the school onto a wall in a dark school corridor. The pictures emerged as part of a session when one girl's best (boy)friend lay on the floor and projected video footage upwards onto her body, feet, legs and face, showing her composure and his creative use of images of the place where they are growing up and forging a relationship with each other. Only later did we find out that in this relationship, the boy was supporting her struggle with mental well-being and she was supporting his emerging gay identity. These aspects of their relationship cannot be fully known to the audience, yet the images somehow capture an ineffable trace of a union, which could be read as belonging to a place and borne of trust, intimacy, feelings of belonging and reciprocal support. Furthermore, juxtaposing a tree, a head and a young girl does not easily build into 'a' message; instead, the projection technique animates a multiplicity of discordant images. This is just one of the many images that made it into the film. The apparatus/camera created a 'cut' in the flow of movement-time that resonated back to create potentially new experiences, meanings, insights and possibilities.

### Impromptu body-forming workshops

The next example from a body-forming workshop emerged unexpectedly. We return to the girl who was struck by an album cover by The Smiths that appeared in one of the local newspapers and mentioned earlier. It is an iconic image of a 1960s' woman, hands on hips, legs wide, standing tall and backgrounded by an active/inactive post-industrial landscape. This album cover picture was pasted into the newly purple-coloured pulped *Skint* headlines. In a further workshop, her body forming became a queer Peter Pan figure, with aspirational slogans of adventure and freedom, located in the body. Other images seem to flow out into the surrounding space. The feet were rooted firmly in grass made from cuttings of local maps of the area. The collage seems to capture an adventurous spirit rooted in place, becoming more than place. This image was made by a friendship group who referred to themselves as 'outsiders' to the normative cultures of their school. Once again, the process was accompanied by an outburst of collective singing. Lyrics from their favourite, non-mainstream band were sung loudly and joyously as they cut paper and ground their spoons round and round in an orange bucket of paper mulch and ink. We speculate that this is a proto-politics of paper-making, belonging and resistance. They selected a single line each and collectively co-created with Emma what later became a *Metal Mash-Up* poem by the 'angry 12 year olds'.

### Cutting place together and apart

These examples capture the complexity of how place came into view anew. Media representations and the *Skint* series feed a voyeuristic tendency to project difficult emotions, such as loss and abandonment, onto some places. These places become symbolic dumping grounds for general fears of, for example, worklessness, poverty and decline. Some estates become places where these projections come to stick, they become dark attractors. The young people were fully aware of the stigma attached to the place they call home. For example, Barry's personal, spontaneous, affectionate view of his street was superseded by the dominant representation of his street as "crap".

In some ways, *Graphic Moves* takes the more intimate and fragile representations of the place, such as the one that Barry gave when he was taken by surprise, and made them visible. These examples point to the multiple strata of place buried beneath the more dominant discourses and representations. The art activities seemed to unearth other layers, perhaps revealing more intimate connections and more hidden makings of place and gave them creative form. Dominant and pathologising images proliferate through the well-resourced machinery of public media, and are in danger of constantly regulating what can be thought about a place. This is how stigma of place is perpetuated. Our film, *Graphic Moves*, was an attempt to 'speak back' to the *Skint* series by capturing the place through layers of projected images in different ways, ways that spontaneously emerged as young people cut, ripped, soaked, stuck and coloured their way into a 'feeling-forth' of place.

We suggest that the workshops created spaces where counter-images of the estate were able to emerge. The material affordances of paper, ink, water, film and projection, as well as the techniques used to compose sections of the film and set them to music, hint at hidden, precarious and affective ties to place. The images created by young people did not simply counter one flat image of place with another. Instead, they created counter-folds of juxtaposing images that both amplified nascent expressions and created channels, or passages, for feelings of belonging to be reaffirmed. In processes of making, art worked as *a way* for sedimented layers of the history and future potentialities of place to find expression.

The arts-based, film-making processes reflected back a place stigmatised in the media, especially by the Channel 4 series *Skint*, to reveal a place where deep feelings of belonging exist, some joyous and some painful. Multiple layers of visual and auditory sensorial architecture became the film *Graphic Moves*, which cuts real-life footage of streets, parks and buildings of Merthyr together, and apart, with artworks, colour and visuals projected in layers and soundscapes (see also Ivinson and Renold, 2016). The effect has been to diffract the place through multiple assemblages that defy verbal articulation. The sequences of *Graphic Moves* work through aesthetic and affective intensities that create a multiplicity of rippling effects and affects in audiences.

The processes and micro-dynamics that emerged in workshops are retained as traces in the images, sounds and artefacts in *Graphic Moves*.[13] The film and the young people's artefacts are forms of resistance to the multiple systems of everyday regulation and stigma that come with poverty (Massumi, 2015). They contain the residues, fluxes and affects of creative workshop encounters that are the micro-political effects, random movements and paint splashes that counter power and control (Deleuze and Guattari, 1987: 216). *Graphic Moves* created a generative proliferation of layers of hybrid representation that cannot be condensed into one counter-image. Instead, it proliferates a multiplicity of diffractions that have an aesthetic and affective power to move.

## The more-than of regulation and resistance

The Productive Margins programme set out to explicitly work with people on 'the margins' of society in order to enable alternative voices to be brought into current political debate about the regulatory aspects of democracy and participation in times of austerity in the UK. Furthermore, it started from the premise that 'citizens can and do exercise agency within mainstream political spheres through obstruction, challenge, exit, ignoring or bending the "rules"'.[14] The groups at the margins in the 4Ms project were the young people living with legacies of an industrial past that no longer provided a raison d'être for community 'beingness' (Walkerdine, 2010), and we were interested in how it is possible to make sense of a place, its 'matters of concern' (Latour, 2004) and its utopian imaginings with and for young people. Our chapter, we hope, has offered a glimpse at how the 4Ms team attuned to, and worked with, the experiences of some of the young people living in Merthyr who have inherited and must navigate the multiple, contradictory and imperceptible forms of regulation that come with living in this post-industrial place.

This was not a project that held onto predefined research questions, methods or outcomes with a vice-like grip, leaving little wiggle room to reroute when events and experiences emerged that required a change of approach. Rather, our project specifically drew upon arts-based, co-produced practices and activist politics to open up new ways of attuning to, understanding and responding to place-based concerns and how what comes to matter gathers significance in unpredictable ways. What we are beginning to understand from our multi-phased project is that resistance as well as regulation are not stable states of being, but processes that are dynamic and transitory. Our arts-based practices and 'runaway methodologies' (see Renold and Ivinson, 2019) followed a rhizomatic (Deleuze and Guattari, 1987) rather than a linear and systematic approach, and are based on openness, invention and creativity. By offering opportunities to subvert GIS technologies of surveillance and by gifting experimental arts-based workshops, we hoped to enable young people at the margins to communicate anew and to release their capacities to 'use this energy to co-produce new ways of envisioning and engaging regulation'.[15] While we did not know in advance what would emerge from many of the workshops and activities that we orchestrated with artists, teachers, youth workers and Citizens Cymru, we had a strong sense from our previous work of using inventive and speculative methodologies (Lury and Wakeford, 2012) that as new ways to express feelings and moments emerged, we might begin to find out which and how 'regulative frameworks' come to traverse young people's lives. Indeed, the experimental arts-based practices seemed to offer multiple possibilities to disrupt repressive regimes and enable the communication of a wide range of expressions, such as hope, frustration, anger, fear, hurt, belonging and desire.

Mapping the mobilising processes of making in our activist-research confronted us with navigational, ethical and pragmatic issues and practices that we are only now beginning to explore and theorise, with others, in forums and exhibitions,[16] in papers (cited throughout this chapter), and in performances (for example, Ivinson et al, 2017a, 2017b; Renold et al, 2018a, 2018b). The young people's films, poems and artefacts from the 4Ms project continue to act back on us and wider publics as they are shared and infect forums, festivals, meetings and policy agendas with affects that 'cut' their place and their experience together, and apart, differently (Barad, 2007). We continue to share these practices and artefacts as we work to create conducive contexts with and for other young people in Merthyr and further afield so that we/they might continue to find new ways to obstruct, challenge, bend and rewrite the rules in macro-political (the Zebra-crossings and the Relationship Matters projects) and micro-political ways (*Graphic Moves*). We continue to source and assemble, where possible, creative reservoirs that might regulate for and make productive, marginalised and minority ways of knowing and being visible.

## Notes

[1] For further reading on participatory research-activist scholarship, see Fine and Vanderslice (1992), Hale (2008), Wardrop and Withers (2014), Kara (2017), Huckaby (2018), Sandwick et al (2018) and Fine et al (2018).

[2] The artists for the 4Ms project included Jên Angharad, Seth Oliver, Rowan Talbot and Heloise Talbot-Godfrey.

[3] The 'art' in 'pARTicipatory' is emphasised to illustrate how arts-based methodologies (for an overview, see Leavy, 2017) are embedded in participatory research practices (see Renold et al, 2008; Bradbury, 2015).

[4] To read more about the qualitative GIS method, see Innes (2014) and Thomas (2016).

[5] The purpose of Estyn is to inspect and regulate the quality of and standards in education and training in Wales.

[6] See: www.citizensuk.org/cymru

[7] See: https://youtu.be/tZ3Jkq8QlF8

[8] View written evidence here: http://data.parliament.uk/WrittenEvidence/CommitteeEvidence.svc/EvidenceDocument/Women%20and%20Equalities/Sexual%20harassment%20of%20women%20and%20girls%20in%20public%20places/written/79670.html

[9] See: https://esrc.ukri.org/news-events-and-publications/impact-case-studies/transforming-relationships-and-sexuality-education/

[10] See: www.productivemargins.blogs.bristol.ac.uk/projects/mapping-making-mobilising/

[11] The image of the collage, along with many other images taken in-situ cannot be included in this chapter because the quality of the images do not meet the requirements of the publisher. To see some of the images explored in this chapter, please go to: www.productivemargins.blogs.bristol.ac.uk/projects/mapping-making-mobilising/ and view the film, Graphic Moves, here: https://vimeo.com/233439593

[12] Orchard Street is a fictional name.

[13] See: https://vimeo.com/233439593

[14] See: www.productivemargins.blogs.bristol.ac.uk/projects/mapping-making-mobilising/

[15] See: www.productivemargins.ac.uk

[16] See: www.productivemargins.blogs.bristol.ac.uk/projects/mapping-making-mobilising/

# 8

# Regulating engagement through dissent

*Greg Leo Bond, Daniel Balla, Ari Cantwell and Brendan Tate Wistreich*

## Introduction

The Productive Margins research programme was formed in the belief that the people and communities excluded from participating in the regulatory regimes that impact upon their daily lives have the expertise and experiential knowledge to be politically productive. The Productive Margins' mission statement is that these regimes can be redesigned and harnessed for engagement, ensuring that communities at the margins are engaged in regulatory processes and practices. The challenge is therefore to experiment with new systems of engagement that enable creativity and increase agency. One of the selected themes that the research programme set out to explore was *spaces of dissent*. This chapter focuses on the work co-produced with Coexist, one of the programme's community partners, in response to this theme.

Coexist is a social enterprise set up to create a space where different communities and individuals can grow, share, collaborate and learn what it is to live in coexistence with each other. In 2008, Coexist acquired the lease of Hamilton House in central Bristol, creating a place where the cross-pollination of progressive ideas could emerge by offering low-cost rent to artists, well-being practitioners and social enterprises. Coexist combines elements of radical practice with a distinct mindfulness approach as a means of enabling new forms of social relations within the space. The more dynamic aspects of the organisation's practice are offset by the need to pay rent and fulfil its legal obligations. Therefore, Coexist performs the role of regulator, responsible for the safety of the users of the building and ensuring that the project is economically sustainable.

In the period covered by the research, Coexist discovered problems reconciling its core purpose and values – being open to all and providing space for the community – with the challenge of managing the unequal power relations that make this vision potentially unachievable. It found that its commitment to 'solution-focused' forms of engagement between its various groups meant that it was unable to adequately deal with dissent and conflict. There is a risk within projects with egalitarian ambitions that – in the desire to create a space for 'everybody' and 'celebrate difference' – projects neglect to address latent power relations that perpetuate exclusion and privilege.

Here, we foreground notions of *dissent* not only as a practical question facing Coexist, but also as a means of addressing wider issues of privilege, disagreement and other difficult aspects of socially engaged work. We follow critical theorists who contest that any attempt to pull together different community groups and individuals into a unitary space of consensus will simply reaffirm wider societal hierarchies and social exclusion (Fraser, 1990; Warner, 2002). We also draw on literature from geography which argues that disagreements between groups can provide a basis for connection, and that shows the value of political agonism over consensus (Amin and Thrift, 2005; Barnes and Sheppard, 2009; Staeheli, 2010).

Foregrounding dissent as a form of engagement presented a new trajectory within Coexist's regulatory processes. A distinguishing feature of our co-produced project was the desire to articulate dissent as a series of embodied acts. With this notion, dissent is understood not only as an expression of resistance voiced through language, but also as an opportunity to reconfigure how bodies relate to one another and their material environment. We wanted not merely to expand *who* Coexist engages with, but also to experiment with *how* Coexist exists in different spaces. In other words, the impetus was not to *increase*, but to *diversify*, spaces of engagement in order to see what new social relations might be formed. Dissent is therefore imbued with a transformative potential: disrupting habitual ways of existing in space with the possibility of discovering something new.

The transformative potential of dissent is further inflected by the decision to experiment with arts practice. The Productive Margins programme aligns with more recent critical trajectories in the social sciences, where arts practice is understood not only as a knowledge-*communicating*, but also as a knowledge-*generating*, practice (Allegue et al, 2009). With our co-produced project, we harnessed the unique capacities of arts practice to create spaces of dissent in the form of transient spatial disruptions. This included street art, social sculpture, film, immersive installations and live performances. We were thinking about notions of dissent *through* arts practice, realising that art can generate ephemeral ruptures from everyday ways of thinking and being

(Phelan, 1993; O'Sullivan, 2006; Grosz, 2008; Hawkins, 2013). The initial aim was to create spaces of dissent where a 'new world, a way of seeing and thinking this world differently', could emerge (O'Sullivan, 2006: 1). The long-term challenge would be to translate these creative interventions into a stable strategy for engagement.

## Regulating Hamilton House

Coexist is a registered community interest company (CIC) formed in 2008 by a small group of social entrepreneurs to manage the derelict former office block of Hamilton House on Stokes Croft in central Bristol. The opportunity to lease the 55,000 square foot building on a long-term basis arose when property developers Connolly and Callaghan abandoned plans to convert the space into private housing after the global financial crisis of 2008. Coexist have regenerated the building into a functioning community centre as a means to realise its core purpose to 'co-create spaces that best provide for the communities that surround us' (Coexist, 2016). Moving between the different floors of the building, one encounters artist studios, dance studios, theatre groups, well-being and therapy rooms, a community kitchen, an events space for theatre productions, a charity bike organisation, and so on, with the rest of the building made up of shared office space for social enterprises, charities and independent workers (see Figure 8.1).

The Hamilton House building now possesses a strong DIY aesthetic that evokes the grass-roots approach that Coexist adopted in the regeneration of the once-dilapidated building. Coexist has translated aspects of radical practice into a sustainable economic model in which Coexist rents space in an official capacity. Coexist implements prefigurative politics, meaning that its modes of organisation reflect the future society that it wants to help create. It therefore utilises consensus decision-making tools, flat-hierarchical governance structures and a DIY approach in its practice. The tools and systems of engagement that Coexist utilises are significant given that, as a CIC, it performs the role of regulator within the Hamilton House space. Renting space has enabled Coexist to act as an umbrella organisation to a diverse range of economically precarious practices and labour for which stability offers a lifeline. Offering stability can be viewed as a potential antidote to the struggle for independent workers to acquire a sustainable existence within these so-called times of austerity (Bain and McLean, 2013). By handling a more conventional economic relationship with the property-owners, Connolly and Callaghan, Coexist is able to practise more alternative economic practices elsewhere in the project. Coexist's

**Figure 8.1:** Composition created by Coexist showing the different spaces and activities contained within the Hamilton House building

Source: Coexist, 2016

economic model is designed to enable the low-cost hire of spaces for meetings and workshops in order to encourage the cross-pollination of ideas. Coexist offers space on a sliding scale, while often gifting space and services to socially engaged activities and groups with little to no money.

For Coexist to continue to provide stability, it has a long-held ambition to purchase the Hamilton House building, an ambition that has been consistently reaffirmed by founding director, Jamie Pike, as integral in the organisation's quest to build resilient communities and the only sure way to counteract the market-led development of urban areas. There is a risk that in prioritising economic sustainability, it may become difficult to sustain the more value-led and radical elements of the Coexist project. In their quest for economic sustainability, alternative and non-capitalist organisations will often adopt the 'familiar path from charisma to regularised routine, from inventiveness and passion to bureaucracy, hierarchy, and instrumental reason' (Walker, 1994: 141). This process is often referred to as *institutionalisation*, in which a collective's initial visions and principles are co-opted by the demands of working within an official capacity (Pruijt, 2003; DeFilippis, 2004). Grass-roots organisations and alternative economic practice still contend with the same issues that exist in conventional or big business. Studies have exposed gender inequality (Gregson and Rose, 2000; Oberhauser, 2005), labour exploitation (Samers, 2005; Smith and Stenning, 2006) and racial–class privilege as being prevalent (Hodkinson and Chatterton, 2007; Hanson and Blake, 2009).

## Diversifying spaces of engagement

The approach to co-production implemented for this specific research project aligns with participatory action research methods that engage everyday tensions with academic theory as an iterative process of action and reflection, theory and practice (Brydon-Miller et al, 2003). In this respect, the co-produced research project between the University of Bristol and Coexist was an attempt to articulate theoretical frameworks around engagement in a way that supported Coexist's goal of effecting positive social change. There was an explicit desire from Coexist to experiment with new forms of engagement. A three-year residency working as an 'in-house researcher' enabled a perspective not only of Coexist's organisational practice that accounts for its formal structure and its stated ambitions, but also of the many other tacit practices required within grass-roots action: the emotional investments and conflicting intentions; the idealistic optimism; the self-exploitation and inevitable burn-outs; the evolving attitudes, new knowledges and dominant discourses; and the haphazard and chaotic assemblages clashing with formalised and legal obligations. As an organisation, Coexist embodies and evokes all the troubles, tensions and conflicts that anything close to 'coexistence' will inevitably necessitate. During its more formative years, Coexist was able to maintain most of its egalitarian ideals; the stated intention to 'respond to the callings of the community' (Coexist, 2016) was easier to practise when it had an excess of space waiting to be utilised. In more recent years, as activities and users of the space have increased, so too have the responsibilities of the core Coexist team.

To enable the Hamilton House building to function at its most efficient and economically viable level, organisational practices have been streamlined with the incorporation of a larger core team and separate departments, with each person holding more distinct job roles and responsibilities. The boundaries between Coexist and the licensees renting space have become less amorphous and reflect a more conventional customer–provider relationship. The ossification of roles and responsibilities has made it harder for the team to respond to developing issues and tensions that surround the building, such as gentrification, exclusion, diversity and the increased regulation of public space. The more structured and restricted practice now employed is understood by some Coexist members as an inevitable phase of any organisation. The process of 'Forming, Storming, Norming, Performing' (Tuckman, 1965) has been quoted by some of the longer-serving Coexist directors. However, other team members would prefer to see the collective perform 'more radically and shut down next year' rather than plateau for the next 20 years (weekly meeting, field notes, 22 May 2015). It was through evaluating Coexist's current regulatory processes and governance structure that we began considering how it might be possible to use arts practice as a space that could fulfil some of the more experimental and non-hierarchical forms of engagement.

The adoption of an embedded researcher offered a critical perspective that made it possible to identify a growing concern, and indeed frustration, among team members. The rise in responsibilities and diminishing capacity was restricting the team's ability to construct spaces of critical reflection within their regulatory processes and limiting their engagement strategies with external stakeholders. The opportunity to interrogate decisions on pressing issues within weekly meetings was proving untenable given the number of other operational tasks and *firefighting* that must be addressed. In the past, when certain pressing issues have required further reflection, Coexist had constructed additional ad hoc meetings. However, a rapid increase in team members and responsibilities has made it logistically more difficult to organise this on a regular basis.

Another area of concern was how the frustration and anxiety arising from financial pressures could cause some team members to question the *value* or *use* of more experimental spaces and egalitarian practice. This can then manifest in a situation in which some team members feel that they must either choose a conventional hierarchical business model or succumb to the so-called 'tyranny of structurelessness' (Freeman, 1970; see also Chapter 2, this volume). It is vital to disrupt this assumed dichotomy between conventional business practice and structurelessness. The purpose of utilising arts practice as a space for critical engagement and dissent is therefore not only to *increase* the number of spaces, but also to *diversify* the kind of spaces in which team members, other building users and external stakeholders can engage with one another – to construct more distinct and structured spaces with specified intentions, thereby reaffirming the stance that an organisation need not be viewed as a *place* where people are organised, but can instead be seen as a 'set of fluid processes whereby needs and desires are cooperatively formulated and met ... through a rich multiplicity of means' (Reedy, 2014: 641).

Facilitating a series of interventions – or *spaces of dissent* – through artistic practice enabled us to move beyond situating dissent as a process of consultation, in which data are gathered *by* Coexist *from* stakeholders. Instead, we wanted to approach dissent as an embodied act: an opportunity to reconfigure how Coexist as an entity exists in different spaces. Crucially, we did not merely want to reinforce Coexist's systems for 'measuring' social impact. The purpose of diversifying spaces of engagement was to facilitate situations in which something different could emerge. What this *something different* might manifest to be we were not always sure. It might be different ideas, different behaviour, different ways of relating to other people or different ways of combating social tensions. Arts practice was therefore utilised as a transient intervention to disrupt habitual ways of thinking and being in order to enable space for something new to emerge.

It was important to identify which aspects of Coexist's existing regulatory processes were causing tensions. A salient aspect of weekly meetings that generates tension is the dominance of a *solution-focused* approach to engagement. The solution-focused approach is indicative of a mindfulness discourse that permeates much of Coexist's internal discussions, whether encouraging team members to use the phrase 'yes and' when responding to someone else's suggestion or outlining in their approach document that team members should try to implement *openheartedness* within their practice. A solution-focused approach is not problematic per se, but when it is combined with a lack of capacity for adequate critical engagement, it can create a situation in which disagreement or dissent is positioned as being unnecessarily difficult or obstructive. If there is not adequate time for dissent to be voiced, acknowledged and accounted for, this can contribute to feelings of frustration and disempowerment expressed by team members. This has led to some team members commenting that they have experienced 'passive aggression' in needing to agree with the wider team with a lack of means to register dissent (field notes, 13 May 2015); others have expressed that team members often feel a lack of agency from their ideas being consistently 'hen-pecked' by the wider team (field notes, 1 July 2017).

The impetus to create new spaces of engagement was, then, partly motivated by the need to enable *spaces of dissent* within a particular growing organisation. In doing so, the intention was not to criticise any one specific aspect of Coexist's approach, but to offer balance. The mindfulness discourse of Coexist is a defining feature of its practice and demonstrates its own innovative approach to prefigurative politics. Coexist team members are highly sensitive to the performativity of language. It is embodied in their decision to call themselves 'Coexist' and also in their first act after acquiring Hamilton House in 2008 to hang a banner that simply read 'Everybody' on the front of the building. Each act denotes a performative use of language, making bold statements of intent in their efforts to achieve a potentially unachievable vision. What is problematic is when a clear disparity emerges between the egalitarian ambitions of the language that Coexist implements and the actual systems of decision-making and regulation that it practises. Therefore, the impetus is not to negate Coexist's solution-focused approach, but instead to elevate the importance of dissent and the inability for this to exist within Coexist's current weekly operational meetings. Dissent and critical engagement are an opportunity to converge, challenge and, indeed, transform the codes of behaviour currently practised. This is a vital process of any organisation or collective with ambitions to enable positive social change. Moreover, it is vital for any alternative organisation that does not want to replicate the qualities of larger-scale business practices that they are attempting to refute.

## Facilitating spaces of dissent through embodied arts practice

We explored the theme of *spaces of dissent* as a way of (re-)imagining how we might understand and approach processes of engagement. We harnessed embodied arts practice – social sculpture, street art, film and immersive installations – as a means to engage Coexist stakeholders and team members with everyday social tensions and political issues. Arts practice can increase agency because art has the ability to generate ruptures with habitual ways of thinking and being (Phelan, 1993; O'Sullivan, 2006; Grosz, 2008; Hawkins, 2013). The way in which art creates a rupture has been theoretically situated as producing *encounters* (O'Sullivan, 2006). The term 'encounter' is used to describe the moment when 'something in the world forces us to think; something that is an object not of recognition but of a fundamental *encounter*' (Deleuze, 1994: 139 [emphasis added]). An encounter enables new ways of seeing and thinking the world differently, thereby increasing the capacity to act. Our emphasis on embodiment was inspired by Coexist's own use of embodied facilitation, a theatre-inspired approach to learning that affirms that the body contributes to knowledge production. Our contention was that dissent should be articulated as a series of embodied encounters, where the dominance of language and different systems of knowledge give way to sensation and felt realities. Finding new ways to think about and act with the body can help us access those experiences of the world that are at the edge of thought (Harrison, 2000).

Our intention was that these more expressive and expansive forms of engagement – these *spaces of dissent* – could inform how Coexist facilitates and regulates the Hamilton House building or any other spaces that it might inhabit in the future. Over the course of three years, we facilitated a series of events experimenting with the notion of spaces of dissent. It was conducted as an iterative process of action and reflection, thinking with theory through practice and continuously refining our approach to enable new ideas, social relations and possibilities to emerge. While the actions did not always follow a linear line of progression, it is possible to demarcate three distinct phases within the development of our project. Within our first phase, we were motivated by the relatively simple desire to make *public* interventions; to experiment with the notion of *engagement through dissent* as a way to explore how Coexist might exist in spaces away from the Hamilton House building. It was a crucial juncture during the project's inception, with Coexist gently pushing at the boundaries of what might constitute research, while negotiating how much influence the community partner was entitled to within the co-produced research.

### Interventions phase 1

The first significant intervention came in the form of a 2014 Candy Chang-inspired sticker installation 'I wish this was …'. The artist Candy Chang has produced a series of interactive public interventions in which participants are encouraged to respond to a provocative question. Using a template available on Candy Chang's website, we created an installation against a Grade II listed building nearby. The installation engaged with a contentious issue regarding the future of this vacant, derelict building. The installation stimulated participation by leaving pens available next to the provocative question 'I wish this was …' (see Figure 8.2).

The intervention enabled us to immediately confront pertinent questions concerning the power relations embedded within Coexist by conducting acts of engagement in new spaces, namely: 'What *role* would Coexist be adopting by facilitating spaces of dissent?'; 'How would the parameters of *dissent* be set?'; and '*Who* would be engaging

**Figure 8.2:** Sticker Installation, Carriage Works, Bristol (2014)

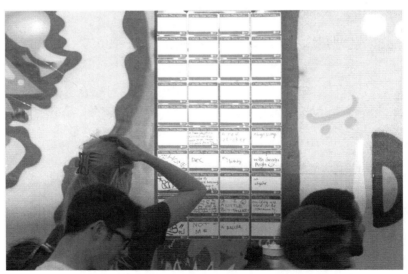

Source: Greg Leo Bond, 2014

*whom*?' The limit to what extent dissent can be contained was made palpable during the sticker installation by people's readiness to alter the parameters. While compliant contributions were made, such as a person writing within one box that they wished the building was 'a home', others were quick to mould the situation to accommodate their own needs. Several participants altered the question from 'I wish this was ...' to simply 'I wish ...', with one contributor earnestly offering: 'I wish I was not addicted to smack'. Another person spread their message across multiple boxes – 'I wish Palestine was free' – seemingly evoking the proportional level of plight suffered by a nation compared with an individual. It demonstrated that while we can set the initial parameters, there must always be space for something more. While engagement can be produced through a notion of dissent, who possesses or owns this engagement is not fixed. This was expressed with how others sustained the site – removing pens and cups when all stickers were filled – and also with the confrontation that occurred when we began removing the installation. We told two concerned passers-by that it was alright for us to remove it because we were the ones who created the installation, unconsciously qualifying our actions through a claim of ownership. The response from one passer-by was simple but clear: "Yes, but *we* like it being there."

The installation – or space of dissent – had become a microcosm for much larger social actions. The situation reaffirmed the role of facilitators: how something grows beyond that of those who 'manage' or 'own' space. The facilitators might agitate a social situation but the direction in which it develops is determined by those who participate. The specific public intervention echoes wider ethical questions regarding the Hamilton House project and who 'owns' it once a project is set in motion. Does control lie with: the property developers Connolly and Callaghan who still own the physical structure; Coexist who set the spark and adapted the space; or the people who frequently use the space and participate as part of the Hamilton House community?

## Interventions phase 2

Our second phase was specifically driven towards how engagement through dissent could be integrated within Coexist's everyday regulatory processes, and what arts practice could offer that is not attainable through more discursive practices alone. It was in this phase that the co-produced project first started to turn its focus directly upon Coexist, explicitly encouraging dissent towards different aspects of the project by foregrounding tensions that manifest within Coexist's everyday practice. If our first phase demonstrated members of Coexist testing the co-production relationship, this second phase therefore represented a counter-proposition: testing to what extent Coexist members were willing to welcome challenges to their own practice.

What emerged during this phase was a more defined understanding of how the unique capacities of arts practice could be utilised to engage with wider social tensions and political issues. A shared vision for the role of arts practice arose through the co-production of the 2015 film *Keyhole Whispers* (see Figure 8.3). In terms of subject matter, we co-produced the film in response to discussions surrounding security in the Hamilton House building. A theft had occurred in one of the studios after a person gained access beyond the secured doors at the front of the building. The theft that occurred was relatively low impact – a bag and a phone had been stolen from one of the event spaces – yet it nonetheless required the Coexist team to raise the possibility of increasing security measures during their weekly operational meeting. This relatively mundane issue of security offered a tangible access point to a wider ethical dilemma that Coexist regularly experience as an organisation, namely, how can a relatively small core team approach making decisions that will impact a diverse range of stakeholders and an estimated 10,000 weekly building users. It is clear that some team members are more sensitive to the pressure of performing efficiently and in line with conventional business practice when it comes to issues

**Figure 8.3**: Still taken from the 2015 film *Keyhole Whispers* showing the coded double doors at the front of Hamilton House and a user of the space on the outside

Source: Greg Leo Bond, 2015

of security and fulfilling the requirements of insurance policies. Other team members prefer to address issues within Coexist's practice from an ethical perspective: *who* should be involved in decisions regarding the Hamilton House building and is Coexist attempting to *provide* a space *for* or *create* a space *with* users of the space? The value of arts practice – in this case, film – proved to be the ability to engage with the less tangible tensions attached to these wider, more difficult questions, in which reaching a clear decision or resolution is not necessarily appropriate.

The co-produced film does not offer an accurate representation of the different perspectives and opinions held regarding issues of security and exclusion in Hamilton House. The impetus is not to *represent* dissent, but to *present* dissent. The first way in which this is achieved is by elevating the materiality of the doors and evoking an embodied experience. The film is made up of two still shots from either side of the coded doors at the front of the Hamilton House building (see Figure 8.3). The camera holds as users of the building go in and out through the doors. Accompanying the everyday sounds of the Hamilton House entrance is a commentary from two people discussing the need for security in a community building that aims to provide a space for 'everyone'. One disembodied voice of a Coexist director questions the less perceivable, and potentially exclusionary, effect that the secure doors have on day-to-day interactions, while another voice of an artist who rents space asserts the need for Coexist as an organisation to take responsibility in providing a safe space. The film constructs a dynamic by editing the commentary in time with the opening and closing of the door, meaning that the viewer is only able to hear the commentary when the door is momentarily open. The slamming door cuts through the voices on the soundtrack, evoking the way in which decisions are made *behind closed doors* so to speak. The viewer is 'shut out' from conversations. The heightened sound of the door slamming elicits an embodied response from the viewer: the slamming door obstructs the speakers' voices, not allowing for any form of resolution, but instead creating space for disagreement to exist. The intention of this filmic space is to act as a space of dissent, enabling the dissonance of ideas and opinion.

The co-produced film elicited what is at stake when thinking through arts practice and notions of dissent within processes of regulation. Conducting interviews and participant observation studies is a valuable entry point into ongoing issues and everyday tensions. It is an opportunity to *map* different perspectives and ideas attached to a subject matter before creating an arts practice. However, one must not misconstrue the function of arts practice as merely communicating what qualitative data have been attained. The information should serve the art and not the other way around. In this case, we were *thinking through film*: the observations and ideas pooled together during the research and development process informed the artistic decision-making. This phase of the co-produced project revealed the potential for arts practice to go beyond language and to hint at something less easily perceived, at the edge of consciousness. Rather than seek resolution, the film presents the incongruence between a group's ideals with issues of representation and exclusion inherent to hierarchy.

## Interventions phase 3

Our third phase was when *regulating engagement through dissent* became a Coexist strategy, with the aim of embedding a sustainable, rigorously tested format within Coexist's regulatory processes. The format that we developed was to create spaces of dissent every two to three months as an opportunity to engage Coexist's stakeholders with the most pressing big topics that had surfaced within Coexist's everyday operational meetings and wider practice. We would facilitate creative public interventions with diverse stakeholders, where new ideas, thoughts and emotions could be shared. We would then integrate what was experienced directly into Coexist's regulatory spaces, holding two-hour workshops that team members, building users and other relevant community organisations would attend. Any actions or materials produced during this process would be disseminated and exhibited in the gallery space downstairs at the front of the building in order to increase awareness of Coexist's engagement strategy.

Articulating dissent as a series of embodied encounters enabled new forms of engagement that are able to account for the less tangible and less easily perceived textures of the everyday. The spaces of dissent that we facilitated were in stark contrast to the more discursive, operational spaces of engagement created elsewhere in Coexist's practice. The value of such an approach is that we can reconfigure how we approach social tensions or political issues, as was demonstrated when we implemented social sculpture and immersive arts practice to engage with issues of gentrification in the Stokes Croft area of Bristol. Gentrification can be defined as the production of space for progressively more affluent users (Hackworth, 2002). A central concern has been the displacement of lower-income groups and more vulnerable individuals at the expense of these processes. The issue of gentrification is a prominent concern among grass-roots regeneration projects in general, but it has become an increasing point of focus for how the Stokes Croft area is represented in online and public newspapers (Gales, 2014; Harris, 2015; Harrison, 2017; Frenzel and Beverungen, 2017). There is a well-rehearsed narrative regarding the role of grass-roots organisations within processes of gentrification that is often ascribed to Coexist. The narrative posits a situation in which grass-roots regeneration projects will inevitably attract the very same market-led development that they first sought to resist: by attempting to present an alternate approach to urban development, they merely accelerate the displacement of lower-income residents and vulnerable communities. It has been documented that affluent groups are attracted to the *edginess* that activist and artist groups give to an area (Hackworth, 2002; Lees, 2008). Concurrently, council-driven 'creative city' initiatives attempt to sell a sanitised version of subversive culture as a means of increasing investment and tourism (Chatterton, 2000; Erdem, 2014). The rapid change of the Stokes Croft area has placed Coexist's own existence within the Hamilton House building under threat due to the increased market value of the property, thus leaving Coexist to perform the contradictory roles of both victim and perpetrator of gentrification. Yet, these disembodied narratives do not account for the more felt realities of Coexist's team members and stakeholders. Narratives that represent space as an empty container filled with distinct individuals, groups and organisations cannot adequately inform how Coexist might regulate their practice. What is vital is the ability to engage with such issues in a way that *increases* the capacity to act.

Facilitating a creative intervention in the form of a social sculpture, 'Conversations in Thread', held in 2016 in the Bearpit underpass in Stokes Croft, Bristol, enabled us to directly engage with the everyday dynamics of the gentrification phenomenon. In recent years, this contested space has experienced a combination of council-driven development and grass-roots regeneration. The rapid change and the contrasting desires for what kind of change is needed has caused tensions between the new cafes, pop-up shops and ping-pong tables, and the well-established street-drinking and homeless culture that exists in the space. The development and regeneration of the space has done little to improve the lives of the homeless community, the street drinkers or the drug users who frequent the area. What the development has produced is more restrictions on vulnerable communities. Public toilets are closed earlier, leading to more instances of public urination and defecation, which, in turn, leads to police sanctions. Surveillance has increased, with shopkeepers and the police working in tandem to monitor behaviour. A palpable sense of tension

## Imagining Regulation Differently

engulfs the space, manifesting in small-scale confrontations on a daily basis.

Adopting an embodied arts practice such as social sculpture enabled a reconfiguration of space. The term 'social sculpture' was coined by the performance artist Joseph Beuys and refers to an expanded conception of art. Similar to how one might sculpt clay, there is an emphasis on *manipulating the social fabric* through this process. We facilitated the social sculpture as a means to reconfigure how bodies relate to one another and their material environment. The 2016 social sculpture 'Conversations in Thread' invited passers-by to continue a thread of conversation by participating in creating a *lemniscate* between two points. In algebraic geometry, a lemniscate is any of several figure-of-eight-shaped curves, commonly associated with the infinity symbol. The word comes from the Latin '*lēmniscātus*' meaning 'decorated with ribbons'. Participants were invited to weave a ribbon – or, more specifically, gold-coloured thread – in a figure-of-eight formation between two lamp posts in the centre of the Bearpit. As participants moved through the space, unravelling the roll of golden thread in their hand, we recorded some of the ideas and experiences they shared regarding the rapid change that has occurred both in the Bearpit and in the wider Stokes Croft area. The social sculpture manipulates the social configurations of a space, entwining material and discursive relations into the social fabric.

**Figure 8.4:** Photograph of the 2016 social sculpture 'Conversations in Thread' held in the Bearpit underpass in central Bristol

Source: Greg Leo Bond, 2016

Our aim was to engage with how changes to material landscapes affect individuals' felt reality. Importantly, we deliberately avoided using common terms such as 'gentrification' and instead encouraged participants to focus on their own daily experiences. We would also ask participants to reflect on certain words, such as 'disruption' and 'development'. A member of the homeless community reflected on how they experience the space: "The minute we wake up ... we're disrupting normal society." It was evident that the blunt assessment of their own existence was directly influenced by the well-intentioned actions of the grass-roots project tasked with regenerating the space. The participant continued:

> 'All they ever want to do to enable any sort of community bonding, is one ping-pong table and a couple of plants.... All this stuff there is pretty and nice, but it's never gonna be appreciated because most people walk around when they see us lot. So, the only way you're ever gonna get any appreciation for any garden or art is to move us lot out.'

In one respect, the material changes of the space affected collective resilience among the vulnerable communities. Yet, more worryingly, other members of the homeless community expressed an intense sensation of paranoia from being continuously under surveillance by the newly established shopkeepers. A member of the regeneration project Bearpit Improvement Group lamented the predicament: "They're feeling that they're being pushed out. But that's not our intention or never has been. Our intention is just to make it more diverse and more welcoming to everybody." While well-meaning, this statement is indicative of how attempts to create space for 'everybody' inevitably reaffirms wider societal hierarchies and social exclusion. Ultimately, the arrival of the regeneration project was responsible for constructing an 'us and them' dichotomy with some of Bristol's most vulnerable communities.

Once a public intervention is facilitated, the concern is then how this engagement can be more directly connected to regulatory processes. The social sculpture was revealing through its very reconfiguration of space and social roles. The distinct groups that inhabit the Bearpit space – cafe workers, regeneration project workers, drug users, homeless people, commuters and so on – were all able to participate in the same process. By facilitating new kinds of interactions within the space, the everyday power relations were temporarily disrupted. An increased sense of agency was co-produced through this intervention. We were not objectively assessing a social tension at a critical distance. Instead, we embraced the notion that our 'social-material enactments … contribute to, and are part of, the phenomena we describe' (Barad, 2007: 26). As facilitators, we were not separate to, but a part of and contributing to, the gentrification phenomenon. The purpose of engagement and the possibilities of Coexist's regulatory processes were thus transformed. We were conscious not to reduce this experience when we integrated it back into Coexist's everyday practice. With the subsequent workshops we held, we did not want to *represent* or *disseminate* the 'data' we had gathered. It was important that we continued to create *live* spaces. We therefore facilitated the subsequent workshop as a series of immersive installations. The intention was to present some of the felt realities and embodied sensations generated during the social sculpture so that the new set of participants – Coexist team members, building users and other community groups – could engage with these experiences first-hand, and contribute their own thoughts, feelings and ideas.

The first immersive installation constructed for the workshop presented the double-screen film *Conversations in Neon* (2016), created from audio and video recordings generated during the 2016 'Conversations in Thread' social sculpture. The film was projected across two walls. The film's audio track is made up of polyphonic voices generated during the social sculpture, evoking the sensations of anxiety, frustration and guilt expressed during the intervention. The space was demarcated by translucent screens lit by red floor lights. Elsewhere participants were confronted with a room covered in text written about Hamilton House by academics, journalists and online commentators, much of it critical of Coexist and other grass-roots initiatives for their role within processes of gentrification. The final space was a live performance of two people holding a conversation behind translucent screens (see Figure 8.5). The people were chosen because of their direct experience of working with and being a part of communities that have sometimes experienced issues of exclusion and privilege within the Hamilton House space. Participants of the workshop were encouraged to write down any thoughts, feelings, memories or ideas triggered during the immersive installations.

The immersive installation workshop interrogating processes of gentrification enabled participants to confront and reject the less easily perceived yet restrictive aspects of the cultural phenomenon – the anxiety, guilt and frustration – and instead focus on the more astute affirmative changes that might be made. In response, Coexist team member Gem stated: "I'm so bored of 'gentrification' … this word.

**Figure 8.5:** Photograph of a live performance of two people holding a conversation while a Coexist team member makes notes

Source: Greg Leo Bond, 2017

This is a political fight. This is not a fight about gentrification. This is about politics and about socialist ideals and communities."

The rejection of the word 'gentrification' was itself a rejection of inadequate narratives being ascribed to one's own lived experience. The workshop created space for participants to demand more and instigate new trajectories for the Coexist project. The discussion asserted that unless an organisation is content with only producing ephemeral disruptions, then they must seek ownership of a space at the very start of their existence. It was agreed that such precautions would be added into Coexist's core purpose and approach document.

Some spaces of dissent do not always produce such tangible outputs, and short-term and long-term outcomes are not always overtly visible or easily measured. Within these spaces of dissent, it was possible to identify clear moments when participants were able to reclaim a sense of agency. The social sculpture created an activity within the Bearpit space that offered members of the homeless community a new outlet, unlike most development of the space that simply further restricts their behaviour. The workshop space also showed moments where Coexist team members were able to confront any lingering sense of guilt relating to their role in processes of gentrification and turn this into expressions of defiance, as Ari contributed:

> 'It's uncomfortable because you're a part of the process ... but you're also not the same as multinational corporate

development. It is not the same. Working in arts organisations and acting and responding, creating in an area, is not the same as a multinational organisation coming in and making profit only, I do think it's different. But we pave those stones for that thing to happen. And, in fact, what happens is this organisation is blamed ... which I think it's absolutely fine to have that blame ... but then we forget to blame properly the multinational corporations that are finally, clinically, determining the future of the area. That's what happens ... the scapegoat gets blamed for these huge systemic problems and we don't reflect about it enough in our practice.'

It is difficult to measure what kind of long-term impact such moments of defiance might have on future practice. There is an inherent risk that because some outcomes are not always obvious or tangible, these creative and reflexive aspects of practice will be the first to be cut when charities and social enterprises come under economic strain.

## Conclusions and reflections

Experimenting with spaces of dissent as a form of engagement has enabled us to reaffirm the contention that disagreement and difference are more suited to combating unequal power relations than idealistic notions of consensus (Amin and Thrift, 2005; Barnes and Sheppard, 2009; Staeheli, 2010). The co-produced research articulated dissent as a series of embodied acts produced through arts practice. The value of arts practice in regulation is that 'art struggles with chaos but it does so in order to render it sensory' (Deleuze and Guattari, 1994: 205). It is able to do this because art is itself regulation – in the way in which art organises materials, form, movement, words and so on according to an internal system (Grosz, 2008). It does this to produce intensities and sensations that are not instantly recognisable. In doing so, one creates access points to cultural phenomena and social tensions that can otherwise be overwhelming, while foregrounding less easily perceived aspects that are at risk of being excluded.

Within these spaces of dissent, dominant discourses, normative codes of behaviour and conventional systems of knowledge were disrupted.[1] The consistency between all these spaces is that they facilitate new ways of thinking and new ways of relating to one another. What is ultimately at stake is that if adequate time is not given to engagement in which all participants can creatively engage with the big issues of society, then charities, social enterprises and other grass-roots projects will only ever be able to perform *firefighting* or crisis management. Regulating engagement through dissent can increase agency; therefore, if one wants to effect positive social change, there must be space for dissent.

## Note

[1] The future of Coexist and Hamilton House was in flux during the final years of the programme and during the writing of this book. Coexist was evicted from Hamilton House in December 2018 (see https://thebristolcable.org/2018/12/photoessay-coexists-last-48-hours-at-hamilton-house/).

# 9

# The role of community anchor organisations in regulating for engagement in a devolved government setting

*Eva Elliott, Sue Cohen and David Frayne*

## Introduction

In Wales, devolution signified an opportunity for the Welsh government to do politics differently. In particular, there was a focus on public participation as a mechanism for improvements to the economy, social outcomes and public services (Welsh Government, 2004). In ambition, at least, the devolution experiment in Wales anticipated the development of regulations *for* the engagement of its citizens. This chapter considers the role of community anchor organisations in the 'flagship' regeneration programme of the National Assembly for Wales,[1] 'Communities First', launched in 2001 and later terminated in March 2018. The programme started as a 'bottom-up' initiative for engaging with disadvantaged communities at the margins, setting up regulatory structures to deliver that vision; became a reduced and more competitive programme from 2008/09, with more defined outcomes; and then entered its final phase in 2012, with 'clusters' of communities that were expected to deliver government-driven outcomes on health, learning and, in particular, employability through a system of results–based accountability (RBA). In the process, regulation *for* engagement shifted to regulatory structures and processes that controlled engagement: the regulation *of* engagement.

Other research has traced the evolution of the programme (Pearce, 2012; Dicks, 2014) in the context of a bold policy experiment in a devolved context while the programme was still live. This chapter, however, unpicks the story of its evolution and demise from the perspectives of community development advisors and community development practitioners, the latter based in two community organisations in South Wales: South Riverside Community Development Centre (SRCDC) in Cardiff and 3Gs Community Development Trust in Merthyr Tydfil. Both organisations were involved in the Productive Margins programme and in the design and analysis of this research. Both pre-existed the Communities First programme and were charged with its delivery to local people. We look at the regulatory context in which these organisations found themselves and how they negotiated the demands of the state-funded programme, on the one hand, and their accountabilities to the communities that they believed they represented, on the other. A key question remains as to whether the involvement of community organisations in state-funded programmes can facilitate regulation for engagement for social change or whether their power to improve the well-being of the communities they represent might better be served in providing alternative modes of living.

## Research rationale, design and analysis

Indications that Communities First would be terminated came through an announcement in October 2016 when the Communities Secretary stated that he was 'minded' to phase out the programme. Given their role in delivering the programme at a local level, the two Welsh community partners in the Productive Margins research programme were shaken. Having committed substantial resources to that delivery, it looked as though their capacity to continue as organisations was now threatened. The announcement coincided with the research timetable of the Productive Margins programme, which had one more project to deliver in Wales. It felt inconceivable to community development workers and academics alike that the last research project should be anything other than one that explored the role of community grass-roots organisations in the Communities First programme. The research would also bear witness to the ways in which the organisations weathered the proverbial storm as state funding was withdrawn and redirected. The question that concerned all at the time was how community organisations could mediate the needs and aspirations of their communities while taking advantage of the resources and opportunities that a state programme had to offer, particularly one that initially appeared to be underpinned by values of citizen engagement and inclusion.

The community organisations referred to in this chapter are both within what is now described as the Cardiff Capital Region: SRCDC in a diverse and rapidly shifting inner-city area of Cardiff and 3Gs in a post-industrial area within Merthyr Tydfil, where the population is largely static but physical, economic and social resources have migrated through years of economic neglect. SRCDC has its origins in the late 1970s, when local activists harnessed local people in activities responsive to challenging housing issues. The second community organisation, 3Gs Development Trust, was set up in the late 1990s in an attempt to bring three local areas (Old Gurnos, New Gurnos and Galen Uchaf) together through their tenant and resident organisations in order to build bridges between communities and improve collective resources for people living locally. Both were set up as community development trusts, with structures that enabled them to manage and administrate funded projects similar to that of a small- to medium-sized company. Interestingly, both community organisations gave their local communities names that did not exist as a way of making visible communities that may not have been mapped in terms of administrative boundaries or places. While SRCDC did not directly employ staff as part of the Communities First programme in the first six years, staff within the organisation had already prepared the ground in readiness for taking on a leadership role when the opportunity arose. This opportunity came in 2007 when they were offered 'employer status'.

Following a small workshop in November 2016 that involved the academic lead (EE) and three community partners (two from SRCDC and one from 3Gs), the research questions and preliminary research design were scoped out. It was also agreed that: a working group would be set up and meet monthly[2]; SRCDC should employ an academic researcher to conduct interviews as well as ethnographic observations as the organisations responded to government and local authority decisions; and that artists would be engaged in order to capture the emotions and metaphors that were ubiquitous in the stories, accounts and explanations that community workers provided. All the working group meetings were recorded not only as data in themselves, but also as forms of collective real-time reflective analysis of change and its implications for the organisations themselves. What this did was to provide a co-produced analytic lens for the interpretation of events and data presented in this chapter.

Interview data consisted of 25 interviews, including with people working or volunteering in the organisations, two academic government advisors in community development, and key personnel from the Welsh government who were associated with the Communities First programme. Welsh government interviews were largely conducted by one of the academic members of the working group who was conducting related and relevant research on Welsh government understandings of evaluation and impact. It was agreed that interview data be shared. In addition, two values workshops took place as a way of drawing out ideas for the future development of the community organisations themselves. The names of all interviewees have been changed to hide their identities.

## Communities First: the 'community' as a driver for bottom-up regeneration

Indicating the possibilities of a polycentric state, Morgan (2007) saw devolution in the UK as opening up multiple spaces for deliberation, empowerment and engagement in national and regional contexts. However, England, Scotland and Wales developed these experiments in democracy and policy development with communities at the margins (economically and politically) in different ways. The Communities First programme was perhaps *the* exemplar of the participative approach that the new Welsh government wished to take, placing 'community' centre stage in dialogue with the state.

The need for the state to be in a *dialogical* relationship with communities in order to address marginalisation and inequality was stressed early on in a review of best practice in community regeneration (Adamson et al, 2001). This review highlighted a number of themes, principles and actions that would be needed to inform the design and development of the Communities First programme. The principal organisational engine for programme delivery at the local level was the 'partnership', based on what became known as the 'three thirds principle' (the statutory, voluntary/business and community sectors comprising the three thirds) (National Assembly for Wales, 2001). The model was formally adopted in this and other Welsh national programmes as a form of meta-governance to ensure that minority groups and voices at the margins were included in decision-making (Bristow et al, 2008).

This was a bold innovation as the partnership, with 'community' as the lead and driver, was to be the engine for local regeneration in the context of national ambitions for social and economic change. The difficulties in creating a formal role for community in a national regeneration programme were many. In this context, 'community' presupposes a relational idea of place with porous boundaries. However, communities are also shaped by, and are dependent on, territorial and bounded ideas of place (Morgan, 2007; Massey, 2011). The authors of the best practice review (Adamson et al, 2001) recognised that the informal, permeable, self-declared nature of community was at odds with the formal, spatially bounded ideas of place that underpin institutionalised democratic processes and methods of public service delivery. They called for a framework that would mainstream the three thirds partnership approach and clarify roles and responsibilities.

Adamson et al also warned of the dangers of communities themselves being co-opted into the agendas of government or other professionals and public services. In particular, the authors warned that although community should be seen as an entity and driver for the programme, it should not be 'a vehicle for transferring responsibility for structural disadvantage to communities' (Adamson et al, 2001: 10). They emphasised the need for government responsibility for the structural causes of poverty and inequality, seeing the local partnerships as 'ameliorating the negative consequences of some of these structural areas in parallel with affirmative action by government at the national level' (Adamson et al, 2001: 10). Only the state itself could be responsible for anti-poverty-oriented changes to wage legislation, taxes, welfare and economic development (some of which were also beyond the powers of the Welsh Assembly government). They also warned against dependency on state sponsorship, calling for formal arrangements that would enable 'communities' (as relational entities) to interact with the territorial administrative and democratic arrangements. They therefore emphasised the need for regulatory structures that would enable these different constructs of place to work productively to empower communities.

A major recommendation was that the programme be developed incrementally on the basis of local experience and capacity. However, as highlighted later, this strategy was not built into the programme. Nevertheless, the existing structures of community-led governance and multiple partnerships of 3Gs and SRCDC placed them in a good position to exemplify the regulatory practices of participatory governance for social change.

## Community anchor organisations

The term 'community anchor' is not one that the organisations would have used in their promotional literature and its usage was discussed at length in the working group meetings. Although the term had previously been used by some of the community development workers in describing their organisations, more than one of the community representatives queried a term that not only left out people, but also failed to reflect that the organisations in question felt distinctly unanchored and precarious at the time. However, as the research progressed, it became seen as potentially useful terminology, with symbolic value in making claims for legitimacy, recognition and resources. It was considered especially useful where the state avoided or dismissed the value of community-based accountability and authority. As a consequence, SRCDC is now exploring the collective worth and value of community anchor organisations in a study across Wales in the context of current policy developments.

In his contribution to the parallel work referred to earlier, Todd (2018), building on the work of Stoker and Young (1993), traces the emergence of the terminology of 'community anchors' back to the rapid proliferation of 'third force organisations' (TFOs) during the late 1970s and 1980s. Todd notes that they were defined as 'spontaneous community initiatives; rooted in a "local" that is self-defined; governance drawn from a local population; and, a fragility of existence due to uncertain income levels and sources' (Todd, 2018: 12). However, they could also be seen as stemming from the cooperative movement and, in Wales, the collective forms of local mutual support born out of cooperatives, the workers' institutes and trade unions. Community anchors are born of necessity and then establish themselves through distinct forms of local governance. The UK government's 'Firm foundations' framework (Civil Renewal Unit, 2004) also used the term 'community anchor organisation' as part of their framework for community capacity building, and it was perhaps the first mainstream policy agenda that enmeshed a role for community anchor organisations in the social economy and public service modernisation strategies.

More recent interest in community anchors could be seen as both responding to, and as a critique of, the Big Society conception of civil society development needing to be separate from the state. Community organisations themselves have developed in ways that have gained recognition in local governance settings, and austerity has generated a language around community resilience and what that might look like in terms of resource and asset maximisation. Building on a think-piece on community anchors (Henderson, 2018), What Works in Scotland has recently published a research report on the role of community anchor organisations (Henderson et al, 2018). The report suggests that such organisations could play a distinctive role in place-making, mitigating threats to local social and economic well-being, and (perhaps naively, as some might argue) in influencing structural forms of social change.

Anchors could also be regarded as embodying the renaissance of community in a context where communities may find themselves disconnected from political and economic structures, forced to live with varying degrees of disruption and distress (Mulligan, 2015; Byrne et al, 2016). Local anchor organisations may provide democratic structures *for* belonging, providing the organisational possibilities for affirmation, legitimation and voice. However, this strength also makes them intensely vulnerable to the powers of co-optation by the neoliberal state, and of abandonment as policy agendas shift.

Henderson (2018) asserts that community anchor organisations are distinct from other third sector organisations, on the one hand, and small community organisations, on the other. The latter may not call themselves anchors as such, but could be part of a wider local ecosystem, with community anchor organisations providing a core local infrastructure role. In their report, they see community anchors as being (or aspiring to be): community-led or -controlled, with associated governance structures and processes; 'holistic, multi-purpose or inherently complex'; and responsive and committed to local community and context (Henderson et al, 2018: 6). These characteristics would certainly have been associated with the organisations taking part in this research.

## Capacity building: the challenge for communities and civil servants

We now turn to the Communities First programme as it was seen from the perspective of those working in community development. It could be argued that the first dislocation from the Community First's grand vision was at the very beginning when the programme was announced in 2001. Instead of starting incrementally with existing organisations as the basis for learning, development and expansion, the ministers made a very late decision to announce 100 ward-level, place-based Communities First areas based on the extent of deprivation across Wales, rather than on the basis of organisational potential and capacity. Including a number of communities of interest and sub-ward-level places, this amounted to 142 Communities First partnerships, which had to constitute themselves rapidly. This was in the context of widespread inexperience of the community development and organisational skills needed to deliver the imagined programme in many locally disadvantaged communities.

While much is made of capacity building for the community sector in the first phase of Communities First (2001–08), very little focus is placed on capacity building for those who regulate engagement. Capacity building was an issue not only for community infrastructures, but also for some civil servants who had little experience of centrally managing community development programmes because of redeployment. Community development experts had the sense that key people within the civil service felt that the programme was 'messy' and vague given that both civil servants and people working in local authorities began to express concern about what could not be controlled and measured. Being committed to democratic principles, community workers could be considered unmanageable and 'out of control'. Government had an aversion to risk and messiness. It was messy because it was diverse, could not be centrally contained, was too variable and could not be predicted in terms of outcomes that many civil servants would recognise. Social science researchers, politicians and funding bodies alike have a tendency to 'repress the mess' in order to both manage and control the outcomes (Law, 2003).

Nevertheless, for community organisations involved in the programme from the start, the programme offered resources and hope for the communities that they served. As an established community organisation, 3Gs experienced the programme as open and liberating for the first few years. They were successful in attracting additional funding and they enjoyed, as did SRCDC, productive research and funded project partnerships with universities and other organisations. However, what the organisations did not experience was the power and influence to make changes to mainstream services in ways that transformed the landscape of public sector delivery and budgetary priorities. As John (a community worker in Merthyr involved in this first phase of Communities First) reflected, many service delivery agencies failed to give space to those voicing community issues:

> 'They did nothing at all about changing the culture within the delivery agencies. So, like, we used to go to meetings and they'd look at us as if to say, "Well, what's it got to do with you?" Like, you know, "We've got to do this. This is what we're doing."'

Yet the experience of some participants suggests that there was sometimes not a grand clash of values between the government, public services and communities. Sometimes, it is civil servants working in silos with no effective communication systems; sometimes, it is the lack of consistency when staff are effectively unanchored and moved from one role to another, very different government department. In addition although, for community organisations at the local level, there was a sense that they felt that they were responding to, and accountable to, their community, they did not have the power to ensure the same from their statutory partners.

## Regulating engagement under austerity

After the first seven years the impact of the global financial crisis, together with concerns about Communities First and its uneven development, resulted in fundamental changes. The second phase of the programme (from 2008/09) came with deep funding cuts and a focus on outcome measures defined by national policy. While the partnerships were still in place, the power was now more firmly with the local authorities. There was no longer mention of capacity building, but rather talk of outcomes to be overseen by the Welsh government (Pearce, 2012). The programme was scaled locally but steered centrally (Dicks, 2014; Pil and Guarneros-Meza, 2017), with compliance as a regulatory constraint on participation.

From 2009, the experience of the community organisations was of firefighting. Some felt that they were merely filling a gap in public services where statutory services failed to deliver, or providing services that arose as a consequence of austerity cuts and welfare reform. Community staff talked about signposting people to food banks, assisting people claiming benefits after they have been sanctioned, supporting refugees lost in state bureaucracy (SRCDC specifically), helping the homeless or championing and encouraging young people rejected by their schools (3Gs). In many cases, community organisations had come to represent a 'second safety net' after the welfare state; in some cases, they were the 'only safety net':

> 'I guess you can have the most brilliant community development, but benefit changes come along, job changes come along or the job market shrinks and you're knocked. You're really knocked. And then there's a lot of damage-limitation projects just to keep people from sinking. You're not actually developing any more. You're just stopping people from drowning. And that was sad to me – towards the end of my time with 3Gs, I could see much more of that firefighting and damage limitation, and stopping people going under. What funding you had was just being used to save people.' (Rhian)

The importance of this work intensified in parallel with austerity. Community anchor organisations can be invaluable in this regard but there is also a sense in which, in a better world, the crisis-management aspect of community work would not need to exist.

## From communities to clusters

It could be argued that in its original version as a bottom-up, community-led regeneration programme, the Communities First programme came, all but in name, to an end in 2012. At this point, 52 local authority-led clusters were created. The clusters were usually two or more Communities First areas merged together to create areas that were often unrecognisable and meaningless places from the perspectives of the people living within them. The three thirds partnership structures – statutory sector, voluntary/private sector and communities – disappeared and local authorities became the dominant regulatory force, usually employing staff directly (though not in 3Gs or SRCDC). Any notion of partnerships that placed communities in a position of power and influence over budgets and decisions had disappeared. For the two community organisations in this chapter, it meant that in order to maintain funding, they had to become a different kind of place-based community organisation charged with supporting and representing communities with which they had no historical roots (though individual staff may have been employed from the newly attached areas who did have these connections). Their responsibilities were not only wider in terms of geographical representation, but deeper as result-based accountability meant that they needed to demonstrate often, and in detail, how they had impacted on the lives of individuals in three priority anti-poverty arenas: learning, employment and health.

In a case study of local governance through partnerships in Cardiff, Pil and Guarneros-Meza (2017) highlighted how the processes of national austerity resulted in the dumping and downloading of risk and responsibility in the local implementation of state priorities. SRCDC became part of their neighbourhood partnership, a mechanism that was intended to coordinate state and non-state actors at the local level (Pil and Guarneros-Meza, 2017), while the local authority in Merthyr Tydfil saw 3Gs as a very separate organisation and at arm's length from the local authority. However, both organisations felt the acceleration of demands from results-based accountability, which got in the way of relationship-building and the micro-level, face-to-face community work that was at the heart of community development approaches. One community development worker tried to describe the tensions in managing conflicting ways of talking about what they do. They had to be conversant with both the regulatory logics of the state programme and the community logics that were still at the heart of their organisational practices:

> 'So, instead of Maslow's hierarchy of needs is the programme's hierarchy of demands … and how that feeds out because the line is down there in terms of the contact with community and population and we are having to consistently rephrase how we talk about things.… There are certain things you can and cannot say, you have to be careful what you say and how you say it.… So, there's dynamics and regulation and power there.' (Rhys)

## The end of Communities First

The wind-down of Communities First started in October 2016 with the public signal that the Welsh government had little intention of supporting the programme in the future. The announcement that the minister in charge was 'minded' to phase out Communities First came as a shock, even though it was no secret that the Welsh government was unhappy about the programme. It was felt to be more than the loss of over 800 jobs in Wales; it was the loss of people and a way of working that had been woven into the fabric of everyday life. In 3Gs, 20 out of 22 staff almost immediately became redundant after the announcement and SRCDC slowly lost most staff as the programme came to an end in March 2018.

The 'failure' of the programme was seen to be an attack on the very principles by which community anchors operated. Moreover, the irony that the programme had failed on the basis that they had been unsuccessful in addressing poverty was not lost on those who remembered that the programme had never started out as an anti-poverty programme. Community development workers became the scapegoats for the presumed failure of those outcomes. As Sam from 3Gs commented: "One of the things that has driven me insane is the notion that it was supposed to change or stop poverty. Now that is completely bizarre. Poverty is a structural problem, you know; people aren't poor because of something that's not happening in Penywaun." One community representative felt that designating the programme an 'anti-poverty' programme had created a convenient opening for the government to label it a failure. The question that he and others asked is: can area-based initiatives ever remedy poverty? You cannot strictly fail at something if the task set for you is impossible. As Sam further reflected:

'If you think about it, the way I look at it is if you're looking at government interventions into poverty, you've got three main policy levers which fall into their hands, really. They've got rates levels, they've got taxation and then there's the welfare system. But all these three are far and above the control of community workers.'

## Re-describing the 'failure' of Communities First: the politics of evaluation

The official representation of Communities First as a failed programme is problematic for a range of reasons. First, there is the departure of the programme from the initial grass-roots principles and recommendations of the original report (Adamson et al, 2001) used as the basis for designing the programme. Later on, there is the lack of scrutiny as to whether area-based initiatives were equipped to 'tackle poverty' in the first place. Most importantly, there is the significant and regrettable oversight of what we have called the 'hidden value' of community anchor organisations: the slow, close, flexible and often immeasurable work that goes on at ground level.

Re-describing the 'failure' of Communities First means grappling with the politics of evaluation. Who gets to decide whether the programme 'failed'? On what values and measurement tools is this assessment based? Are the real successes and value of the programme unaccounted for by evaluations, or are they well accounted for and simply ignored? There is the difficulty of accounting for slow change. Impact, as one respondent described it, is like 'ripples on a pond' and hence hard to evaluate.

While it could be argued that evaluations that rely on qualitative accounts of those who are close to the ground will not provide a disinterested and comprehensive picture of change, there was a frustration that evaluative processes gave an account of neither the everyday micro-processes of change, nor the more sustained changes for individuals and the wider community. Williams et al (2007: 206) argue that Marris and Rein's (1974) use of the term 'demonstrable rationality' is a more powerful way of understanding the development, implementation and evaluation of social interventions than what they saw as the 'eviscerated concept of "evidence based"'. It implies a 'looser, more multifaceted and potentially more contextually aware' (Williams et al, 2007: 206) approach to understanding the success of programmes, both in terms of if they work and what counts as working, and in terms of if they matter and whether it matters if they work. Such a framework would have the structures of power and values at the heart of the evaluative process.

## The hidden value of community anchors

So, what was it that the community organisations did that went unrecognised and how did they manage to sustain their practices in the face of increasing state scrutiny and command? What were the activities that were valued by community workers and community members, and yet hidden? The people that were interviewed described the work that they did much as one would a craft: work that had value in and of itself; work that required a multiplicity of skills that had to be applied intuitively; and work that developed, and was applied slowly, with attention to the subject and not external targets (Sennett, 2013). As the philosopher Alisdair MacIntyre (1981) argued, such orientations hold and perform 'virtues internal to practices'. Whereas the goals of the state-led programme became more employment-focused over time, the activities that community workers cared about were often crafted in terms of what they thought was possible in relation to the particular local context in which they worked.

This is not to say that all community development workers thought or operated in this way; indeed, some may have responded more directly to the target-driven goals that shaped the extent to which they were perceived as successful or not. However, this was considered more difficult in community organisations where there was a historically rooted connection and obligation to the community. Evaluation as a form of regulation was therefore resisted in community organisations, which was seen as legitimate in terms of doing what needs to be done to respond to the things that mattered to communities (Sayer, 2011). Organisational structures, regulatory practices and values were oriented towards community interests. Community development workers in both communities had emotional and historical ties to the people who they had worked alongside. The activities that they valued were more social, emotional or relational. They were about improving people's everyday lives or making the area a good place to live. Targets were achieved through stealth. In other words, the ways of working had to be practical, worthwhile and meaningful if they were to work for the people involved. The community workers learned how to 'play the game' while knowing that the real support 'went underneath the wire'.

They also talked about the disconnect between policy and the job descriptions that emerge, on the one hand, and community needs and the job that the community worker needs to do, on the other.

The craft of the community worker is to 'make it into what needs to be done' and it derives from the embedded knowledge that comes from noticing, giving recognition to and being able to respond to the people that they work with every day. This knowledge is rooted in the particularity of places. The skilled community worker, as other craft workers, develops a sense of the texture and nuances of place, and how to respond accordingly. Jasmin works in SRCDC, though she was also very familiar with Butetown, which became part of the Communities First cluster after 2012. The area is mobile and highly diverse. Jasmin became a fluent reader and navigator of the community:

> 'I can walk into the Mosque, take my shoes off – obviously cover myself – and then go and speak to people. Or, I can be on the corner of a football pitch with a group of football players. Or, I can be sat teaching a group of Syrians. Or, I can be in a room teaching a mixture of Syrians, Iraqi people, Somalis, all different languages. Then I could be teaching a class of children. All this can happen in one day.'

However, it is slow work and a number of community workers talked about the frustration that the changes that they observed in particular people, families, groups of people or particular spaces (the development of abandoned spaces into allotments and the creation of heritage walks for communities and visitors alike) go unnoticed in the temporal metrics of monitoring or in the time-limited gaze of traditional evaluation.

Respondents often described their work as street work, and the significance of encounters outside of public buildings. The described a walk across the places they were working as places where they: maintained relationships with people; acquired information about subtle local changes and concerns; and communicated their own information or advice in relation to provision or support. Such ways of working created spaces of sanctuary from the harsher dictates of conditionality and thereby offered forms of resistance to community workers in the production of welfare locally. For community workers, it often meant being available at all times: the boundary between public and private life was hard to discern. They continued to do what they had always done, and/or re-imagined new possibilities in enabling communities to empower themselves. They did not 'turn off'. Jasmin reflected on this in terms of the type of community work that is embodied in the everyday:

'So, yeah, I don't turn off. And I cannot envisage a time where that won't be part of my life now. And I think, probably, every community development worker would feel the same way as I do. It's hard because it becomes almost like a vocation. It's not like a nine-to-five job. You know, they're slamming the doors closed in March but you can't do that in real life. You can't do that with people that you've worked with. You can't say 'I won't be there for you, I won't be able to answer the phone to you and give you information when you need it. I won't be able to support you in that.' You can't do that. That's just not ... well, I can't.'

Workers at SRCDC emphasised the importance of assets: well-equipped, well-maintained, accessible buildings, used for projects and by community members for self-organised activities. In metropolitan areas like Cardiff, increasingly commercialised, semi-privatised and exclusive, there is a sense in which a 'place for everyone' has become a rare and important thing. Many research participants described the success of the anchor organisations in creating this sense of a shared place. One community representative recalled a family walking into the foyer of 3Gs when there was a local fire – as if that is where people naturally felt safe – while another spoke of local youths guarding the SRCDC warehouse at night because the door had been left open – testimony to the idea that the building belongs to everyone. Regulatory controls matter. One community development worker's detailed account of key-holding, booking systems and zoned alarms at SRCDC contributes to the idea of a collectively owned space, enabling community members to use the buildings with minimal fuss.

---

### Box 9.1: Anchor people

The hidden work of anchor organisations also conceals the hidden value of those working within those organisations. We began to define them as 'anchor people'. It is 'anchor people' who bring buildings and organisations alive: 'community' becomes visible and of practical value through their work. One of the ways in which this happens is through the complex web of interactions that are forged and strengthened by workers on the ground. Community organisations cannot be anchored without the connectors that make those 'threads' – between people and organisations – real and active in the very practices of community work.

In addition to the workers, there are the leaders who give credibility and legitimacy to the community organisations from the perspective of government and non-government funders and policy leads. This is where the ability to communicate an understanding of wider non-community agendas becomes the stuff of leadership: understanding the agendas (and logics) of the state or other public institutions while being seen as succeeding in speaking for local people. Anchor people are brokers, mediators and translators (see also Chapter 10, this volume). This also requires a sense of when and how to challenge. One community worker at 3Gs remembered a widely admired community manager from the past. Asked why he was so respected, Angie reflected:

'Some of the council, the officers in the council, hated him because he was very clever. He was very creative in the way he wrote the bids. Very creative. But, well this is the difference as well and it's just coming to me. [He] would write the bid with input from every member of staff right.... He would challenge Welsh government as well. He would challenge it. It's about challenging others who challenged what was going on. Like I just said, now officers in the local authority didn't like him. He'd challenge everything. Whereas other leads wouldn't, they'd accept.'

In Cardiff, the multiplicity of partnerships and networks meant that leadership meant negotiating the community's interests through complex sets of relationships at many different levels. 'Anchor people' became hybrid actors (Pil and Guarneros-Meza, 2017) working through the tensions generated by organisational boundaries and being alert to the dangers of being co-opted, while acknowledging the limits of positive action (Newman, 2012).

'Anchor people' in economically disadvantaged communities are workers and leaders who demonstrate their 'craft' through their repair work, having developed a 'quiver' of skills (Sennet, 2013) through their close work with the material and emotional lives of the people they support. As a result, they also have embedded knowledge grounded in the everyday contexts of people's lives and are aware of the degree to which time changes the textures and nuances of community life. Too many are hidden from view.

*Anchor Peoples* was an installation of artworks that came out of the research project. It placed 31 figures, each about seven feet high, for two weeks in the Senedd in November 2018, home of the National Assembly for Wales. The portraits of community workers and volunteers stood majestically: they filled the public space and were impossible to ignore. They stood in different poses, with expressions suggesting a variety of emotions and characteristics: bravery, anger, defiance, humour, tenderness and generosity. The standing portraits were accompanied by a narrative soundscape from the interview data[3] on headphones that spoke of the work that anchor people do and their anger and sadness at their work being misunderstood and rendered invisible. The installation literally made the invisible sensorially visible.

Standing at the entrance to *Anchor Peoples* was *People's Palace*, an artwork that draws inspiration from René Magritte's 1953 *Golconda*, with the anchor people seemingly raining down on the Senedd, the seat of political power in Wales (see Figure 9.1). In Magritte's original image, multiples of the conservative moniker of a bowler-hatted gent rain down upon a line of lifeless terraced houses. The dislocation and juxtaposition in the image conveys the idea of social control in a poetic sense, like a descending blanket of conservatism, threatening to suffocate an already-lifeless community within which windows of buildings are vacant. The artists, Glenn Davidson and Chris Coppock from Artstation utilised the graphic formality of the Magritte image, bringing it into play with the contemporary research themes of regulation and community. *The People's Palace* comes from the name given by the great socialist Sir Leslie Martin – architect of the Royal Festival Hall – to celebrate the Festival of Britain in 1949.

**Figure 9.1:** *People's Palace: after Magritte*

Source: Glenn Davidson and Chris Coppock, Artstation, 2018

## Freedom from the regulatory controls of state funding

As the programme increasingly came to operate against the principles that anchor people embodied, their work became more exhausting and more challenging. Community development practices and state demands were in opposition to each other. It is perhaps not surprising, then, that the phasing out of Communities First has brought a certain amount of relief in that the programme was felt to impose impossible demands on time, as well as on the agility of organisations to work with the 'changing landscapes of poverty' imposed by austerity. The increasing demands of reporting left little time for the relational, street-level community building that they felt was at the heart of their practice (Blakely, 2010). As Gareth, a community development worker from SRCDC, reflected:

> 'The pressure of Communities First, in various ways, has inhibited our ability to fundraise … it doesn't give you time for reflective practice, it doesn't give you thinking time either, you know. You've got to really struggle in your working day to find the time to think things through, you know.… it's not healthy for your mind, you know, because you're just turned into like a robot, you know, just delivering and delivering all the time.'

Working outside the metrics of top-down regulatory controls can become a point of resistance and pride – it is what allows many anchor people to do their job well and in accordance with their values. While these spaces of resistance to policy hegemony were, to different extents, sanctioned by community organisations under the Communities First programme, freedom from the programme has meant that there is an opportunity for the organisations to be more explicit about their values and plans. However, many years of dependence on state funding has meant that they are having to rebuild anew.

Coming out of the Communities First programme, SRCDC and 3Gs are, at the time of writing, working to resurrect community-based infrastructures. While the difficulties in rebuilding core organisational structures and networks cannot be underestimated, their contributions to social change and the design of community-centred programmes may well lie in their independence from the controls of majority state funding, for in spite of all the devastation, some also conceptualised the crisis as an opportunity.

## Conclusion

The Communities First programme was a bold experiment in redesigning the democratic process of regeneration through a structure that explicitly aimed to regulate for inclusion and engagement. However, the three thirds partnership structure that was meant to drive the programme at the local level was eventually abandoned. That this partnership structure failed to work demonstrates, among other things, a failure to understand community as anything more than a 'collection of activated bodies, rather than an active, collective body' (Dicks, 2014: 293). The Welsh government failed to recognise the distinctive contribution of these anchor organisations and anchor people, both in its original implementation of Communities First and throughout the programme. The community organisations could have evolved and been positioned in a different way had anchor organisations been the focus of programme development from the outset. The strategy may also have freed them from subservience to the requirements of government outputs and monitoring in favour of developing and cementing their relationship and structures of accountability to the community. They did the best they could but the energy in maintaining their position in the programme depleted their capacity to maintain the regulatory structures for engagement that anchored them into communities in the first place. While there were some examples of mismanagement across Wales (which the press and politicians used to denigrate the programme and the idea of grass-roots regeneration as whole), the lack of capacity building and support, particularly in the latter phases, cannot be overestimated.

Community as an active body, in which the knowledge of poverty is accumulated and the capacity for action is collective, is nowhere to be seen in the later iterations of the programme. The despair of community development workers who saw the futility of employability programmes in the context of insurmountable labour market inequality, discrimination, competition (in the context of Cardiff) and a labour market wasteland (in Merthyr Tydfil) was palpable. Yet, it is also possible that in their stories of individual change and growth, the community organisations themselves started to embody the language and approach of individualism, rather than of collective change and the transformation of place.

Sandwiched between a government programme and community needs, community anchor organisations find themselves in a tricky position. Some worry that reliance on government funding results in a loss of independence and self-sufficiency. They become tethered to government-led agendas rather than anchored in the community. There is a sense in which community workers felt that they had been increasingly forced to work 'on' rather than 'with' communities, and they often drew on metaphors to describe the way in which Communities First had squeezed them, sucked them into a black hole, forced their ideas through a funnel or taken the jazz out of their work.

For all the hurt and damage caused by the sudden closure of this state-funded programme, some of the people that we have met and worked with have also described a taste of freedom as they go back to first principles, set their reports aside and reclaim some space for reflection. For the first time in years, there is time to think, to the extent that anchor people are already re-imagining and reinventing, creating reflective responses to the changing times.

Perhaps the key task will be for community anchor organisations themselves to collectively develop a shared identity as an anchored type of grass-roots civil society 'actor', on the one hand, and a mutual resource for knowledge and skills, on the other. While such member organisations exist in England, Scotland and, until recently, in Wales, we suggest in Chapter 10 that there is perhaps an opportunity to reassess what kind of collective resources are needed at a time when austerity too often results in processes of co-option, downloading and offloading, with time to think about the infrastructures for regulating for engagement in a context of marginalisation and inequality.

Following a referendum in March 2011, Wales has had the power to legislate without permission from Westminster in the 20 devolved areas for which it is responsible. Subsequently, the Wellbeing of Future Generations (Wales) Act 2015 created a legal obligation for all public bodies, including the Welsh government, both individually and collectively through public service boards, to consider social, economic and cultural well-being now and for future generations in relation to seven well-being goals.[4] In addition, one of five ways of working in order to implement the Act requires public bodies to involve citizens in the achievement of these goals. Regulating *for* engagement will be critical to public participation, achieved not by top-down control, but rather by investing in participatory ways of working. Many community development workers – anchor people – have developed their craft in regulating for engagement. Where they have had the time and capacity to mature and embed themselves locally, anchor organisations offer rich, 'on-the-ground' knowledge on how policy and services might work locally. However, they have not always been trusted guests at the 'public sector table'. Perhaps the focus should be on how public bodies themselves acquire the knowledge and experience to regulate for engagement rather than the other way around.

## Notes

[1] The National Assembly for Wales was created to take over key powers from Westminster in the wake of devolution in 1999. The Welsh Assembly government was established in March 2002 to distinguish the actions of the minister (the executive) from the Assembly as a whole.

[2] This included representatives from the two community organisations and academic members of the Productive Margins team. Three additional academics from Cardiff University were also invited as they had relevant academic knowledge and interests, as well as knowing one or both of the community organisations.

[3] Anonymised data were gathered from a mix of community members from both communities.

[4] See: http://futuregenerations.wales/about-us/future-generations-act

# 10

# Conclusion: Towards an organic model of regulating for engagement

*Bronwen Morgan, Morag McDermont and Martin Innes*

## Introduction

Regulation scholarship has typically been domain-specific, focusing on a particular industry (such as financial services) or a specific legislative domain (such as health and safety). Even when theorising at a general level, it has drawn its theoretical insights from domain-specific research. By contrast, the imaginative heart of each of the explorations laid out in the preceding chapters has been the holistic lived experience of diverse groups of citizens, many of whom described themselves as excluded from regulatory systems. In those experiential spaces, as this book has subsequently shown, multiple regulatory domains criss-cross, fragment and overlap. The specialised knowledges of each domain tend not to talk to each other, and even if they are linked through practices such as 'joined-up policymaking', these are often unintelligible to the citizens caught up in this regulatory web.

In generating exploration from the starting point of the lived realities of these citizens, it is fitting that 'expertise-by-experience' has been at the conceptual heart of the Productive Margins research programme. Correspondingly, the technocratic specialised expertise of specific regulatory domains has been more in the shadows, though this final chapter does seek to find points of fruitful dialogue with it. However, it is key to the findings of the whole research programme that expertise-by-experience is both sidelined and valuable. It is sidelined by current approaches to regulation, and it is valuable for redressing the limitations of those approaches documented in Chapter 1.

Two examples may bring to life the force of this general point. The first concerns the collectively written novel created by the research project *Life Chances* (see Chapter 6). This creative methodology involved participants developing characters from lived experience.

This meant that it was possible to meld into one coherent narrative the everyday experience of negotiating with asylum and immigration officials, teachers, social workers, homelessness officers, and other regulatory officials. These multiple fields typically operate according to particular siloed logics, but by putting the experience embodied by relational subjects at the centre of the novel's narrative, this particularity moves into the background, melding into cross-cutting ripples of an individual life instead.

A second example also draws on the generative arts-based methodologies utilised in the programme: the Alonely monologues produced in the course of research on older people's experiences of isolation and loneliness (see Chapter 4). These monologues blended real-life interview data with the lived experience of the community researchers who gathered the data. The resulting theatrical experience communicated an integrated sense of how older people's experience was shaped by very diverse regulatory fields: the impact of retirement from work; planning policies that could create housing environments where older and younger people could support each other; the double-edged capacity of digital spaces to both exclude and include; and the effects of social care and health service regulatory regimes.

The insights gained from these examples are invisible from the viewpoint of both officials and academics. Many scholars of regulation and governance offer sectorally siloed approaches, and many officials fail to conceptualise their domain as a species of regulation. Yet, the lived experiences of citizens were certainly constituted through multiple layers of regulation. The gulf between the documented experiences of our research participants and the perspectives of the officials whose decisions shaped those experiences is considerable. As a result, the project findings run against the conceptual grain of regulation theory per se, especially its self-presentation as a complex of generalised and generalisable institutions, routines and practices that apply across many domains.

This chapter seeks to build inductively from the findings of the research projects discussed in previous chapters, summarising their collective implications to answer the question: *what makes it possible to regulate for engagement?* We argue that the answer is a processual one. A threefold dynamic process underpins effective regulation for engagement, constituted by three factors that build upon and support each other: a holistic appreciation of place; the power to reframe the key narrative underpinning a regulatory regime; and the capacity to surface invisible or tacit rules. Together, these three facets challenge the technocratic conceptions of regulation that were subjected to critique in Chapter 1, suggesting instead a much more organic conception of regulation with expertise-by-experience at its heart, holding a space for messy, incremental and often formally ill-defined processes.

In what follows, we first elaborate on this threefold process, drawing on micro-illustrations from the preceding chapters. A more detailed understanding of those examples can be gained by returning to Table 1.1 in Chapter 1 and the chapter commentary that follows, as well as to the project-specific chapters. We follow by acknowledging the limits and perils of these dynamics, especially if they are institutionalised through traditional regulatory policy or legally enforceable programmes. Responding to these limits is the aim of the third and final section of the chapter, where we argue that embedding these practices and processes in *experientially sensitive infrastructure* is the key to preserving and stabilising their creative potential. This pathway is not without challenges, but we conclude with a sense of optimism about the benefits that could flow from meeting such challenges head-on.

## What makes it possible to regulate for engagement?

### Attention to place and/or a holistic system

The first factor highlighted as a collective implication of the diverse research projects explored in the Productive Margins programme is that of holistic attention to the place and systemic context of the practices and lifeworlds being regulated. At a very general level, the way in which this enhances the process of regulating for engagement can be illustrated with reference to *Live Model*,[1] a film made by Close and Remote, artists-in-residence during the programme's final 18 months. The artists' brief was to critically and creatively respond to the problems and possibilities of regulation as perceived by the academics and community organisations working on the programme.

The film is a creative riff on what regulation means by reference to a journey through urban space. In doing so, it provokes some important, critical questions about the meaning and practices of regulation. It takes local residents, councillors, activists and people associated with the research programme on a walk through three urban areas, inviting them to reflect on the myriad ways in which regulation is encoded in the built environment, the signs around them and the relationship between text and place. The film shows walkers handling tablets that speak to them in a sepulchral, mechanical voice, and it is clear from watching the film that the walkers acquire a new relationship to an otherwise familiar place, and that the enhanced understanding of regulation that they acquire throughout the walk is embodied, lateral and indirect. In this way, the film is a performative representation of the first step of the threefold dynamic in effective regulation for engagement. Aesthetically as much as content-wise, it enacts the embodied, material perspective that provides a foundation for that process.

This first step in the threefold process is at its heart about widening the lens of regulation, moving away from the perspectives of regulatory officials or specialist expertise that typically dominate. Once taken seriously, citizen-focused perspectives constantly pushed the conceptual and topical boundaries of what they understood to be the regulatory context. Sometimes, this widened lens incorporates an embedded relational sense of the geographical place and setting of their practices; at other times, it brings in a holistic understanding of context and perspective, even if not materially embedded. The most powerful (or productive) combination is when both of those dimensions are present.

Chapter 5 illustrates a widening of the lens in relation to issues concerning the regulation of the consumption of food. Narrower concerns of nutrition, access and cost were reframed into two different urban planning issues relating to accessing affordable, healthy food. In inner-city Easton, the concern was with licensing decisions that allowed a high density of fast-food takeaways within the vicinity of local schools. In more peripheral Knowle West, the problem was perceived to be the planning decisions of supermarket chains that left the area with few shops with only a very limited range of relatively expensive food.

Chapter 3 extends this widening to encompass a holistic appreciation of the context. In exploring the potential for engaging Muslim communities in the governance of the Prevent agenda, the Bristol approach to this agenda allowed women to look at broader systems of representation in mosques that regulated their own potential for engagement. Here, women sought ways to move out of the roles ascribed to them by government (as bearing upon the behaviour of their sons), instead considering the need for their active involvement in the life of the mosques.

Chapter 4's exploration of experiences of loneliness and isolation in older people is an instance of widening the lens in a highly place-sensitive way. Here, photo-essays created through walking tours enabled an exploration of connections and disconnections in the local community, so excavating 'the impact of natural and urban landscapes on a community's sense of its own isolation and loneliness'. This identified the focus on personalisation and individualisation in the 'care' system as contributing to the widely held belief that loneliness is an individual experience rather than a result of wider social and economic systems, often producing a degree of self-blame on the part of isolated older people.

In a final example, place, holistic context and a wider lens all converge. In Chapter 7, the young people's project used geographic information system (GIS) mapping to directly elicit understandings of their sense of safety in relation to the places they inhabit on a daily basis. As told in the chapter, one of the young people involved gave an instinctively positive picture of his street that had been profiled in a negative way on TV, but when asked on public record, reverted to calling the street "crap". Working through the medium of film, this project recovered the 'more intimate and fragile representations of ... place ... that lie buried beneath the more dominant public images of the place' (see Chapter 7), giving creative form to a much more textured and evocative sense of place.

In short, widening the lens of regulatory practice in ways that are sensitive to the specificities of place, especially its history and aesthetics, is at the heart of this first factor of the threefold dynamic of regulating effectively *for* engagement. Rather than linking networks of regulators in a professional technocratic way, paying attention to this factor helps respond to and re-imagine the embodied shared understandings and lived experiences of the regulated.

## *Telling a different story*

The first step makes possible a second. Paying attention to specificities of place and holistic understandings of the system produces narratives that weave together citizens' experiences of multiple regulatory mechanisms piled on top of each other. This, in itself, helps to 'tell new stories' and to create conceptual room for a new narrative about a regulatory system. For example, the Somali women from Easton working together with low-income white British families from Knowle West collectively reframed issues of food production and consumption as a broader story about urban planning, temporal family rhythms and advertising, producing the 'Ten principles for the community-led design of urban food systems' (see Figure 5.2, Chapter 5). The researchers specifically noted how this experience of collective naming, which they saw as a form of commoning, generated convivial energy between otherwise very disparate groups who rarely interacted.

Similarly, the loneliness research stressed the emergence of a 'common and public language' as a result of the processes described earlier, one that drew attention to the 'person in relation' (with the environment, with services and with each other) rather than the 'person in isolation' (see Chapter 4). The Bristol approach to the government's agenda to tackle extremism, which brought Muslim participants into the heart of agenda-setting through a partnership advisory group headed by a Muslim chair, told a different story through the choice of name: Building the Bridge instead of Prevent (see Chapter 3).

The *Life Chances* project (see Chapter 6) also conveyed several new stories articulated by the research participants. The visual reconfiguring of a white, heteronormative family in government-sponsored graphics for their *Life Chances* programme into images of a black family, a Muslim woman in a hijab with a child and a single father and his children conveyed political critique and an implicit alternative narrative. Meanwhile, the long-form freedom of a novel provided room for the imaginative construction of more critical details of regulatory exclusion, as well as an elaboration of the possible futures that could be constructed from that new identity. The narration of new identities and concerns is powerful, especially when the identities produced in the new story *overlap with* the standard story. In the young people's project (see Chapter 7), for example, the initial theme of harm and safety overlapped with the fresh story generated by the young women in the project: the pervasiveness of sexual harassment was not an expected theme, but still related to the concerns about harm and security of the police and education system.

### Surfacing 'invisible rules'

The two factors identified earlier work to begin to produce a sense of collective agency. Place and holistic context animate shared meanings and understandings. The articulation of new stories brings those to life and engages and involves others in these understandings. However, the process of surfacing 'invisible rules' works to lay the foundations for a more *enduring* sense of collective agency and is thus a crucial part of the threefold dynamic. Engaging with the dynamics of place and the energies of new stories through the prism of rules helps to codify and generalise what has been learnt. Yet, codification and generalisation have limits: as will be argued, it is vital that the process of surfacing invisible rules preserves the nuance of once-tacit understandings.

## Conclusion

The food project (see Chapter 5) developed a particularly elegant account of invisible rules, arguing that they:

> comprise the forms of regulation that influence food production and consumption at levels that we may be unable to control, such as globalising economic processes, labour processes, dynamics of supply and demand, advertising, and marketing.... [as well as] the 'cultural' rules that — often in implicit ways — dictate who can use which spaces, how it is appropriate to shop or cook, and who may associate with whom.

In one sense, this account echoes the widening lens of the first step, but the idea of articulating this as a set of general rules or principles provides tools for the collective agency unleashed by the new stories. In other words, the process of making invisible rules visible directly alters the sense of agency held by participants in the different projects.

For example, the question posed directly by the food project's title, 'Who decides what's in my fridge?', shifts the focus from an individual householder with purchasing power to an understanding of how broader patterns of advertising, street design, food-labelling practices and life rhythms combine to shape these decisions. This much more holistic context provides many more leverage points for potential change in the overall regulatory system.

Across the projects, we found that arts-based methods enabled open-textured creative spaces that seemed to be key to research participants freeing themselves from the negative, oppressive sense of regulation. They allowed for nuance and silence as much as voice, which are important buffers for communities at the margins, who may 'voice hesitancy' and need regulators 'to use their imaginations to fill in gaps that can sensitise them to emotional complexity', all opportunities provided by arts-based approaches (Iossifidis, 2016, n.p.). In many of the research project settings, participants did not always want to convey the whole story; fiction or drama provided space to construct characters based on aspects of their story that they felt safe to share.

Another way to surface invisible rules emerged through the notion of 'running with' the newly visible rules to create a new artefact, organisation or initiative that can then travel further out into different regulatory spaces. This might be a dramatic performance, a novel or a social enterprise. The interaction between the research and the experience of research participants did, in fact, create such artefacts that have since been further deployed (performed, sold, disseminated) by the research participants, in part, as an outcome of the project. Perhaps these are instances of using the collective agency generated by the threefold dynamic to create a 'business model', for the potential for commodification is indeed a danger, as Chapter 6 exploring the *Life Chances* project makes clear. In that chapter, the authors document an artistic response to the 'neoliberal' rhetoric of 'life chances' which may ironically and critically produce the very objective of the Conservative government's *Life Chances* project through the enacted methods of the project: an empowered, economically active individual engaged in creative-entrepreneurial endeavour. The crucial aspect of this is the agency rather than the business model per se. Rather than being engaged regulatees, people grasped at the opportunities to engage through collective economic action: new social enterprises in the form of community interest companies (CICs)[2] arose out of the food project (Somali Kitchen CIC) and *Life Chances* project (Creating Life Chances CIC), though it is not clear how enduring these developments will be in the medium to long term.

Together, these three elements – attending to space and a holistic system, telling a story differently, and surfacing tacit rules – *recover a sense of collective agency* that constructs a subjectivity able to speak into the regulatory space. That sense of collective agency is an overarching precondition of regulating for engagement. However, a crucial question is how such agency can endure. Should conscious effort to encode collective agency into enforceable legal and policy regimes necessarily follow from the threefold process that we have described thus far? This is a question that raises limits and perils.

## Limits and perils of regulating for engagement

### Encoding collective agency into enforceable legal/policy regimes

Securing the gains of the threefold process described thus far is no simple task. The food project (see Chapter 5) articulated most clearly the desirability of encoding the hard-won collective agency into some form of enforceable action. One pathway towards this is to formalise its implications into clear legal or policy rules that can be invoked against or by the state. While the limitations of the research process meant that the food project itself did not do this, it identified certain aspects of planning law that, if altered, would considerably improve the situation of food production and consumption for local residents.

An example of engagement resulting in a recoding of formal legal regimes is Muslim engagement in the Prevent agenda in Bristol, which resulted in a new formal arrangement for consultation between statutory agencies and the Muslim community in the setting up of Building the Bridge (see Chapter 3). However, we would acknowledge that the social relations in Bristol were very particular, which enabled this form of recoding to take place but made it unlikely that it would be widely reproduced. While the macrostructural potential of formal rule changes is an issue that we return to later, it is worth highlighting on their own terms some of the important formal rule changes secured by some of the project members (working with other actors) during the life of the project. The Muslim engagement project succeeded in securing a more equal gender representation in mosque governance. Others sought to take the creative outputs into the heart of policymaking, for example, the researchers on the loneliness project took the Alonely monologues to the Houses of Parliament in Westminster, London (see Chapter 4). In the case of the young people's project, the steps noted earlier led to a formal change in the school curriculum to cover the issue of sexual harassment (see Chapter 7). Of course, none of these gains is hard-wired. After 2011, the Prevent programme reverted to regulation without engagement, a top-down programme of training front-line workers as the eyes and ears of surveillance (or 'sous-veillance', as O'Toole terms it in Chapter 3), demonstrating that bottom-up is not always progressive. However, ongoing struggle is not surprising.

Perhaps more notable is that this 'strategic' step of encoding was not widely or vividly present in the projects as a whole. Indeed, there was a general absence of a desire to create statutory entitlements, nor was there much focus on the idea that clear regulatory entitlements create effective rights for citizen engagement. However, the *Life Chances* project (see Chapter 6) did focus on the statutory rights of parents in relation to their interactions with social workers. Through the course of workshops with a social work academic and a practicing lawyer, participants explored the 'rules of the game' in these interactions and clarified the legal framework around the rights of parents to query the record of case conferences and to make their own recordings of meetings with social workers.

Alternative foci did emerge, stressing that there are easier ways to bridge the gulf between citizens and officials. In the young person's project (see Chapter 7), for example, digital technologies (such as when the young people's projects carried out surveys embedded in GIS mapping) were recognised as providing an easier way to collect generalisable (or at least more extensive than anecdotal) data than resource-intensive individualised interviews. These data can reveal patterns hitherto invisible to regulatory officials, which may catalyse state responses or at least dialogue.

Overall, however, the project findings tend to highlight open-textured and institutionally fragile practices for forging collective agency. In other words, many of the practices that were most successful in fostering engagement were nonetheless not embedded in enforceable legal or policy regimes, and were thus institutionally fragile. The lack of formalised, conscious steps to encode these practices in enforceable legal or policy regimes is likely to be a function, at least in part, of the prefigurative nature of the practices, as well as their institutional and cognitive distance from the 'ways of seeing' of institutionalised regulatory officials. However, it may well be that the relative absence of this step reflects an intuitive understanding of its *costs* for the citizens co-producing the research in each project. In other words, the pursuit of enforceable policy and the formal collection of generalisable data could undermine the openings for engagement created by the practices outlined earlier. It could, one can easily imagine, work against the grain and ethos of place sensitivity, particularly for historical and cultural ways of embodying this sensitivity. This would have flow-on effects for the power and capacity to tell new stories. Invisible rules could still be surfaced, but not in ways that underpin a sense of collective identity. In other words, there is a sense of constraint on the possibility of regulating for engagement, though this is present in the data in a general albeit inchoate way. In the next section, we articulate this constraint more explicitly.

### Bureaucratic formalisation and power politics

A significant constraint on efforts to achieve strategic effectiveness by encoding collective agency into enforceable rules is that the productive practices that we have identified run the risk of bureaucratic formalisation. In Chapter 9, it is suggested that the Welsh government's anxiety about the messiness of community development practices was a factor in their decision to end the Communities First programme: 'Being committed to democratic principles, community workers could be considered unmanageable and "out of control". Government had an aversion to risk and messiness.'

Of course, bureaucratic formalisation has multiple benefits. In particular, it provides support, stability and resources for state practices that institutionalise social protection and help ameliorate inequality. However, the important question is whether these productive implications of bureaucratic formalisation reach those at the margins.

For example, the third stage of the Prevent programme (see Chapter 3) narrowed the focus of activities in ways that aligned with powerful elites and provided generous funding that spawned a professional compliance industry for a top-down 'securitised' approach. This was damaging to the open-ended approach supportive of marginal communities that had been developed in Bristol in earlier stages of the programme.

Effective policy formalisation can all too often suffocate the more elusive spirit of much of what was valuable in co-producing regulation at the margins. However, this is not inevitable. For example, through developing the 'Ten principles' (see Figure 5.2, Chapter 5), the food project explored creative ways to temper and challenge perceived incompatibilities between a nuanced sense of place and the articulation of relatively formal rules. The 'Ten principles' acknowledge 'food as always more-than-food: as contexts, socialities and spaces'. The isolation and loneliness project also developed ten overarching principles that need to come to the fore to ensure a 'care-ful', co-produced approach to knowledge production (see Chapter 4).

This shows that it is quite possible, at least in principle, to develop a formalism that leaves open the possibility for creativity, emergence and risk. However, it is worth acknowledging the salience of realpolitik and the reality that regulation for engagement can be blocked by the intentional mobilisation of power and money against groups at the margins. The post-2011 version of Prevent demonstrated a strong thread of this (see Chapter 3). The formalism of the professional compliance programme was a top-down one that closed down possibilities. This closing down was not an unintended side effect of formalisation, but rather precisely a rejection of a more open-ended and tolerant interpretation of Prevent, that Bristol and other local authorities had enacted, by an incoming government with different policy priorities. Similarly, the Welsh government shut down the Communities First funding entirely, leaving community organisations throughout Wales stranded in their attempts to engage the citizens at the margins that they had worked with for years (see Chapter 9).

In light of this, it is clear that formal bureaucratisation, particularly if legally entrenched, can be explicitly beneficial for those on the margins as it can help to prevent a policy rollback of this nature. However, as the framing of the research programme as a whole makes clear, a necessary condition for success is that encoding and formalism must take place in such a manner that develops the co-produced nature of knowledge production. If not, as this section has outlined, there are significant attendant risks and costs. More constructively, however, the project findings also support the idea that there is an alternative pathway to supporting the open-textured and institutionally fragile practices for forging collective agency that we have identified here. This pathway focuses not on bureaucratic formalisation or on legal rights per se, but instead on infrastructure. Infrastructure, built carefully, can help to give institutional heft and longevity to the emerging collective agency without diluting the constructive qualities that make it responsive to groups at the margins.

## Experientially sensitive infrastructure

Regulatory complexity has given rise to an increasing role for intermediaries. In the standard regulation literature, which has a somewhat linear model of regulation, 'intermediaries' provide 'assistance to regulators and/or targets [that is, the regulated organisations], drawing on their own capabilities, authority, and legitimacy' (Abbott et al, 2017: 6). This approach tends to focus on inter-organisational communication between large-scale entities, privileges technocratic expert knowledge and consigns citizens to the margins, considering them as end users or beneficiaries at best (Koenig-Archibugi and Macdonald, 2017). However, if there is to be a possibility that regulatory systems will truly engage with communities in the manner envisaged in the Productive Margins programme, then the crucial need is for intermediation, translation and brokering between communities at the margins and those organisations and systems that regulate their daily lives.

We want to argue for the need to support and maintain an *infrastructure* that can enable the engagement of those generally excluded from regulatory systems. Here, we are envisaging infrastructure understood in a socio-political way (Larkin, 2013; Amin, 2014), with a particular focus on the connectedness of social action rather than its isolation or exclusion via technical management. Understood as such, infrastructure supports endurance, articulated by Berlant (2016: 395) as the reproduction of forms of life, or 'ongoingness'. In the context of the Productive Margins programme, we suggest that 'experientially sensitive infrastructure' makes possible regulating for engagement, specifically through networks of organisations that can act as brokers, intermediaries and umbrella or 'in-between' entities that support and curate the work of smaller, focused groups or enterprises.

In contrast to the self-description by one of the community organisation partners in the programme that they were "experts in nothing very much", those who constitute experientially sensitive

## Conclusion

infrastructure organisations are more like 'experts in everything'. Particularly in Chapter 9, with its focus on the idea of community organisations in Wales as 'anchor' organisations, we can see their multiple functions and roles. They run community centres, translate between local communities and citizens and regulators, and can call on other experts as needed (for example, picking up the phone and talking to the right person in the local authority). Through the legal encoding of these organisations (generally as companies limited by guarantee and as charities) these organisations can support the organic development of hyper-local action, as in the case of BS3 Community (BS3C) (originally Southville Community Development Association). BS3C enabled the group of peer researchers that took part in the Alonely research (see Chapter 4) to form a Bristol-based Local Isolation and Loneliness Action Committee (LILAC). LILAC were keen to get on with doing the work of an action committee, and therefore sought not to be a registered association of any form, or to spend their time working out administrative, technical and legal issues. This was made possible because BS3C was able to bid for funding for a worker to work with the LILAC team and to administer the monies subsequently received, allowing LILAC to remain an unincorporated entity and get on with *action*.

Similarly, Coexist (see Chapter 8) is an organisation in Bristol that originated to provide an infrastructure for a wide range of community organisations, largely in terms of space. Originally invited by the owners of Hamilton House, a large dilapidated building in the centre of Bristol, to come in and see how the building might be repurposed, Coexist set up a social enterprise, opening their doors to see what would happen. At first, many small businesses nearing bankruptcy in the post-2008 context came to them. Soon, a range of organisations were using the space, including dance studios, a well-being centre, a cookery school, people in recovery, young people and a gallery-and-shop space for selling products made in the building. Coexist has been one element in the regeneration of the local area, which became populated with a vibrant local set of independent shops.

Coexist helped to support the various ways in which these smaller initiatives were already engaging with regulatory systems as part of their day-to-day activity, such as brokering arrangements between their tenants and the local council concerning the payment of business rates. Their role here was highly strategic. Deploying expertise 'explicitly geared to process issues, they can facilitate, mediate and negotiate, nurture networks, and deploy cultural knowledge and local knowledge in ways that enable traditionally "silent" voices to be heard along with the articulate, persistent and powerful' (Larner and Craig, 2005: 417–18).

Infrastructures are described in the literature as constantly needing maintenance and repair (Jackson, 2015), reminding us that they are fragile entities themselves. In terms of community organisations, a key practice of maintenance is finding enough monetary funds to endure. The organisations in the Productive Margins programme rely on funding from a wide range of sources, not just from the state. For instance, BS3C runs two day nurseries, enabling it to provide support to a myriad of local groups in its large repurposed school building. Illustrating the site-specific nature of these organisations, these nurseries are only possible due to BS3C's location in an area with a significant middle-class population, opening possibilities that would be unlikely to exist in other areas of high economic deprivation (see Chapter 4). Similarly, as a CIC and umbrella organisation, Coexist was able to provide facilities that enabled over 200 artists, social enterprises and other 'alternative' entities to flourish (see Chapter 8).

Critical resources can be found in property as well as grants. Coexist's occupation of Hamilton House was only workable when the property was considered to have low value. The organisation has shifted from thriving to being unsustainable now that the (economic) opportunity costs for Hamilton House have been driven up by neighbourhood gentrification.[3] In the context of the withdrawal of Communities First funding, both 3Gs Development Trust and South Riverside Community Development Centre owned the buildings that they operated from, enabling them to have sustainable futures beyond the withdrawal of state resources.

The fragility of infrastructure poses a dilemma, intensified by the implicit assumption that infrastructures need to be independent; as a worker in one of the Welsh organisations said: "I see this place as independent infrastructure – it's not run by the council and it's not run by politicians." Statutory funding could buttress infrastructural organisations from fragility but can lead to them getting root-bound. The Welsh organisations (see Chapter 9) experienced a sense of relief when Communities First funded ended, relief from constantly having to meet targets, leaving no time to think, re-imagine or reinvent. State funding also leaves them very vulnerable to changes in the political winds. If funding is reduced, eliminated or tied to new and unacceptable conditions, it may not be easy to rapidly amass a range of non-statutory sources of funding. Thus, statutory funding may temporarily reduce fragility but at the cost of losing agility. In short, community infrastructures may benefit from remaining agile, yet fragile, despite the necessary labour that this requires.

## Formality/informality

The experientially sensitive infrastructure described earlier works to support regulation for engagement over the long term because of its capacity to absorb and enact a nuanced balance between formality and informality. The dilemma of fragility and agility is one instance of this broader conundrum. As noted in their special issue, Boudreau and Davis treat informality as a productive site: 'Vibrant residues of informality', they argue, 'offer a distinctively fertile resource that is often overlooked by state actors' (Boudreau and Davis, 2017: 154). They sketch several positive responses by state actors to informality and its potential: embracing ambiguity in grey regulatory areas; creating space for interactive personalised relations that blur the borders of legal authority; and even accepting the ways in which excluded groups may stubbornly defend existing practices, notwithstanding illegality.

While regulatory officials can learn from the perspectives of the citizens at the margins, embracing informality does not mean dispensing with rules altogether. Indeed, as discussed in Chapter 2, our experiments in co-production demonstrated that we tend to become more unsure and uncomfortable without rules. Co-production itself regulates practice (Innes et al, 2018) and, indeed, requires the making of new rules; otherwise, existing rule systems will dominate. The lesson would be that we should not be afraid of making rules; rather, it is in the processes by which rules are made that the possibilities for engagement can be reframed. Thus, while infrastructure is a critically important resource for balancing formality and informality, for regulatory systems to engage communities at the margins as actors within the systems rather than subjects of regulation, there is a need to focus on the structures and processes required to enable, support and translate expertise-by-experience into possibilities for engagement. Infrastructure must be experientially sensitive in carrying out its tasks of intermediation, translation and brokering, and the practices of co-production can be a key mechanism for sensitising regulatory systems to experience.

## Co-production as a crucial method for building infrastructure

As we progressed through the programme, in what often felt like slow and painful steps, to collaboratively produce new ways of seeing and knowing regulatory systems, we realised that much of our focus and energy was directed towards the doing of co-production. We often asked ourselves: had we lost sight of regulatory systems? However, as we show in Chapter 4, the 'care-ful' application of principles of co-production led us to insights that have important implications for regulatory systems. In that chapter, researchers came to see that the terminology of isolation and loneliness (which, by that time, had become entrenched in Westminster government in the form of a 'Minister for Loneliness') was associated with an individualistic attitude towards the social problem that led older people to feel that they were somehow to blame for their isolation. What the collaborative production of knowledge enabled was a switch in language to 'disconnections' and 'connections', which provided a positive potential for action – for understanding loneliness as a cross-generational experience, and for seeing the potential for intergenerational action as the solution – leading to Tech and Talk cafes that bring older people and younger, tech-savvy people together in informal settings for learning. Co-production, then, enables new ways of seeing and knowing that can move regulation away from the problems that we identified in Chapter 1. The professional practices of 'community development' embodied similar understandings and practices that we were developing under the banner of 'co-production'. It is partly this realisation, and the knowledge of the practices of the organisations involved in the programme, which makes us suggest that a sustainable network of community organisations would provide valuable infrastructure for regulation *for* engagement.

One of the many lessons that we learnt from this programme was the need to leave space for emergence. Much of what arose from our research programme could not have been anticipated at the start. Indeed, that must surely be the point of good research, good community development or, indeed, good engagement. In Chapter 1, we analysed a principal problem with regulatory systems: that they were not allowing space for expertise-by-experience. We suggest that this can only be addressed if existing systems are made *open* to experimentation rather than being stuck in the technocratic mindset of the all-too-familiar experts, allowing space for 'situational spontaneity that pushes back against established state regulations and the constraints of the law' (Boudreau and Davis, 2017: 155).

Of course, we acknowledge that a shift towards collaborative production, with its requirement for substantial time and other resource investment, will be a hard move for policy developers, especially under conditions of austerity. Its short-term costs are probably higher but, we would argue, are more likely to deliver long-term tractable change.

We also recognise that experiments do fail – not everything we tried in the research programme worked – and that experiments can appear uncomfortable or even induce harm to some participants. However, we would point to the difficult road navigated by those setting up Building the Bridge as a collaborative approach to the top-down anti-extremism policies of Prevent (see Chapter 3). Despite anxiety within the local authority and the police that this would be handing over power to local communities (who might be the 'wrong' people), the trust developed between the participants meant that Building the Bridge survived beyond the withdrawal of central government funding.

## Concluding thoughts: towards the idea of organic regulation

Organic regulation, while being messy in the manner outlined earlier, can still be defined. The concept is analogous with Innes's (2014) notion of 'organic social control', where he expounds the idea that influencing behaviour and conduct can be accomplished through relatively spontaneous and informal arrangements that arise through people's direct interactions, as opposed to just 'manufactured' forms delivered by state institutions. It can hold a space for messy, incremental and often formally ill-defined processes, pulling back from requiring prescriptive definition of outcomes at the start. Organic modes of regulation allow space for new ideas and solutions to *emerge*. This can lead to outcomes that are (perhaps surprisingly) productive for citizens at the margins, in particular, to a sense of collective agency that is crucially important for building innovative responses in the context of increasing austerity and institutional complexity at the level of the state.

However, a formalisation that is fully sensitive to the dynamics of co-produced knowledge is a real challenge for regulation. A preoccupation with formalising social processes is endemic to state modernisation processes. Boudreau and Davis (2017: 152) describe this as the 'conquest and reshaping of "untamed" spaces and practices through social and spatial integration', in order to impose order on messiness. This aesthetic is mirrored in the common etymology of 'regulation' and 'regularity'. Huising and Silbey (2015) also stress the importance of relational regulation.

All we are doing here is gesturing briefly to the potential relationship of this book's finding to other literature – this chapter has focused on synthesising the research *findings* into a consideration of their implications for regulation writ large. As was argued in Chapter 1, traditional regulation is strained and cracking at the edges. Truly engaging citizens at the margins rests upon regulation incorporating marginal understandings of its own nature. This chapter has articulated three especially important dimensions: a sense of place, new narratives, and surfacing invisible rules. The implications of these dimensions for regulation are likewise threefold. We suggest that regulation must embrace and balance informality, the need for infrastructure and an openness to organic change and development.

Our aim from the outset of the programme has been to explore how regulatory systems can engage citizens and communities at the margins. All the projects have been driven by concerns for enabling communities to articulate what regulatory systems would look like and act like in order to promote social justice. However, this is not some abstract idea of social justice, but rather points to developing ways in which inequalities and injustices, perceived by and in communities, can be tackled. The emergent patterns of the research projects point to the potential of 'mutually-productive interactions, adaptation, and flexibility' (Boudreau and Davis, 2017: 162) to push back at inequalities and injustices. Of course, as with so much about collective existence on a finite planet, these possibilities are Janus-faced. This is why any new approach to regulation has an ongoing responsibility to maintain a critical edge and a commitment to emancipation, however fleeting that may often feel in the cracked interstices of a fraying modernity.

There is a sense – very evident across the chapters – that the regulatory systems that we experience make no place for social justice. The challenge is one of becoming involved in the design and implementation of a radically different infrastructure that is sensitive to experience, to open up a place for forms of social justice that can be contextually understood. Yet, the question remains as to whose social and whose justice is represented and performed in these contexts. There are no easy answers here. While co-production methods allow conceptions of social justice generated within communities – rather than government or corporations – to come to the surface, the knottier issue is how to both identify each strand of contextually specific social justice concepts and to thread these conceptions back into the complex warp and weft of regulatory systems.

## Notes

[1] See: www.closeandremote.net/live-model/

[2] The UK legislated for the formation of hybrid social enterprises known as community interest companies in 2005 through the Companies (Audit, Investigations and Community Enterprise) Act 2004, brought into force by the Community Interest Company Regulations 2005.

[3] The future of Coexist and Hamilton House was in flux during the final years of the programme. Coexist was evicted from Hamilton House in December 2018: see https://thebristolcable.org/2018/12/photoessay-coexists-last-48-hours-at-hamilton-house/

POSTSCRIPT

# Engaging the university?

*Janet Newman*

## Introduction

This postscript offers both a celebration of the achievements of the Productive Margins (PM) research programme and an attempt to set it in the broader context of contemporary political possibilities – and constraints. My particular focus is on attempts to transform universities into instruments of engagement and connectedness – to turn them inside out. This is an attempt to take the 'productive' emphasis of the programme seriously, and to ask how far, or in what ways, the engagement of 'communities at the margins' has the potential to transform university hierarchies of knowledge and power.

In addressing this question, the programme raises a number of issues that, if pursued in future work, have a transformative potential. However, it raises further questions that remain unresolved, and that may limit the impact of transformative agendas:

- The politics of co-production: is it possible to co-produce research across inequalities of power and divergent objectives?
- The politics of policy: how can research that retains a commitment to notions of complexity and emergence persuade policymakers of its utility and legitimacy?
- The politics of the academy: how can researchers manage the tensions between the demands of their institutions, their own values and the requirements of publishing and career advancement?

I will return to these questions at various points (especially in the later section on 'Working the borders'), but I first want to highlight the distinctiveness and importance of the PM programme.

One of the objectives of the programme was 'to shift the way research in higher education is conducted in order to bring in and acknowledge the expertise and experience of communities at the margins into the whole research process, from programme design to data collection through to analysis and dissemination' (Productive Margins, 2018). This objective has three features that mark it out from other forms of innovation in research. First, it is concerned with *bringing in* excluded forms of knowledge and expertise, rather than disseminating it after the event (though, as Chapter 10 suggested, the latter also matters if the intention is to effect a change in the thinking and practice of policymakers). Second, it references the *whole research process*, rather than engagement in one aspect (for example, data collection or dissemination). The tensions raised – notably, between the temporal priorities of university staff and those of activists/community organisations, between a focus on emergence over time and operational tightness, and between financial security and precarity – defeat any simple notion of 'co-production' as a necessarily progressive development and open out important challenges for future experiments in engagement.

Third, the programme sought to engage 'communities at the margins', those communities with little voice in or influence over the making of public policy. This also opened up difficult questions: here, about the term 'community' and about the meaning of being 'at the margins'. The programme chose to work with neighbourhood-based, identity-based and faith-based organisations, as well as with social enterprises experimenting with new ways of living and working. As such, it draws on and contributes to a wider tradition of community development – a tradition now somewhat both sidelined in terms of the literature on public engagement, and displaced in government discourse by weaker notions of 'partnership', 'user involvement' and 'consultation'. In distancing itself from these heavily compromised terms, the PM programme opened up greater possibilities for the transformation of university practice and entrenched hierarchies of knowledge and power.

The PM programme was, then, much broader in scope and ambition than the focus on engaging specific categories of students, stakeholders, partners or service users. This scope meant that difficulties arose as different communities brought different priorities and agendas. However, despite this breadth, the programme's achievements have been remarkable. Chapter 1 showed how it has challenged taken-for-granted assumptions about the politics of regulation. Often viewed as oppressive, distant and a symbol of a discredited view of the interventionist state, regulation is, rather, essential to the well-being of communities and the flourishing of civic life. This is an important intervention in a climate in which regulation serves as something of a political football – opposition to European Union

(EU) regulations formed a central plank of the campaigns for Britain to leave the EU, which tended to set up 'distant technocrats' and 'ordinary people' as antagonistic forces. Demonstrating the value of regulation in such a context is an important outcome. However, also significant was the ways in which the researchers situated regulation in alternative conceptions of policy and governance – ones that reflect the interconnectedness of the lives and experiences of citizens and are driven by their participation in the local polity, rather than organised around the specificities of 'siloed' departments of government.

## The productive capacity of border work

Universities, of course, also have 'siloed' departments, embedded systems of governance and entrenched hierarchies of knowledge and power. These were all challenged by the programme's emphasis on the importance of co-production. It sought to draw on the expertise and knowledge of different communities and explored the innovative possibilities of working with 'communities at the margins' – precisely those communities that have little voice in public policy or presence in university life. However, it also shows the difficulty of aligning the priorities of university staff and those of the civic and community groups that they seek to engage. The latter tend to operate within the short time frames of funding regimes, as opposed to the five-year time horizon of the PM programme. They have to demonstrate the value of research in the context of the urgent demands of those in desperate need of support, and their values and politics often differ markedly from those of university staff.

Community groups seldom offer a unitary voice but are themselves cross-cut by political conflict and competing priorities, and much the same can be said for the universities that seek to engage them. All of this makes simplistic ideas of 'co-production' rather hollow. Like earlier notions of partnership and participation, it is a term that carries associations of warmth and consensus and implies an equality that fails to recognise the multifaceted dynamics of power. It tends to overlook – or ignore – differences of capacity (both temporal and financial), and so fails to address the substantial challenges of engaging groups and voices 'at the margins' (see also Facer and Enright, 2016). This is why I want to offer the idea of *border work* to signify the ways in which relationships have to be negotiated across difference and brokered by mediating actors who can forge relationships – or at least institute conversations – across different perspectives, interests and voices.

Newman (2012) traced the ways in which border workers are not simply situated at the boundaries between organisations. Rather, they operate across, and draw on the resources of, multiple regimes of organisational, political and social power: public/private, bureaucratic/community-based, governmental/activist and so on. As such, their work is that of negotiating between contradictory rationalities and translating between different discourses and vocabularies of meaning. Such skills – relational and political – are often acquired through work in community and activist groups or are honed in what tend to be 'non-traditional' career routes that span multiple organisations and projects. Such skills and forms of labour are of great value to institutions seeking change but tend to be found on the margins of institutional life, job descriptions and reward structures.

Several forms of border work were evident in the PM programme. It involved working across academic departments and disciplines (multidisciplinary working was crucial to its success), as well as the different histories and cultures of the two sponsoring universities and the communities that they served. These were situated in England and Wales, respectively, and so faced different local, institutional and governmental challenges. However, working across these differences served to broaden the perspectives of research staff and brought new axes of learning into both institutions. Relationships with funding bodies were also complex: the Economic and Social Research Council (ESRC) and Arts and Humanities Research Council (AHRC) brought different expectations, and the award was made after iterative negotiations. The subsequent focus on demonstrating effectiveness to both arts and social science funders produced some tensions in terms of methods, but the previous chapters demonstrate the value of creative and visual practice in shaping a diversity of research outcomes.

More potentially troubling was the tension between the goal of co-production and normative expectations of what a research process should look like: set research questions before deciding on methods; rely on researchers well versed in established techniques; view case studies as a one-way process of knowledge extraction; and produce papers with tidy conclusions. This programme has shown something of the messiness of its own evolving practice (see Chapter 2). It brought together different forms of experience and expertise (inducting community actors in research methods, or exposing university staff to the conflict-resolution techniques used by some of the community organisations). It had to work with different meanings of key terms – most notably, regulation itself. It also had to confront the very different politics of institutional life, cooperative working and activist projects.

Border work is, then, riven with contradictions and tensions; however, these can be exploited to create new possibilities and opportunities. This has a generative or productive potential, and the chapters of this volume offer ample evidence of the transformative impact of border work on university life, theoretical work, policy models and norms of public engagement. However, without attention to the tensions inherent to such work, the issues raised at the beginning will impede this productive potential.

## The politics of co-production

It is evident that beginning with normative assumptions about the benefits of co-production and trying to impose these on potential collaborators and partners is likely to fail. Many of the groups that the programme sought to work with were already well versed in handling conflicts between different political stances and normative values. They were not, however, versed in the language of co-production. There may be a need for academics to suspend previous assumptions about collaborative practice and to address the dynamics of conflict and collaboration from the outset. This may mean not attempting to work with models of consensus which assume that value conflicts – and conflicts of priorities – can necessarily be resolved.

## The politics of policy

Trying to produce policy guidance that, on the one hand, simplifies the complexity of the outcomes of research or that, on the other hand, suspends the need for policy 'answers' that can be applied in the short term and across divergent contexts is perhaps not helpful (though such guidance might, of course, help to legitimate research with funders and stakeholders). However, the role of the university in educating future policy actors, civil servants, politicians and professionals in alternative ways of thinking about public policy and social action is nonetheless crucial. Universities might also give thought to how to support mediating actors – including the community groups debated here – in their own educational activities, as well as in policy evaluation exercises.

## The politics of the academy

'Bringing the outside in' is clearly of value for academic programmes of transformation, exposing universities to innovative perspectives, offering alternative forms of expertise and challenging entrenched norms. However, the enrichment of universities as institutions often tends to be at the expense of the individuals 'working the borders', often with little recognition, and may impoverish the civil society cultures and community organisations on whose knowledge and skills they draw. This is where positive leadership within higher education is crucial, an issue I turn to later.

## The politics of possibility

Here, I want to look beyond the PM programme to highlight some of the limits and possibilities of transforming universities in ways that enable them to serve wider social and political purposes. In higher education, success in demonstrating public engagement is increasingly tied to the award of research funding, to career and promotion prospects, and to wider public and governmental legitimacy. However, it often takes narrow, instrumental forms, prioritising impact on public policy or business. For those seeking radical change, there is a certain ambiguity about the value of public engagement. As others have argued elsewhere, public engagement marks an uneasy confluence of moves towards a more 'progressive' governance and the emergence of new governmentalities: orders of rule that draw on the knowledges and resources of individuals and communities to enhance the legitimacy of ruling relations (Newman and Clarke, 2008).

However, such grand theoretical assertions obscure the ways in which multiple forces are played out in particular sites, and, moreover, tend to generate a pessimism that squeezes the potential for radical experimentation. This is why empirical studies such as those reported in this volume are so significant – not least because of the range of cases on which authors draw: some offering evidence of the co-optation of radical approaches in the roll-out of new governmentalities (for example, see Chapter 3); others offering more ambiguous depictions of the progressive potential of experiments.

However, experiments and projects, while important, are perhaps not enough unless they are located in and help drive wider programmes of transformation. As Munck et al (2014) note, higher education is facing not only a funding crisis, but also a crisis of perspectives, with commercial interests overriding more public-facing goals. In the contemporary UK, university missions tend to be oriented towards global competitions for students, research funds and reputational capital. Such tendencies are exacerbated by central government funding and performance regimes, not least the notoriously flawed research assessment exercises. Yet, in the current climate of austerity, in which local resources have been hollowed out and community initiatives have been starved of funding, there is surely a need for something more. As an alternative strategy, Munck et al (2014) propose a 'third mission', alongside teaching and research, oriented to community. The PM programme was not, of course, unique in its focus on community engagement and development: the Universities of Sydney and Chicago have a long tradition of establishing research centres that sought to include community partners as active participants in research, and together produce *Gateways: An International Journal of Community Research and Engagement.*[1]

It is also common for universities to have publicly stated missions that offer fine words about the role of universities in building resilient communities, and as agents of social – as well as economic – development. However, can these be more than fine words? Why do such ambitions so frequently fail to materialise in substantive change? One reason is that university missions work across, and perhaps seek to mask, deep and persistent conflicts of values and ideology. This makes it notoriously difficult to embed the stated mission in material systems, relationships, resource flows and infrastructure. Moreover, a focus on missions implies that change inevitably flows from and is driven by the 'top' of university hierarchies, and can be translated into action plans that flow 'downwards' to departments, teams and units.

This is why attempts to build on the productive capacity of forms of engagement that not only reach out to support vulnerable or marginal communities, but also seek to bring the outside in, are so vital. The value of the PM programme lay in its emphasis on the productive role of 'marginal' or excluded forms of knowledge and expertise, productive not only for public policy, but also for sponsoring universities. It has brought community activists into university life, co-producing empirical research and programme events/outputs. It has tackled 'real-world' problems and opened up new relationships between theory and action. It has troubled established forms of power/ knowledge and taken staff out of their comfort zones. As such, it has pointed to the permeability of the boundaries between inside and outside, between theory and policy, between the centre and the margins – all the very essence of border work.

However, the capacity of such work to bring about transformative change is fragile, subject to the whims of university restructuring programmes, funding priorities and performance regimes, and perhaps the loss of key 'champions' at senior levels of the hierarchy. University staff are constrained by the wider cultures and reward structures that shape the conditions of possibility for transformative work. Such institutional constraints shape the capacity for innovation, potentially squeezing the potential for cross-disciplinary research and for work at the 'margins'. They may also limit the further development of theory and methods. The authors of this volume have refused to offer simple lists of research outcomes in the form of policy recommendations, instead offering challenging models of complexity and emergence – vocabularies that do not feature significantly in the bullet-point action plans that pervade conventional transformation programmes.

My focus on the productive capacities of border work means that universities cannot stand alone as agents of transformation. However, the resilience – even the survival – of many of the organisations involved in the programme is currently being challenged by the withdrawal of funding. While this may free some from constraints, it is ultimately destructive. There is a need for universities to help sustain the infrastructure of mediating and activist organisations in order to enable new networks to emerge and voices to be heard – and to be agents in the co-production of future transformative programmes.

These are rather general points that can be applied to any programme of change, but they nevertheless serve as important considerations for the two universities sponsoring the PM programme as they attempt to embed the learning that it has generated. The programme has helped shift the culture within the University of Bristol, with the 'co-creation' of knowledge now being viewed as a central strategy, and a commitment to local communities – and understanding of their formation through wider social/political forces – implicit in its ambition to become a 'global–local' university. It has also helped shape work towards the setting up of the Social Justice Project in conjunction with community and private sector partners in the city of Bristol to serve as an access point for community and third sector organisations and social enterprises to engage in collaborative research, and as a space for the co-production of new ideas, perspectives and projects. The university has also founded the Brigstow Institute, which links university researchers and a range of partners across the city. Cardiff University has established Community Gateway, which aims to 'develop meaningful and long-term relationships with local communities, enabling the sharing of community and university expertise to achieve common goals' (Productive Margins, 2018). Community Gateway's pilot project is in Grangetown, one of the most culturally diverse districts of Cardiff.

Of course, causality is difficult here. Such commitments may be as much a product of emerging strategies and shifting power blocs as the result of a specific programme. However, the confluence of emergent trends and positive, reputation-enhancing experiments seems to have had positive results, not least in the embedding of networks of innovators, boundary spanners and influencers within and beyond the universities.

This all matters in the current political culture. The PM programme was set in a political climate in which universities and other public institutions were becoming demonised as repositories of elite, expert power. In such a context, there is an urgent need to restore public trust and democratic legitimacy, to show how universities are capable of responding to contemporary questions and needs, and to demonstrate their value and relevance. To counter these challenges to legitimacy, universities require something beyond the current orientation towards consumerist models of education. While I remain pessimistic about prospects for transformative change, reading this volume has reminded me about the importance of looking in detail at the potential of particular and emerging forms of political, community and civic engagement. It has also generated an excitement about the possibility of alternatives to consumerism, neoliberalism and austerity. Perhaps the legacy of the programme will be as a form of symbolic capital on which others can draw in future experiments and transformative projects.

## Note

[1] See: https://creativecommons.org/licenses/by/4.0

# References

Aabe, N., Abdullahi, S., Ahmed-Shafi, A., Bashir, K., El Dieb, S.J., Kaurser, T., Kauser, S., Lewicki, A., O'Toole, T., Raja, R., Rana, S., Saker, F. and Saliem, T. (2015) 'Enhancing spaces for Muslim women's engagement', Bristol Policy Brief: 10/2015. Available at: www.bristol.ac.uk/policybristol/policy-briefings/muslim-women/ (accessed 31 January 2019).

Abbott, K.W., Levi-Faur, D. and Snidal, D (2017) 'Theorizing regulatory intermediaries: the RIT model', *Annals of the American Academy of Political and Social Science*, 670(1): 14–35.

Abel, T. and Cockerham, W.C. (1993) 'Lifestyle or lebensfuhrung? Critical remarks on the mistranslation of Weber's class, status, party', *The Sociological Quarterly*, 34: 551–6.

Adamson, D., Dearden, H. and Castle, B. (2001) *Community Regeneration. Best Practice Review*, Cardiff: National Assembly for Wales.

Allegue, L., Jones, S., Kershaw, B. and Piccini, A. (eds) (2009) *Practice as Research in Performance and Screen*, London: Palgrave Macmillan.

Allen, C. and Guru, S. (2012) 'Between political fad and political empowerment: a critical evaluation of the National Muslim Women's Advisory Group (NMWAG) and governmental processes of engaging Muslim women', *Sociological Research Online*, 17(3): 17. Available at: www.socresonline.org.uk/17/3/17.html

Amin, A. (2014) 'Lively infrastructure', *Theory, Culture & Society*, 31(7/8): 137–61.

Amin, A. and Thrift, N.J. (2005) 'What's left? Just the future', *Antipode: A Radical Journal of Geography*, 37: 220–38.

Anderson, K. and Smith, S.J. (2001) 'Editorial: emotional geographies', *Transactions of the Institute of British Geographers*, 26(1): 7–10.

Arendt, H. (1998) *The Human Condition*, Chicago, IL: Chicago University Press.

Ayres, I and Braithwaite, J. (1992) *Responsive Regulation: Transcending the Deregulation Debate*, New York: Oxford University Press.

Bain, A. and McLean, H. (2013) 'The artistic precariat', *Cambridge Journal of Regions, Economy and Society*, 6(1): 93–111.

Bang, H. (2003) 'A new ruler meeting a new citizen: culture governance and everyday making', in H. Bang (ed) *Governance as Social and Political Communication*, Manchester: Manchester University Press.

Barad, K. (2007) *Meeting the Universe Halfway: Quantum Physics and the Entanglement of Matter and Meaning*, Durham, NC: Duke University Press.

Barnes, T. and Sheppard, E. (2009) '"Nothing includes everything": towards engaged pluralism in anglophone economic geography', *Progress in Human Geography*, 34(2): 193–214.

Barry, A. and Born, G. (eds) (2013) *Interdisciplinarity: Reconfigurations of the Social and Natural Sciences*, London: Routledge.

Barthes, R. (1977) 'Rhetoric of the image', in S.T. Heath (ed) *Image – Music – Text*, New York, NY: Hill and Wang.

Beasley, C. and Bacchi, C. (2007) 'Envisaging a new politics for an ethical future. Beyond trust, care and generosity – towards an ethic of "social flesh"', *Feminist Theory*, 8(3): 279–98.

Bellacasa, M.P. (2017) *Matters of Care: Speculative Ethics in More than Human Worlds*, Minneapolis, MN: University of Minnesota Press.

Bennett, J. (2010) *Vibrant Matter*, Durham, NC: Duke University Press.

Berlant, L. (2016) 'The commons: infrastructures for troubling times', *Society and Space*, 34(3): 393–419.

Berne, E. (1958) 'Transactional analysis: a new and effective method of group therapy', *American Journal of Psychotherapy*, 12: 735.

Bevir, M. (2016) 'Decentring security governance', *Global Crime*, 17 (3/4): 227–39.

Birt, Y. (2009) 'Promoting virulent envy?', *The RUSI Journal*, 154(4): 52–8.

Bishop, C. (2006) 'The social turn: collaboration and its discontents', *Artforum*, 44: 178–86.

Black, J. (2001) 'Decentring regulation: understanding the role of regulation and self-regulation in a "post- regulatory" world', *Current Legal Problems*, 54(1): 103–46.

Black J. (2002) 'Critical reflections on regulation', *Australian Journal of Legal Philosophy*, 27, 1–37.

Blackwood, L., Hopkins, N. and Reicher, S.R. (2012) 'I know who I am, but who do they think I am? Muslim perspectives on encounters with airport authorities', *Ethnic and Racial Studies*, 36(6): 1090–108.

Blakely, H. (2010) '"A second chance at life": labour, love and welfare on a South Wales estate', PhD thesis, Cardiff University.

Boudreau, J.-A. and Davis, D.E. (2017) 'Introduction: a processual approach to informalization', *Current Sociology*, 65(2): 151–66.

Bourdieu, P. (1977) *Outline of a Theory of Practice*, Cambridge: Cambridge University Press.

Bourdieu, P. (1986) 'The forms of capital', in J.G. Richardson (ed) *Handbook of Theory and Research for the Sociology of Education*, New York, NY: Greenwood.

Bourdieu, P. (1992) *The Rules of Art*, Cambridge: Polity Press.

Bourdieu, P. (1993) *Sociology in Question*, London: Sage.

# References

Bourdieu, P. and Passeron, J.C. (1979) *The Inheritors: French Students and Their Relation to Culture*, Chicago, IL: University of Chicago Press.

Bousetta, H. (2001) *Extending Democracy: Participation, Consultation and Representation of Ethnic Minority People in Public Life*, Bristol: Centre for the Study of Citizenship and Ethnicity, University of Bristol.

Boyle, D., Slay, J. and Stevens, L. (2010) *Public Services Inside Out: Putting Co-production into Practice*. Available at: https://media.nesta.org.uk/documents/public_services_inside_out.pdf

Boym, S. (2001) *The Future of Nostalgia*, New York, NY: Basic Books.

Bradbury, H. (ed) (2015) *The Sage Handbook of Action Research*, Thousand Oaks: Sage.

Bresnihan, P. and Byrne, M. (2014) 'Escape into the city: everyday practices of commoning and the production of urban space in Dublin', *Antipode*, 47: 36–54.

Bristow, G., Entwistle, T., Hines, F. and Martin, S. (2008) 'New spaces for inclusion? Lessons from the "three-thirds" partnerships in Wales', *International Journal of Urban and Regional Research*, 32(4): 903–21.

Brown, K. (2008) 'The promise and perils of women's participation in UK mosques: the impact of securitization agendas on identity, gender, and community', *British Journal of Politics and International Relations*, 10: 472–91.

Brydon-Miller, M., Greenwood, D. and Maguire, P. (2003) 'Why action research?', *Action Research*, 1(1): 9–28.

Brydon-Miller, M., Coghlan, D., Holian, R., Maguire, P. and Stoecker, R. (2010) 'Covenantal ethics for action research: creating a new strategy for ethical review', in J. Boulet (ed) *Proceedings of 8th World Congress 2010: Participatory Action Research and Action Learning*, Australia, 6–9 September, Sidney: ALARA.

Brydon-Miller, M., Aranda, A.M. and Stevens, D.M. (2015) 'Widening the circle: ethical reflection in action research and the practice of structured ethical reflection', in D. Coghlan and M. Brydon-Miller (eds) *The Sage Handbook of Action Research*, London: Sage.

Burlet, S. and Reid, H. (1998) 'A gendered uprising: political representation and minority ethnic communities', *Ethnic and Racial Studies*, 21(2): 270–87.

Byrne, E., Elliott, E. and Williams, G.H. (2016) 'Performing the micro-social: using theatre to debate research findings on everyday life, health and wellbeing', *Sociological Review*, 64(4): 715–33.

Cameron, D. (2016a) 'PM: families are the key to ending poverty', press release 10 January. Available at: www.gov.uk/government/news/pm-families-are-the-key-to-ending-poverty

Cameron, D. (2016b) '"Passive tolerance" of separate communities must end, says PM', press release, Prime Minister's Office, 18 January. Available at: www.gov.uk/government/news/passive-tolerance-of-separate-communities-must-end-says-pm

Caretta, M.A. and Riaño, Y. (2016) 'Feminist participatory methodologies in geography: creating spaces of inclusion', *Qualitative Research*, 16(3): 258–66.

Carey, J. (2013) 'Urban and community food strategies: the case of Bristol', *International Planning Studies*, 18(1): 111–28.

Carolan, M. (2013) *The Real Cost of Cheap Food*, London: Routledge.

Chatterton, P. (2000) 'Will the real creative city please stand up', *City Analysis of Urban Trends, Culture, Theory, Policy, Action*, 4(3): 390–7.

Civil Renewal Unit (2004) 'Firm foundations: the government's framework for community capacity building', Home Office Communications Directorate. Available at: www.scie-socialcareonline. org.uk/firm-foundations-the-governments-framework-for-community-capacity-building/r/a11G000000182i6IAA (accessed 31 January 2019).

Clifford, J. and Marcus, G. (eds) (1986) *Writing Culture: The Poetics and Politics of Ethnography*, Berkeley, CA: University of California Press.

Code, L. (2015) 'Care, concern, and advocacy: is there a place for epistemic responsibility?', *Feminist Philosophy Quarterly*, 1(1), doi:10.5206/fpq/2015.1.1.

Coexist (2016) Coexist strategy document, unpublished.

Coghlan, D. and Brydon-Miller, M. (eds) (2014) *The SAGE Encyclopedia of Action Research*, London: SAGE.

Cohen, S. (1998) 'Body, space and presence: women's social exclusion in the politics of the EU', *European Journal of Women's Studies*, 5(3/4): 367–80.

Cohen, S. and McDermont, M. (2016) 'When things fall apart', in D. O'Brien and P. Matthews (eds) *After Urban Regeneration: Communities, Policy and Place*, Bristol: Policy Press.

Cohen, S., Herbert, A., Evans, N. and Samzelius, T. (2017) 'From poverty to life chances', in A. Ersoy (ed) *The Impact of Co-Production: From Community Engagement to Social Justice*, Bristol: Policy Press.

Coleman, R and Ringrose, J. (2013) *Deleuze and Research Methodologies*, Edinbugh: Edinbugh University Press.

Cornwall, A. and Coelho, V.S.P. (eds) (2007) *Spaces for Change? The Politics of Participation in New Democratic Arenas*, London: Zed.

Dahrendorf, R. (1979) *Life Chances*, Chicago, IL: University of Chicago Press.

# References

Davidson, G. and Coppock, C. (2018) *Peoples Palace: after Magritte*, Artstation.

DCLG (Department of Communities and Local Government) (2007a) *Preventing Violent Extremism: Winning Hearts and Minds*, London: Department of Communities and Local Government.

DCLG (2007b) *Preventing Violent Extremism Pathfinder Fund*, London: Department of Communities and Local Government.

DeFilippis, J. (2004) *Unmaking Goliath*, New York, NY: Routledge.

De la Cadena, M. (2017) 'Matters of method: or, why method matters toward a *not only* colonial anthropology', *Hau: Journal of Ethnographic Theory*, 7(2): 1–2.

Deleuze, G. (1994) *Difference and Repetition*, New York, NY: Columbia University Press.

Deleuze, G. and Guattari, F. (1987) *A Thousand Plateaus: Capitalism and Schizophrenia* (trans Massumi, B.), Minneapolis, MN: University of Minnesota Press.

Deleuze, G. and Guattari, F. (1994) *What is Philosophy?*, London: Verso.

De Sousa Santos, B. (2004) 'The World Social Forum: toward a counter-hegemonic globalization (Part I)', in J. Sen, A. Anand, A. Escobar and P. Waterman (eds), *The World Social Forum: Challenging Empires*, New Delhi: The Viveka Foundation, pp 235–45.

Dicks, B. (2014) 'Participatory community regeneration: a discussion of risks, accountability and crisis in devolved Wales', *Urban Studies*, 51(5): 959–77.

Douglas, A. (2018) 'Redistributing power? A poetics of participation in contemporary arts', in K. Facer and K. Dunleavy (eds) *Connected Communities Foundation Series*, Bristol: University of Bristol and AHRC Connected Communities Programme. Available at: https://connected-communities.org/wp-content/uploads/2018/07/Contemporary_Arts_SP.pdf.pdf (accessed 30 January 2019).

Dumenden, I.E. and English, R. (2013) 'Fish out of water: refugee and international students in mainstream Australian schools', *International Journal of Inclusive Education*, 17: 1078–88.

Edwards, A. (2005) 'Relational agency: learning to be a resourceful practitioner', *International Journal of Education Research*, 43(3): 168–82.

Eitington, J.E. (1996) *The Winning Trainer: Winning Ways to Involve People in Learning*, Houston: Gulf Publishing Company.

Ellingson, L.L. (2017) *Embodiment in Qualitative Research*, London and New York, NY: Routledge.

Ellis, C. (2007) 'Telling secrets, revealing lives: relational ethics in research with intimate others', *Qualitative Inquiry*, 13(1): 3–29.

Erdem, E. (2012) 'The ambivalence of imperceptibility in political economy', *Rethinking Marxism: A Journal of Economics, Culture & Society*, 24(3): 428–35.

Facer, K. and Enright, B. (2016) *Creating Living Knowledge: The Connected Communities Programme, Community–University Relationships and the Participatory Turn in the Production of Knowledge*, Bristol: University of Bristol and AHRC Connected Communities Programme. Available at: https://connected-communities.org/wp-content/uploads/2016/04/Creating-Living-Knowledge.Final_.pdf (accessed 31 January 2019).

Ferguson, H. and Northern Rivers Landed Histories Research Group (2016) 'More than something to hold the plants up: soil as a non-human ally in the struggle for food justice', *Local Environment*, 21(8): 956–68.

Fine, M. and Vanderslice, V. (1992) 'Qualitative activist research', in F.B. Bryant, J. Edwards, R.S. Tindale, E.J. Posavac, L. Heath, E. Henderson-King and Y. Suarez-Balcazar (eds) *Methodological Issues in Applied Social Psychology*, Boston, MA: Springer.

Fine, M., Torre, M.E., Frost, D., Cabana, A. and Avory, S. (2018) 'Refusing to check the box', in K. Gallagher (ed) *The Methodological Dilemma Revisited: Creative, Critical and Collaborative Approaches to Qualitative Research for a New Era*, London: Routledge.

Flaherty, R. (1922) *Nanook of the North*.

Forsyth, A. and Megson, C. (2009) *Get Real: Documentary Theatre Past and Present*, Boston, MA: Springer.

Foster, H. (1995) 'The artist as ethnographer?', in G. Marcus and F. Myers (eds) *The Traffic in Culture: Refiguring Art and Anthropology*, California, CA, and London: University of California Press.

Foucault, M. (2000 [1982]) 'The subject and power', in R. Hurley (ed and trans) *Power: Essential Works of Foucault 1954–1984* (vol 3), London: Allen Lane.

Fraser, N. (1990) 'Rethinking the public sphere: a contribution to the critique of actually existing democracy', *Social Text*, 25/26: 56–80.

Freeman, J. (1970) 'The tyranny of structurelessness'. Available at: www.jofreeman.com/joreen/tyranny.htm (accessed 9 August 2018).

Freire, P. (2001 [1972]) *Pedagogy of the Oppressed* (trans Bergman, M.T.), New York, NY: Herder.

Frenzel, F. and Beverungen, A. (2017) 'Stokes Croft: the saga of one British neighbourhood reveals the perverse injustices of gentrification', *The Independent*, 10 August. Available at: www.independent.co.uk/news/long_reads/gentrification-bristol-stokes-croft-injustices-a7882966.html (accessed 31 January 2019).

## References

Gale, R. (2005) 'Representing the city: mosques and the planning process in Birmingham', *Journal of Ethnic and Migration Studies*, 31(6): 1161–79.

Gales, C. (2014) 'Is this the best way to prevent gentrification?', *Vice*, 17 June. Available at: www.vice.com/en_uk/article/wdaqnz/bristol-town-stokes-croft-is-under-risk-of-yuppification (accessed 31 January 2019).

Gallagher, K. (ed) (2018) *The Methodological Dilemma Revisited: Creative, Critical and Collaborative Approaches to Qualitative Research for a New Era*, London: Routledge.

Geerts, E. (2016) 'Ethico-onto-epistem-ology', *New Materialism: How Matter comes to Matter*. Available at: http://newmaterialism.eu/almanac/e/ethico-onto-epistem-ology (accessed 31 January 2019).

Gibson-Graham, J.K. (2008) 'Diverse economies: performative practices for other worlds', *Progress in Human Geography*, 32(5): 613–32.

Gohir, S. (2010) 'Muslim women are not political pawns', *The Guardian*, 9 April. Available at: www.theguardian.com/commentisfree/2010/apr/09/government-failed-muslim-women

Gottlieb, R. and Joshi, A. (2010) *Food Justice*, Massachusetts, MA: MIT Press.

Grabosky, P. and Braithwaite, J. (1986) *Of Manners Gentle: Enforcement Strategies of the Australian Business Regulatory Agencies*, Melbourne: Oxford University Press.

Gramsci, A. (2005) *Selections from the Prison Notebooks*, London: Lawrence & Wishart Ltd.

Gregson, N. and Rose, G. (2000) 'Taking Butler elsewhere: performativities, spatialities and subjectivities', *Environment and Planning D: Society and Space*, 18(4): 433–52.

Grenfell, M. and James, D. (2004) 'Change in the field – changing the field: Bourdieu and the methodological practice of educational research', *British Journal of Sociology of Education*, 25: 507–23.

Griggs, S., Norval, A. and Wagenaar, H. (eds) (2014) *Practices of Freedom: Decentred Governance, Conflict and Democratic Participation*, Cambridge: Cambridge University Press.

Grillo, R. (2015) *Muslim Families, Politics and the Law: A Legal Industry in Multicultural Britain*, Aldershot: Ashgate.

Grosz, E. (2008) *Chaos, Territory, Art: Deleuze and the Framing of the Earth*, New York, NY: Columbia University Press.

Gunaratnam, Y. (2012) 'Learning to be affected: social suffering and total pain at life's borders', *The Sociological Review*, 60(S1): 108–23.

Hackworth, J. (2002) 'Postrecession gentrification in New York City', *Urban Affairs Review*, 37(6): 815–43.

Hale, C.R. (2008) *Engaging Contradictions: Theory, Politics, and Methods of Activist Scholarship*, Berkeley, CA: University of California Press.

Hall, B., Tandon, R. and Tremblay, C. (2015) *Strengthening Community– University Research Partnerships: Global Perspectives*, Victoria, Canada: University of Victoria Press.

Hanson, S. and Blake, M. (2009) 'Gender and entrepreneurial networks', *Regional Studies*, 43(1): 135–49.

Haraway, D. (2016) *Tentacular Thinking: Anthropocene, Capitalocene, Chthulucene*, Durham, NC: Duke University Press.

Harding, S. (1992) 'Rethinking standpoint epistemology: what is "strong objectivity"?', *The Centennial Review*, 36(3): 437–70.

Harris, J. (2015) 'The Bristol conundrum: gentrification is a danger – and if you're poor, you're really, really stretched', *The Guardian*, 5 November. Available at: www.theguardian.com/cities/2015/ nov/05/bristol-conundrum-gentrification-danger-poor-really-stretched-stokes-croft-george-ferguson (accessed 31 January 2019).

Harrison, A. (2017) 'Make Bristol shit again', *Vice*, 19 September. Available at: www.vice.com/en_uk/article/7xxgj9/make-bristol-shit-again (accessed 31 January 2019).

Harrison, P. (2000) 'Making sense: embodiment and the sensibilities of the everyday', *Environment and Planning D: Society and Space*, 18(4): 497–517.

Hartsock, N. (2004 [1983]) 'The feminist standpoint: developing the ground for a specifically feminist historical materialism', in S. Harding (ed) *The Feminist Standpoint Theory Reader: Intellectual and Political Controversies*, New York, NY: Routledge.

Hawkins, H. (2013) *Creative Geographies: Geography, Visual Arts and the Making of Worlds*, New York, NY: Routledge.

Heath-Kelly, C. (2013) 'Counter-terrorism and the counterfactual: producing the "radicalisation" discourse and the UK PREVENT strategy', *British Journal of Politics and International Relations*, 15: 394–415.

Heath-Kelly, C. and Strausz, E. (2018) 'Counter-terrorism in the NHS: evaluating Prevent Duty safeguarding in the NHS', University of Warwick.

Henderson, J. (2018) 'Think-piece: community anchors', What Works Scotland. Available at: http://whatworksscotland.ac.uk/wp-content/ uploads/2015/11/WWSthinkpiece-Community-Anchors-Nov151. pdf (accessed 31 January 2019).

# References

Henderson, J., Revell, P., and Escobar, O. (2018) *Transforming Communities? Exploring the Roles of Community Anchor Organisations in Public Services Reform, Local Democracy, Community Resilience and Social Change*, What Works Scotland. Available at: http://whatworks scotland.ac.uk/wp-content/uploads/2018/05/WWSExploringThe RolesOfCommunityAnchorOrganisationsInPublicServiceReform. pdf (accessed 27 September 2019).

Hickey-Moody, A. (2015) *Arts, Pedagogy and Cultural Resistance: New Materialisms*, New York, NY, and London: Rowman & Littlefield.

Hill Collins, P. (2000) *Black Feminist Thought*, London: Harper Collins.

Hochschild, A.R. (1979) 'Emotion work, feeling rules, and social structure', *American Journal of Sociology*, 85(3): 551–75.

Hodkinson, S. and Chatterton, P. (2007) 'Autonomy in the city? Reflections on the social centres movement in the UK', *City Journal*, 10(3): 305–14.

Holmwood, J. and O'Toole, T. (2017) *Countering Extremism in British Schools? The Truth about the Birmingham Trojan Horse Affair*, Bristol: Policy Press.

Home Office (2011) *Prevent Strategy*, London: HM Government. Available at: www.gov.uk/government/uploads/system/uploads/ attachment_data/file/97976/prevent-strategy-review.pdf

hooks, b. (2004) 'Choosing the margin as a space of radical openness', in S. Harding (ed) *The Feminist Standpoint Reader: Intellectual and Political Controversies*, New York, NY: Routledge.

Huckaby, M.F. (ed) (2018) *Making Research Public in Troubled Times: Pedagogy, Activism, and Critical Obligations* (vol 2), Sterling, VA: Stylus Publishing, LLC.

Hughes, D. (2009) 'European food marketing: understanding consumer wants – the starting point in adding value to basic food products', *EuroChoices*, 8(3): 6–13.

Huising, R. and Silbey, S.S. (2015) 'Governing the gap: forging safe science through relational regulation', *Regulation & Governance*, 5(1): 14–42.

IETF (Internet Engineering Task Force) (1998) 'IETF working group: guidelines and procedures'. Available at: https://tools.ietf.org/html/ rfc2418 (accessed 9 August 2018).

IMI (Inclusive Mosque Initiative) (2013) 'Summary of research findings: gender and inclusivity in UK mosques'. Formerly available at: http:// inclusivemosqueinitiative.org/wp-content/uploads/2013/05/ in_the_shadow_of_uk_minarets-summary_of_research_findings.pdf (accessed 1 July 2015).

IMI (2015) 'Inclusive Jummah with Dr. Amina Wadud'. Formerly available at: http://inclusivemosqueinitiative.org/2015/02/jummah-congregational-prayers/ (accessed 1 July 2015).

Innes, M. (2014) *Signal Crimes: Social Reactions to Crime, Disorder and Control*, Oxford: Oxford University Press.

Innes, M., Davies, B. and McDermont, M. (2018) 'How co-production regulates', *Social & Legal Studies*, 28(3): 1–22.

Iossifidis, M. (2016) 'Uncertainty, sociology and fiction', *The Sociological Review*. Available at: www.thesociologicalreview.com/uncertainty-sociology-and-fiction/ (accessed 13 September 2019).

Ivinson, G. (2014) 'Skills in motion: boys' trail motorbiking activities as transitions into working-class masculinity in a post-industrial locale', *Sport, Education and Society*, 19(5): 605–20.

Ivinson, G. and Renold, E. (2016) 'Girls, camera, (intra)action: mapping posthuman possibilities in a diffractive analysis of camera–girl assemblages in research on gender, corporeality and place', in C.A. Taylor and C. Hughes (eds) *Posthuman Research Practices in Education*, New York, NY: Palgrave Macmillan.

Ivinson, G., Renold, E. and Angharad, J. (2017a) 'Mobilising run-a-way methodologies for life support', performance, 10–14 July, Summer Institute in Qualitative Research: Putting Theory to Work, Manchester Metropolitan University. Available at: www.youtube.com/watch?v=tNdTX-qlEDE (accessed 31 January 2019).

Ivinson, G., Renold, E. and Angharad, J. (2017b) 'Moving with the not-yet: choreographing the political with young people in space, place and time, generative feminism(s): working across/ within/ through borders', keynote performance at Gender and Education Association Bi-Annual Conference, 21–23 June, Middlesex University. Available at: https://vimeo.com/232354084 (accessed 31 January 2019).

Jackson, S. (2015) '"Repair": theorizing the contemporary', *Cultural Anthropology*. Available at: https://culanth.org/fieldsights/repair (accessed 31 January 2019).

Jones, S., O'Toole, T., DeHanas, D.N., Modood, T. and Meer, N. (2014) 'Muslim women's experiences of involvement in UK governance', *Public Spirit*, 22 January. Available at: www.publicspirit.org.uk/muslim-womens-experiences-of-involvement-in-uk-governance/

Jupp, E. (2007) 'Participation, local knowledge and empowerment: researching public space with young people', *Environment and Planning A*, 39(12): 2832–44.

Kara, H. (2017) 'Identity and power in co-produced activist research', *Qualitative Research*, 17(3): 289–301.

# References

Kester, G. (2005) 'Conversation pieces: the role of dialogue in socially-engaged art', in Z. Zucor and S. Leung (eds) *Theory in Contemporary Art Since 1985*, Oxford: Blackwell.

Khan, K. (2009) *Preventing Violent Extremism (PVE) & Prevent: A Response from the Muslim Community*, Brent: An-Nisa Society.

Kirwan, S., Dawney, L. and Brigstocke, J. (eds) (2015) *Space, Power and the Commons: The Struggle for Alternative Futures*, London: Routledge.

Klassen, L. (2016) 'Research by artists: critically integrating ethical frameworks', in D. Warr, M. Guillemin, S. Cox and J. Waycott (eds) *Ethics and Visual Research Methods: Theory, Methodology and Practice*, New York, NY: Palgrave Macmillan.

Koenig-Archibugi, M. and Macdonald, K. (2017) 'The role of beneficiaries in transnational regulatory processes', *Annals of the American Academy of Political and Social Science*, 670(1): 36–57.

Kopelman, P., Jebb, S.A. and Butland, B. (2007) 'Executive summary: foresight "Tackling obesities: future choices" project', *Obesity Review*, 8(1): vi–ix.

Kundnani, A. (2009) *Spooked! How to Not Prevent Violent Extremism*, London: Institute of Race Relations. Available at: www.irr.org.uk/publications/issues/spooked-how-not-to-prevent-violent-extremism/

Larkin, B. (2013) 'The politics and poetics of infrastructure', *Annual Review of Anthropology*, 42: 327–43.

Larner, W. and Craig, D. (2005) 'After neoliberalism? Community activism and local partnerships in Aotearoa New Zealand', *Antipode*, 37(3): 402–24.

Latour, B. (1986) 'The powers of association' in J. Law (ed) *Power, Action and Belief*, London: Routledge, Kegan and Paul.

Latour, B. (1987) *Science in Action*, Cambridge, MA: Harvard University Press.

Latour, B. (1999) *Pandora's Hope: Essays on the Reality of Science Studies*, Cambridge, MA: Harvard University Press.

Latour, B. (2004) 'Why has critique run out of steam? From matters of fact to matters of concern', *Critical Inquiry*, 30(2): 225–48.

Law, J. (2003) 'Making a mess with method', Centre for Science Studies, Lancaster University. Available at: www.comp.lancs.ac.uk/sociology/papers/Law-Making-a-Mess-with-Method.pdf (accessed 28 January 2019).

Law, J. (2004) *After Method: Mess in Social Science Research*, London: Routledge.

Leavy, P. (2015) *Method Meets Art: Arts-Based Research Practice*, New York, NY: The Guilford Press.

Leavy, P. (ed) (2017) *Handbook of Arts-Based Research*, New York, NY: Guilford Publications.

Lees, L. (2008) 'Gentrification and social mixing: towards an urban renaissance?', *Urban Studies*, 45: 2449–70.

Levitas, R. (2013) *Utopia as Method: The Imaginary Reconstitution of Society*, Basingstoke: Palgrave Macmillan.

Lewicki, A. and O'Toole, T. (2016) 'Acts and practices of citizenship: Muslim women's activism in the UK', *Ethnic and Racial Studies*, 40(1): 152–71.

Lewicki, A., O'Toole, T. and Modood, T. (2014) *Building the Bridge: Muslim Community Engagement in Bristol*, Bristol: University of Bristol.

Libby, G., Chloe, C., Olivia, R. and Renold, E. (2018) 'Making our feelings matter: using creative methods to re-assemble the rules on healthy relationships education in Wales', in N. Lombard (ed) *Routledge Handbook of Gender and Sexual Violence*, London: Routlege.

Lister, R. (2016) 'What do we mean by life chances?', in J. Tucker (ed) *Improving Children's Life Chances*, London: Child Poverty Action Group (CPAG).

Lury, C. and Wakeford, N. (eds) (2012) *Inventive Methods: The Happening of the Social*, London and New York: Routledge.

MacIntyre, A. (1981) *After Virtue*, London: Duckworth.

Manning, E. (2016) *The Minor Gesture*, Durham, NC: Duke University Press.

Marris, P. and Rein, M. (1974) *Dilemmas of Social Reform* (2nd edn), Harmondsworth: Penguin.

Martin, T. (2014) 'Governing an unknowable future: the politics of Britain's Prevent policy', *Critical Studies on Terrorism*, doi: 10.1080/17539153.2014.881200.

Martinson, M. and Minkler, M. (2006) 'Civic engagement and older adults: a critical perspective', *The Gerontologist*, 46(3): 318–24.

Masi, C.M., Chen, H.Y., Hawkley, L.C. and Cacioppo, J.T. (2011) 'A meta-analysis of interventions to reduce loneliness', *Personality and Social Psychology Review*, 15(3): 219–66.

Massey, D. (2011) 'A counterhegemonic relationality of place', in E. McKann and K. Ward (eds) *Mobile Urbanism: Cities and Policymaking in the Global Age*, Minneapolis, MN: University of Minnesota Press.

Massumi, B. (2015) *Politics of Affect*, Cambridge: Polity Press.

Matarasso, F. (1997) *Use or Ornament? The Social Impact of Participation in the Arts*, Stroud: Commedia.

McDermont, M. (2007) 'Mixed messages: housing associations and corporate governance', *Social and Legal Studies*, 16(1): 71–94.

## References

McDermont, M., Cowan, D. and Prendergast, J. (2009) 'Structuring governance: a case study of the new organisational provision of public service delivery', *Critical Social Policy*, 29(4): 677–702.

McFarlane, C. (2011) *Learning the City: Knowledge and Translocal Assemblage*, London: John Wiley & Sons.

McGlone, P., Dobson, B., Dowler, E. and Nelson, M. (1999) *Food Projects and How They Work*, London: Joseph Rowntree Foundation.

McSherry, C. (2001) *Who Owns Academic Work? Battling for Control of Intellectual Property*, Cambridge, MA: Harvard University Press.

Meissner, H. (2014) 'Politics as encounter and response-ability. Learning to converse with enigmatic others', *Artnodes*, 14: 35–41.

Millner, N. (2017) '"The right to food is nature too": food justice and everyday environmental expertise in the Salvadoran permaculture movement', *Local Environment*, 22(6): 764–83.

Minh-Ha, T. (1990) 'Documentary is/not a name', *October*, 52: 77–98.

Mol, A., Moser, I. and Polls, J. (eds) (2010) *Care in Practice: On Tinkering in Clinics, Homes and Farms*, Bielefeld: Transcript Verlag.

Moragues-Faus, A. and Morgan, K. (2015) 'Reframing the foodscape: the emergent world of urban food policy', *Environment and Planning A*, 47: 1558–73.

More, T. (1516) *Utopia*, Available at www.gutenberg.org/files/2130/2130-h/2130-h.htm

Morgan, K. (2007) 'The polycentric state: new spaces of empowerment and engagement?', *Regional Studies*, 41(9): 1237–51.

Mulligan, M. (2015) 'On ambivalence and hope in the restless search for community', *Sociology*, 49: 340–55.

Munck, R., McIlrath, L., Hall, B. and Tandon, R. (eds) (2014) *Higher Education and Community Based Research: Creating a Global Vision*, London: Palgrave Macmillan.

Mythen, G. and Walklate, S. (2016) 'Counterterrorism and the reconstruction of (in)security: divisions, dualisms, duplicities', *The British Journal of Criminology*, 56(6): 1107–24.

Nair, G., Ditton, J. and Phillips, S. (1993) 'Environmental improvements and the fear of crime: the case of the "Pond" area in Glasgow', *British Journal of Criminology*, 33(4): 555–61.

National Assembly for Wales (2001) *Communities First Guidance*, Cardiff: National Assembly for Wales.

Newman, J. (2001) *Modernizing Governance: New Labour, Policy and Society*, London: Sage.

Newman, J. (2012) *Working the Spaces of Power: Activism, Neoliberalism and Gendered Labour*, London: Bloomsbury.

Newman, J. and Clarke, J. (2008) *Publics, Politics and Power: Remaking the Public in Public Services*, London: Sage.

Noorani, T. (2013) 'Productive margins: regulating for engagement scoping study: phase 1', Bristol: unpublished working paper.

Noorani, T. (2014) 'Productive margins: regulating for engagement scoping study: phase 2', Bristol: unpublished working paper.

NUT (National Union of Teachers) (2016) 'NUT Prevent motion'. Available at: http://schoolsweek.co.uk/nut-prevent-strategy-motion-what-it-actually-says/

Oberhauser, A. (2005) 'Scaling gender and diverse economies: perspectives from Appalachia and South Africa', *Antipode*, 37(5): 863–74.

Open Society Justice Initiative (2016) *Eroding Trust: The UK's Prevent Counter-Extremism Strategy in Health and Education*, New York, NY: Open Society Foundations. Available at: www.opensocietyfoundations.org/sites/default/files/eroding-trust-20161017_0.pdf

Ostrom, E. (1996) 'Crossing the great divide: coproduction, synergy and development', *World Development*, 24(6): 1073–87.

O'Sullivan, S. (2006) *'Art Encounters – Deleuze and Guattari: Thought Beyond Representation*, Hampshire: Macmillan Publishers Limited.

O'Toole, T. (2015) 'Prevent: From 'hearts and minds' to 'muscular liberalism'', *Public Spirit*, 12 November. Available at: www.publicspirit.org.uk/prevent-from-hearts-and-minds-to-muscular-liberalism/

O'Toole, T., DeHanas, D.N. and Modood, T. (2012) 'Balancing tolerance, security and Muslim engagement in the United Kingdom: the impact of the Prevent agenda', *Critical Studies on Terrorism*, 5(3): 373–89.

O'Toole, T., DeHanas, D.N., Modood, T., Meer, N. and Jones, S. (2013) *Taking Part: Muslim Participation in Contemporary Governance*, Bristol: University of Bristol. Available at: www.bristol.ac.uk/ethnicity/projects/muslimparticipation/documents/mpcgreport.pdf

O'Toole, T., Meer, N., DeHanas, D.N., Jones, S.H. and Modood, T. (2016) 'Governing through Prevent? Regulation and contested practice in state–Muslim engagement', *Sociology*, 50(1): 160–77.

Pearce, S. (2012) *Constitutional Change and Community Development: Communities First under the Welsh Government*, Sheffield: The Centre for Regional, Economic and Social Research.

Peña-García, A., Hurtado, A. and Aguilar-Luzón, M.C. (2015) 'Impact of public lighting on pedestrians' perception of safety and well-being', *Safety Science*, 78: 142–8.

Phelan, P. (1993) *Unmarked*, London: Routledge.

# References

Pil, M. and Guarneros-Meza, V. (2017) 'Local governance under austerity: hybrid organisations and hybrid officers', *Policy & Politics*, 46(3): 409–25.

Pink, S. (2007) *Doing Sensory Ethnography*, Thousand Oaks: Sage.

Plant, S. (1990) 'The Situationist International: a case of spectacular neglect', *Radical Philosophy*, 55: 3–10.

Pool, S. (2018) 'Everything and nothing is up for grabs: using artistic methods in participatory research', in K. Facer and K. Dunleavy (eds) *Connected Communities Foundation Series*, Bristol: University of Bristol and AHRC Connected Communities Programme. Available at: https://connected-communities.org/wp-content/uploads/2018/07/Up_For_Grabs_SP-1.pdf (accessed 30 January 2019).

Poulter, S., Mellor, S., Evans, N., Hussein, M. and Comrie, A.T. (2016) *Life Chances: A Work of Sociological Fiction*, Bristol: Life Chances.

Prior, L. (2008) 'Repositioning documents in social research', *Sociology*, 42(5): 821–36.

Productive Margins (2018) ESRC large grant: final report. Unpublished.

Pruijt, H. (2003) 'Is the institutionalisation of urban movements inevitable?'. Available at: www.researchgate.net/publication/4990910_Is_the_Institutionalization_of_Urban_Movements_Inevitable_A_Comparison_of_the_Opportunities_for_Sustained_Squatting_in_New_York_City_and_Amsterdam

Rancière, J. (1999) *Disagreement: Politics and Philosophy*, Minneapolis, MN: University of Minnesota Press.

Rancière, J. (2004) *The Politics of Aesthetics*, London: Continuum.

Rasmussen, M.B. (2017) 'A note on socially engaged art criticism', *Field: A Journal of Socially-Engaged Art Criticism*. Available at http://field-journal.com/issue-6/a-note-on-socially-engaged-art-criticism (accessed 8 September 2019).

Reed, P. (2012) 'Co-autonomous ethics and the production of misunderstanding', *Filip*, 16: 27–33.

Reedy, P. (2014) 'Impossible organisations: anarchism and organisational praxis', *Ephemera*, 14(4): 639–58.

Renold, E. (2016) *A Young People's Guide to Making Positive Relationships Matter*, Cardiff: Cardiff University, Children's Commissioner for Wales, NSPCC Cymru/Wales, Welsh Government and Welsh Women's Aid.

Renold, E. (2018) '"Feel what I feel": making da(r)ta with teen girls for creative activisms on how sexual violence matters', *Journal of Gender Studies*, 27(1): 37–55.

Renold, E. (2019) 'Reassembling the rule(r)s: becoming crafty with how gender and sexuality education research comes to matter', in Y. Taylor, T. Jones and L. Coll (eds) *Up-Lifting Gender & Sexuality Study in Education & Research*, Basingstoke: Palgrave Macmillan.

Renold, E. and Ivinson, G. (with the Future Matters Collective) (2019) 'Anticipating the more-than: working with pre-hension in artful interventions with young people in post-industrial communities', *Futures: The Journal of Policy, Planning and Future Studies*, Anticipations Special Issue.

Renold, E. and McGeeney, E. (2017a) *The Future of the Sex and Relationships Education Curriculum in Wales*, Cardiff: Welsh Government.

Renold, E. and McGeeney, E. (2017b) *Informing the Future of the Sex and Relationships Education Curriculum in Wales*, Cardiff: Cardiff University.

Renold, E., Holland, S., Ross, N.J. and Hillman, A. (2008) '"Becoming participant": problematizing "informed consent" in participatory research with young people in care, *Qualitative Social Work*, 7(4): 427–47.

Renold, E., Ivinson, G., Angharad, J. and Oliver, S. (2018a) 'Disrupting the politics of violence: making da(r)ta matter', keynote performance at PhEmaterialism 2: Matter-Realising Pedagogical/Methodological Interferences into Terror and Violence, University College London, 7 June. Available at: www.ucl.ac.uk/festival-of-culture/events/festival-of-culture-thursday-7-june-2018

Renold, E., Ivinson, G., Angharad, J. and Oliver, S. (2018b) 'Life support: disrupting the political with young people', presentation at 'Time & Trust': Working Collaboratively and Creatively with Young People, 5 November, St. Fagans National Museum of History, Saint Fagans, Wales. Available at: www.creativemargins.net/cardiff/

Renov, M. (2004) *The Subject of Documentary*, Minnesota, MN: University of Minnesota Press.

Ringrose, J., Warfield, K. and Zarabadi, S. (eds) (2018) *Feminist Posthumanisms, New Materialisms and Education*, London and New York, NY: Routledge.

Robinson, T.N., Borzekowski, D.L., Matheson, D.M. and Kraemer, H.C. (2007) 'Effects of fast food branding on young children's taste preferences', *Archives of Pediatrics & Adolescent Medicine*, 161(8): 792–97.

Rose, M. (2008) 'Gathering "dreams of presence": a project for the cultural landscape', *Environment and Planning D: Society and Space*, 24(4): 537–54.

Rouch, J. (1967) *Jaguar*.

## References

Rouquier, G. (1946) *Farrebique.*

Rutten, K., Van Dienderen, A. and Stoetaert, R. (2013) 'Revisiting the ethnographic turn in contemporary art', *Critical Arts*, 27: 459–73.

Samers, M. (2005) 'The myopia of "diverse economies" or a critique of the "informal economy"', *Antipode*, 37(5): 875–86.

Sandwick, T., Fine, M., Greene, A.C., Stoudt, B.G., Torre, M.E. and Patel, L. (2018) 'Promise and provocation: humble reflections on critical participatory action research for social policy', *Urban Education*, 53(4): 473–502.

Sayer, A. (2011) *Why Things Matter to People: Social Science, Values and Ethical Life*, Cambridge: Cambridge University Press.

Schirmer, W. and Michailakis, D. (2015) 'The lost Gemeinschaft: how people working with the elderly explain loneliness', *Journal of Aging Studies*, 33, 1–10.

Scott, C. (2001) 'Analysing regulatory space: fragmented resources and institutional design', *Public Law*, 329–53.

Scott-Baumann, A. (2017) 'Ideology, utopia and Islam on campus: how to free speech a little from its own terrors', *Education, Citizenship and Social Justice*, 12(2): 159–76.

Sennett, R. (2013) *Together: The Rituals, Pleasures and Politics of Cooperation*, London: Penguin.

Simoniti, V. (2018) 'Assessing socially engaged art', *The Journal of Aesthetics and Art Criticism*, 76(1): 71–82.

Smith, A and Stenning, A. (2006) 'Beyond household economies: articulations and spaces of economic practice in postsocialism', *Progress in Human Geography*, 30(2): 190–213.

Soja, E.W. (2013) *Seeking Spatial Justice (Vol. 16)*. Minneapolis: University of Minnesota Press.

Sörensson, E. and Kalman, H. (2017) 'Care and concern in the research process: meeting ethical and epistemological challenges through multiple engagements and dialogue with research subjects', *Qualitative Research*, 18(6): 706–21.

Springgay, S. (2008) 'An ethics of embodiment, civic engagement, and a/r/tography', *Educational Insights*, 12(2). Available at: www.ccfi.educ. ubc.ca/publication/insights/v12n02/articles/springgay/index.html

Staeheli, L. (2010) 'Political geography: democracy and the disorderly public', *Progress in Human Geography*, 34(1): 67–78.

Star, S.L. (1988) 'The structure of ill-structured solutions: boundary objects and heterogeneous distributed problem solving', in M. Huhns and L. Gasser (eds) *Readings in Distributed Artificial Intelligence*, Menlo Park, CA: Kaufman.

Star, S.L. (2010) 'This is not a boundary object: reflections on the origins of a concept', *Science, Technology, & Human Values*, 35(5): 601–17.

Stoker, G. and Young, S. (1993) *Cities in the 1990s*, Harlow: Longman.

Strathern, M. (2007) 'Interdisciplinarity: some models from the human sciences', *Interdisciplinary Science Reviews*, 32(2): 123–34.

Taylor, C.A. and Ivinson, G. (2013) 'Material feminisms: new directions for education', *Gender and Education*, 25(6): 665–70.

Theodore, N. (2015) 'Subject spaces: on the ethics of co-producing urban research', university seminar, University of Bristol, Bristol.

Thomas, G.M. (2016) '"It's not that bad": stigma, health, and place in a post-industrial community', *Health & Place*, 38: 1–7.

Thomas, G.M., Elliott, E., Exley, E., Ivinson, G. and Renold, E. (2018) 'Light, connectivity and place: young people living in a post-industrial town', *Cultural Geographies*, 25(4): 537–51.

Thomas-Hughes, H. and Barke, J. (2018) 'Community researchers and community researcher training: reflections from the UK's Productive Margin's: Regulating for Engagement programme', Bristol Law Research Paper Series, ISSN 2515-897X.

Thomson, A.-M. and Perry, J.L. (2006) 'Collaboration processes: inside the black box', *Public Administration Review*, December: 20–32.

Tierney, W. (2004) 'Academic freedom and tenure: between fiction and reality', *The Journal of Higher Education*, 75: 161–77.

Todd, R. (2018) 'Weathering the storm: the hidden value of anchor organisations', paper commissioned by Productive Margins.

Transparency Project (2016) 'Guidance on parents recording meetings with social workers'. Available at: www.transparencyproject.org.uk/guidance-on-parents-recording-meetings-with-social-workers-2/ (accessed 23 February 2018).

Tronto, J. (2009 [1993]) *Moral Boundaries: A Political Argument for an Ethic of Care*, London: Routledge.

Tuckman, B.W. (1965) 'Developmental sequence in small groups', *Psychological Bulletin*, 63(6): 384–99.

Turem, Z.U. and Ballestero, A. (2014) 'Regulatory translations: expertise and affect in global legal fields', *Indiana Journal of Global Legal Studies*, 21(1): 1–25.

Tyler, I. (2015) 'Classificatory struggles: class, culture and inequality in neoliberal times', *The Sociological Review*, 63(2): 493–511 .

Van Der Tuin, I. (2016) *Generational Feminism*, London: Lexington Books.

## References

Veljanovski, C. (2010) 'Economic approaches to regulation', in R. Baldwin, M. Cave and M. Lodge (eds) *The Oxford Handbook of Regulation*, Oxford: Oxford University Press, pp 17–38.

Wadia, K. (2015) 'Women from Muslim communities in Britain: political and civic activism in the 9/11 era', in T. Peace (ed) *Muslims and Political Participation in Britain*, Oxon and New York, NY: Routledge, pp 85–102.

Walker, R.B.J. (1994) 'Social movements/world politics', in L. Amoore (ed) *The Global Resistance Reader*, London: Routledge, pp 136–49.

Walkerdine, V. (2010) 'Communal beingness and affect: an exploration of trauma in an ex industrial community', *Body & Society*, 16(1): 91–116.

Walkerdine, V. and Jimenez, J. (2011) *Gender, Work and Community after De-Industrialisation: A Psychosocial Approach to Affect*, Basingstoke: Palgrave Macmillan.

Wang, Q., Coemans, S., Siegesmund, R. and Hannes, K. (2017) 'Arts-based methods in socially engaged research practice: a classification framework', *Art/Research International: A Transdisciplinary Journal*, 2(2): 5–39.

Wardrop, A. and Withers, D.M. (eds) (2014) *The Para-Academic Handbook: A Toolkit for Making-Learning-Creating-Acting*, Bristol: HammerOn Press.

Warner, M. (2002) *Publics and Counterpublics*, Brooklyn, NY: MIT Press.

Warsi, S. (2017) *The Enemy Within: A Tale of Muslim Britain*. London: Allen Lane.

Watson, D.L., Poulter, S., Mellor, S. and Howard, M. (2016) 'Life Chances: co-written re-imagined welfare utopias through a fictional novel', *Sociological Review Blog*. Available at: www.thesociologicalreview.com/life-chances-co-written-re-imagined-welfare-utopias-through-a-fictional-novel/

Weber, M. (1978) *Economy and Society*, Berkeley, CA: University of California Press.

Welsh, B.C. and Farrington, D.P. (2008) 'Effects of improved lighting on crime', *Campbell Systematic Reviews*, 4(13): 1–51.

Welsh Government (2004) *Making the Connections: Delivering Better Public Services for Wales*, Cardiff: National Assembly for Wales.

Welsh Government (2015) *Good Practice Guide: A Whole Education Approach to Violence against Women, Domestic Abuse and Sexual Violence in Wales*, Wales: Welsh Government.

Whatmore, S. (1996) 'Dissecting the autonomous self: hybrid cartographies for a relational ethics', *Environment and Planning D: Society and Space*, 15: 37–53.

Williams, G.H., Cropper, S., Porter, A. and Snooks, H. (2007) 'Beyond the experimenting society', in S. Cropper, A. Porter, G.H. Williams, S. Carlisle, R. Moore, M. O'Neill, C. Roberts and H. Snooks (eds) *Community Health and Wellbeing: Action on Health Inequalities*, Bristol: Policy Press, pp 119–29.

Willig, C. (2016) 'Reflections on the use of object elicitation', *Qualitative Psychology*. Available at: http://openaccess.city.ac.uk/13575/1/Qualitative%20Psychology%20paper%20version%204.pdf (accessed 23 February 2018).

Wise, T.A. (2013) 'Can we feed the world in 2050? A scoping paper to assess the evidence', Global Development and Environment Institute Working Paper: 13-04. Available at: www.ase.tufts.edu/gdae/Pubs/wp/13-04WiseFeedWorld2050.pdf (accessed 23 February 2018).

Wood, D. and Gray, B. (1991) 'Toward a comprehensive theory of collaboration', *Journal of Applied Behavioral Science*, 27(2): 139–62.

Zola, E. (2004 [1885]) *Germinal*, London: Penguin Classics.

# Index

Note: Page numbers for figures, tables and boxes appear in *italics*. The suffix *n* signifies an endnote.

3Gs Development Trust (3Gs) 26, 168–9, 202
  experiences of and value to Communities First 174–6, 177–8, 179–86
4Ms project *see* Making, Mapping and Mobilising in Merthyr (4Ms project)

## A

Aberfan 35
Adamson, David 170–1, 178
Alonely monologues 37–8, 80–1, 190, 192–3, 197, 201
anchor organisations see community anchor organisations
Anchor people *181–3*
*Anchor Peoples* (artwork) *182–3*
Arts and Humanities Research Council (AHRC) 114
arts-based methods
  as aim of Productive Margins programme 6, 29, 146–7
  art as 'the way' 128–9
  as facilitation methods 28–31, 36
  purpose and value of 142–3, 150–1, 152, 157–8, 164, 195
  social practice art (socially engaged art practice) 106–7, *118–20*
Artstation 183
austerity 13, 37, 94, 127, 142, 147, 172, 175–6, 184, 186, 204–5, 212, 215
asylum and immigration 15–16, 17, 96, 107, 114–15, *116*, 117

## B

Barad, Karen 129
Barthes, Roland 110, *119*
Bedminster (Bristol)
  Greater Bedminster toilet map 20–1, 26
  isolation and loneliness in older people project 69–82
belonging 98, 132, 137, 139, 140, 141
Beuys, Joseph 160
Bevir, Mark 52, 53
Bishop, Claire 106–7
Black, Julia 51, 52, 53
body-forming workshops 140
border work 209–12
boundary objects *8*, 26, 91, 103
Bourdieu, Julie-Anne 203, 204, 205, 206
Bourdieu, Pierre 105, 116–18
Boym, Svetlana 35–6
Brigstow Institute (University of Bristol) 214
Bristol, University of *see* University of Bristol
brokers 182, 200
Brown, Katherine 59
BS3 Community (BS3C) 201, 202
  *see also* Southville Community Development Association (SCDA)
Building the Bridge (Bristol) 55–8, 192, 194, 196–7, 199, 205
bureaucratic formalisation 198–200
Burlet, Stacey 59

## C

Cadena, Marisol de la 40
Cameron, David 59, 108–9
capacity building 173–4
Cardiff University 129, 214
'care-ful' research 67–84
    Alonely monologues 37–8, 80–1,
      190, 192–3, 197, 201
    'care-ful' research model 67–8
    regulation of knowledge exchange
      77–82
    regulation of knowledge production
      72–7
    research project 7–10, 67–72, 194,
      204
    ten elements of 'care-ful' research
      *83–4*, 199
Carolan, Michael 86
Castle, Barbara (Adamson et al) 170–1,
    178
Chang, Candy 153
children and young people
    children's services 120–4
    Convention on the Rights of the
      Child 19
    Making, Mapping and Mobilising in
      Merthyr (4Ms project) see main
      entry
Citizens Cymru 134
Citizens UK 131, 132
Close and Remote 31, 106, 109–10,
    *118–19*, 191
Coalition government 62–3, 108
Coelho, Vera Schatten 58
Coexist 12, 87–8, 99, 145–63, 201–2
Cohen, Sue 35
collective agency 194–200, 205
collective making *30*
command and control (CAC) 3
commoning 90, 193
Communities First
    and bureaucratic formalisation 198,
      199
    evaluation of programme 178–9,
      185

    evolution and demise of programme
      12–13, 167, 170–1, 173, 175,
      176, 177, 198, 199
    experiences of community anchor
      organisations 168–9, 174–6,
      177–8, 184–6, 202
    hidden value of community anchor
      organisations 179–83
'community,' nature of 22*n*, 98, 170–1
community anchor organisations
    167–87
    Anchor people *181–3*
    experiences of Communities First
      168–9, 174–6, 177–8, 184–6,
      202
    as 'experts in everything' 200–1
    funding 202–3
    hidden value to Communities First
      179–83
    nature and use of term 171–3
    research project *9*, 12–13, 168–70
    sustainable network 204
Community Gateway (Cardiff
    University) 214
community interest companies (CIC)
    99, 101, 125, 196, 206*n*
    *see also* Coexist
community researchers 43–6
community safety 131–2
community workers *see* community
    anchor organisations; community
    researchers
Conservative government 108, 109
    *see also* Coalition government
Convention on the Rights of the Child
    19
*Conversations in Neon* (film) 162
'Conversations in Thread' (social
    sculpture) 159–62
Coppock, Chris 183
co-production
    limits of 209
    politics of 211
    as programme method 5–6, 24–5,
      28, 76
    regulating practice 203–5
    and research funding 67

## Index

and social justice 206
understandings of 24, 27
Cornwall, Andrea 58
counterterrorism *see* Prevent
Counter-Terrorism and Security Act
2015 50, 63
Culhane, Anne-Marie 88–9, 99, 100

### D
Dahrendorf, Ralf 109
data protection 121–3
Davidson, Glenn *183*
Davis, Diane E. 203, 204, 205, 206
Dearden, Helen (Adamson et al)
170–1, 178
decentred regulation 3–5
demonstrable rationality 178–9
devolution 19, 167, 170
dissent see spaces of dissent
*doxa* 105, 118, 120
drama exercises *30*

### E
Easton (Bristol), food production and
consumption project 87–102
Easton & Lawrence Hill
Neighbourhood Partnership 44
Ellis, Carolyn 72
encoding 196–8
Escobar, Oliver (Henderson et al) 172,
173
Evans, Nathan 38
experientially sensitive infrastructure
200–5
experts-by-experience and expertise-
by-experience 2–3, 23, 103,
189–90, 191, 203, 204

### F
*Farrebique* (Rouquier) 107–8
fast-food 4, 10, 91–6, 99, 102
female genital mutilation (FGM) 62
feminist approaches 38, 61–2, 67–8,
69, 73, 87, 129

fictional characters *see* game design;
novel-writing
field trips and residential working
*29–30*
film-making 36, 54, 135–7, 138–40,
156–8, 191–2, 192–3
fishbowl exercises *30*, 31
food production and consumption
85–103
affordability 93–6
food justice and spatial justice 90–3
'more-than-food policies' 102–3
research project *8*, 10, 45, 85–9,
192, 193, 195, 196
social dimensions of food 96–102
ten principles for design of urban
food systems *97*, 193, 199
Foster, Hal 108
Foucault, Michel 24
Freeman, Jo 40
Freire, Paolo 40, 89
fridge as installation 87

### G
game design 111, 113–18
gender-based and sexual violence
132–5, 194, 197
gentrification 158–64
geographic information system
mapping technologies (GIS)
128, 129–31, 193
*Germinal* (Zola) 107–8
Gibson-Graham, J.K. 23, 38, 81
Godfrey-Talbot, Heloise 138
*Graphic Moves* (film) 138–40, 141–2
*Graphic Moves* workshops 135–42
Gray, Barbara 40–1
Greater Bedminster Partnership 20–1
Greater Bedminster toilet map 20–1,
26
Grenfell Tower 1
Grillo, Ralph 62
Guarneros-Meza, Valeria 176, *182*
Gunaratnam, Yasmin 105
Gurnos (Merthyr Tydfil) 34–5, 169

239

## H

Hall, Budd (Munck et al) 212–13
Hamilton House 145, 147–50, 152, 153, 155, 156–7, 159, 162, 201, 202
Harding, Sandra 38
Hartsock, Nancy 38
Heath-Kelly, Charlotte 49, 51, 64–5
Henderson, James 172, 173
homeless community 159, 161
housing associations 4
Huising, Ruthanne 205
Hurley, Paul 36

## I

immersive installation workshop 162–4
immigration and asylum *see* asylum and immigration
Inclusive Mosque Initiative (IMI) 61
informality 203
infrastructure *see* experientially sensitive infrastructure
institutionalisation 148
intermediaries 200
Irish, Sharon 30
isolation and loneliness in older people project 67–84
    *Alonely* monologues 37–8, 80–1, 190, 192–3, 197, 201
    'care-ful' research model 67–8
    regulation of knowledge exchange 77–82
    regulation of knowledge production 72–7
    research project 7–10, 67–72, 194, 204
    ten elements of 'care-ful' research *83–4*, 199

## J

*Jaguar* (Rouch) 107–8
jewellery-making 110–12, *113*, *114*, 125
Junior Digital Producers (JDPs) 87

## K

Kester, Grant 106
*Keyhole Whispers* (film) 156–8
keyword exercises 32
Knowle West (Bristol), food production and consumption project 87–102, 192, 193
Knowle West Media Centre (KWMC) 26, 36, 87

## L

Latour, Bruno 40
Law, John 34, 37
Layzell, Richard 36
Leavy, Patricia 123–4
lemniscate 160
Levitas, Ruth 105
*Life Chances* project 105–25
    concept of 'life chances' 108–9
    fiction-writing 107–8, *119*, 194
    game design 111, 113–18
    jewellery-making 110–12, *113*, *114*
    poster workshops 109–10, 111–12, 194
    research project *8*, 11, 17, 105–8, *118–20*, 196, 197
    social work practice 16, 120–4, 197
Live Model (film) 191–2
Local Isolation and Loneliness Action Committee (LILAC) 201
Localism Act 2011 18
loneliness in older people see isolation and loneliness in older people project
low-income families *see* *Life Chances* project

## M

MacIntyre, Alisdair 179
Magritte, René *183*
Making, Mapping and Mobilising in Merthyr (4Ms project) 127–43
    geographic information systems (GIS) 128, 129–31, 193
    *Graphic Moves* workshops 135–42

# Index

Relationships Matter and ruler-skirt activism (gender-based and sexual violence) 132–5, 194, 197

research project 11–12, 127–9, 142–3, 197–8

Zebra-crossings project (community safety) 131–2

Manchester Metropolitan University 129

Manning, Erin 128, 129

mapping exercises 35

Marris, Peter 178–9

McIlrath, Lorraine (Munck et al) 212–13

McSherry, Corynne 91

media representations 109–12, 127, 132, 137, 140, 141

*Medway Council v A & Ors (Learning Disability; Foster Placement)* 121

Merthyr Tydfil *see* community anchor organisations; Gurnos; isolation and loneliness in older people project; Making, Mapping and Mobilising in Merthyr (4Ms project)

mess 33–5, 37, 191, 205

monologues *see* Alonely monologues

mosques 51, 60–1, 192, 197

Munck, Ronaldo 212–13

Muslim civic engagement 49–65

empowerment of women 58–62, 192

under Prevent 49–50, 51–8, 62–5, 194, 196–7

research project 7, *8*, 49–50, 54–5

Myers, Julie 36

## N

*Nanook of the North* (Flaherty) 107–8

National Assembly for Wales *see* Welsh Assembly and government

National Muslim Women's Advisory Group 59

National Union of Teachers 64

neighbourhood forums (NFs) 18–19

New Labour government 51, 52–3, 108

Noorani, Tehseen 37

novel-writing 107–8, 113, *119*, 120, 122–4, 125, 189–90, 194, 195

## O

obesity 95–6

object elicitation *29*

Olden, Matt 29

older people *see* isolation and loneliness in older people project

Oliver, Seth 135–6, 137

Open Society Justice Initiative 64

organic model of regulation 189–206

articulating new stories 193–4

experientially sensitive infrastructure 200–5

holistic attention to place 191–3

limits and perils 196–200

surfacing invisible rules 194–6

organisational governance 147–65

Ostrom, Elinor 27

## P

parental recordings (of meetings with social workers) 121–3

parental responsibility 122–3

pARTicipatory research 128–9

'partner hand' 19–20

Peck, Adam 79

*People's Palace* (artwork) 183

Perry, James L. 40–1

photography 74, 77–8, 192–3

Pike, Jamie 148

Pil, Madeleine 176, *182*

planning regulations and policy 4, 92, 102–3, 190, 192, 196

poetry-writing 29, 140

policing 15, 128, 129–31

pop-up events 100–1

poster workshops 109–10, 111–12, 194

'poverty porn' 127, 136–7

power politics 198–200

praxis 38, 39, 40, 89

Prevent
  Building the Bridge (Bristol) 55–8, 194, 196–7, 199, 205
  empowerment of Muslim women 58–62, 192
  regulation 2007–10 49–50, 51–4
  regulation post 2011 54–5, 62–5, 199
  research project 7, *8*, 49–50, 54–5
Productive Communities Research Forum 23–46
  emotions and values 33–9
  methodology 24–5, 28–33, 40–1
  phases of evolution 26–8
  structure and purpose 6, 24, 25–6, 39
Productive Margins: Regulating *for* Engagement (research programme)
  approaches to regulation 13–22
  border work 209–12
  conclusions see organic model of regulation
  contributions of 21–2, 208–9, 213, 215
  objectives and methods 5–7, 142, 145, 207–8
  overview of projects 7–13
  role of community researchers 43, 44–6
Puig de la Bellacasa, Maria 10, 68, 69

## R

Rancière, Jacques 112–13, 118
Rasmussen, Mikkel Bolt 106
regeneration 158–64
  *see also* Communities First
regulation
  current understandings of 1, 3–5
  organic model of *see* main entry; co-production, regulating practice; isolation and loneliness in older people project; regulation of knowledge exchange; regulation of knowledge production

Productive Margins approaches to 13–22, 24
Reid, Helen 59
Rein, Martin 178–9
Relationships Matter lunch club 132–5, 194, 197
Revell, Philip (Henderson et al) 172, 173
risk-based regulation 4
Rose, Mitch 36
ruler-skirt activism 132–5

## S

savings syndicates 19–20
Schedule 7 policing powers 57
school curriculum 135, 197
sculpture 159–62
security and exclusion 156–8
self-regulation 4–5
semiotic analysis *119*
sexual and gender-based violence *see* gender-based and sexual violence
Siemers, Cheryl 32
Silbey, Susan S. 205
Single Parent Action Network (SPAN) 31, 87–102, 106
*Skint* (TV series) 136–7, 138–9, 140–1
Smiths (band) 137, 140
social enterprises see Coexist; community interest companies (CIC)
social justice 206
Social Justice Project (University of Bristol) 214
social practice art (socially engaged art practice) 106–7, *118–20*
  *see also* arts-based methods
social work practice 16, 120–4, 197
sociological fiction 107–8
Soja, Edward 92
solution-focused approaches 151
Somali Kitchen 88–91, 100, *101*, 196
Somali women 19, 45, 90–1, 95, 96, 99, 102, 117

# Index

South Riverside Community Development Centre (SRCDC) 32, 38, 106, 168–9, 202
experiences of and value to Communities First 174–6, 179–86
Southville and Bedminister, Now and Then map 70
Southville Community Development Association (SCDA) 38
*see also* BS3 Community (BS3C)
spaces of dissent 145–65
*Keyhole Whispers* (security and exclusion) 156–8
organisational governance 147–65
research project *9*, 12, 146–7, 149–53
social sculpture and immersive installations (gentrification) 158–64
sticker installation 153–5
spatial justice 92–3
Sperlinger, Tom 32
Stahl, Susanne 36
sticker installations 153–5
stimulus-response and devising *119*
Stokes Croft (Bristol) 147, 158–61
Strathern, Marilyn 91
Strausz, Erzsebet 64–5
supermarkets 4, 10, 19, 91–3, 95
surveillance 17, 49, 54, 62, 159, 161, 197
*see also* geographic information system mapping technologies (GIS)

## T

takeways (fast-food) 4, 10, 91–6, 99, 102
Talbot, Rowan 136
Tandon, Rajesh (Munck et al) 212–13
Terrorism Act 2000 57
theatre pieces *see* Alonely monologues
Theodore, Nik 38
Thomson, Ann Marie 40–1
Todd, R. 172

toilet provision 20–1, 159
training of community researchers 44–6
transactional analysis *120*
Transparency Project 121–2
Tronto, Joan B. 10, 68
Tuck, Lucy 79–80
Tuckman, Bruce W. 37

## U

United Nations Convention on the Rights of the Child 19
university governance 207, 209–15
University of Bristol 26, 87, 149, 214
University of Chicago 213
University of Sydney 213
urban regeneration 158–64
see also Communities First
*Utopia* (More) 105, 114
*Utopia as Method* (Levitas) 105

## V

values exercises *29*
Violence Against Women, Domestic Abuse and Sexual Violence (Wales) Act 2015 134

## W

Wadia, Khursheed 59
Watkins, Dane 36
Weber, Max 109
Well-being of Future Generations (Wales) Act 2015 186
Welsh Assembly and government 12–13, 133, 134, 167, 170–1, 177, *182–3*, 185–7, 198, 199
*Whose Data* (film) 36
Williams, Gareth 178–9
women
empowerment of Muslim women 58–62, 192
gender-based and sexual violence 132–5, 194, 197

*see also* feminist approaches; Somali women

Wood, Donna 40–1

## Y

young people
 children's services 120–4
 Convention on the Rights of the Child 19
 Making, Mapping and Mobilising in Merthyr (4Ms project) see main entry

## Z

Zebra-crossings project 131–2